DATE DUE

Also by David Howe

Social Workers and their Practice in Welfare Bureaucracies
An Introduction to Social Work Theory
The Consumers' View of Family Therapy
Half a Million Women: Mothers Who Lose Their Children by Adoption (with P. Sawbridge and D. Hinings)
On Being a Client: Understanding the Process of Counselling and Psychotherapy
Attachment Theory for Social Work Practice *
Attachment and Loss in Child and Family Social Work
Adopters on Adoption: Reflections on Parenthood and Children
Patterns of Adoption: Nature, Nurture and Psychosocial Development
Attachment Theory, Child Maltreatment and Family Support * (with M. Brandon, D. Hinings and G. Schofield)
Adoption. Search and Reunion (with J. Feast)
The Adoption Reunion Handbook (with L. Trinder and J. Feast)
Contact in Adoption and Permanent Care (with E. Neil)
Child Abuse and Neglect: Attachment, Development and Intervention *
The Emotionally Intelligent Social Worker *
A Brief Introduction to Social Work Theory *

* Also published by Palgrave Macmillan

Attachment Across the Lifecourse

A brief introduction

David Howe

First published 2011 by
PALGRAVE MACMILLAN

Palgrave Macmillan in the UK is an imprint of Macmillan Publishers
Limited, registered in England, company number 785998, of
Houndmills, Basingstoke, Hampshire RG21 6XS.

Palgrave Macmillan in the US is a division of St Martin's Press LLC,
175 Fifth Avenue, New York, NY 10010.

Palgrave Macmillan is the global academic imprint of the above
companies and has companies and representatives throughout the
world.

Palgrave® and Macmillan® are registered trademarks in the United
States, the United Kingdom, Europe and other countries

ISBN 978–0–230–29359–5

This book is printed on paper suitable for recycling and made from
fully managed and sustained forest sources. Logging, pulping and
manufacturing processes are expected to conform to the environmental regulations of the country of origin.

A catalogue record for this book is available from the British Library.

10   9   8   7   6   5   4   3   2   1
20   19   18   17   16   15   14   13   12   11

Printed in China

24.00

For Elsa and Lucy

Contents

Preface   xii

Acknowledgements   xviii

PART I   ATTACHMENT THEORY, MODELS AND MEASURES   I

1   Attachment Behaviour   3
    Evolutionary beginnings   3
    Danger and staying safe   5
    The origins of attachment theory   7
    The attachment system and attachment behaviour   8
    Attachments and affectional bonds   12
    Protest, despair and detachment   14
    Caregiving   16
    Play and exploration   17
    Safe havens and secure bases   18
    Conclusion   19

2   Emotions and their Regulation   21
    Born to be sociable   21
    The co-regulation of affect   23
    The social brain   26
    The development of the psychological self   27
    Mind-mindedness and mentalization   29
    Conclusion   30

3   The Internal Working Model   32
    Learning through experience and by association   32
    Internal working models and mental representations   33
    Drafts and revisions, beliefs and expectations   35
    Attachment behavioural strategies   37
    Goal-corrected partnerships   38
    Conclusion   39

4 Patterns of Attachment   **41**
   Introduction   41
   Defensive strategies, adaptive strategies and internal
   working models   42
   Measuring attachment in infancy and childhood   48
   Culture, class and attachment   51
   Conclusion   53

5 Attachment in Adulthood   **55**
   Cradle to grave   55
   Adult attachment styles   56
   The Adult Attachment Interview (AAI)   57
   Self-report measures   61
   Conclusion: attachment across the lifecourse   64

**PART II   ATTACHMENT PATTERNS, TYPES AND
            STYLES**   **67**

6 Secure Attachments in Childhood   **69**
   Introduction   69
   Infancy   69
   Resilience   72
   Social skills and emotional intelligence   73
   Growing independence   75
   Middle childhood   75
   Conclusion   78

7 Secure Attachments in Adulthood   **79**
   Introduction   79
   Adolescence   79
   Autonomous adults   81
   Loss   83
   Romantic and couple relationships   85
   Parenthood and caregiving   89
   Physical health   91
   Mental health   92
   Old age   93
   Conclusion   95

8　Avoidant Attachments in Childhood　　**96**
　　Introduction　　96
　　Infancy　　96
　　Middle childhood　　101
　　Conclusion　　104

**9　Avoidant and Dismissing Attachments in
　　Adulthood**　　**106**
　　Introduction　　106
　　Adolescence　　106
　　Adulthood　　107
　　Romantic and couple relationships　　112
　　Parenthood and caregiving　　116
　　Physical health　　119
　　Mental health　　120
　　Old age　　122
　　Conclusion　　123

10　Ambivalent Attachments in Childhood　　**124**
　　Introduction　　124
　　Infancy　　124
　　Middle childhood　　129
　　Coercive strategies　　130
　　School and peers　　132
　　Conclusion　　133

**11　Anxious and Preoccupied Attachments in
　　Adulthood**　　**134**
　　Introduction　　134
　　Adolescence　　134
　　Adulthood　　136
　　Romantic and couple relationships　　140
　　Parenting and caregiving　　144
　　Physical health　　147
　　Mental health　　148
　　Old age　　149
　　Conclusion　　151

12   **Disorganized and Controlling Attachments in
     Childhood**   **152**
     Introduction   152
     Infancy   153
     Organized or disorganized?   158
     Hyperarousal   161
     Preschool and middle childhood   163
     Controlling strategies   164
     Compulsive and coercive strategies   167
     Compulsive caregiving   169
     Compulsive compliance   172
     Compulsive self-reliance   173
     Controlling-punitive and coercive strategies   175
     School and peer relationships   181
     Conclusion   181

13   **Fearful Avoidant Attachments and Unresolved
     States of Mind in Adulthood**   **183**
     Introduction   183
     Adolescence   184
     Adulthood   186
     Romantic and couple relationships   187
     Parenthood and caregiving   188
     Physical health   191
     Mental health   193
     Old age   196
     Conclusion   197

PART III   ISSUES AND DEBATES   **199**

14   **Temperament, Disability and Gender:
     The Interaction of Nature and Nurture**   **201**
     Introduction   201
     Temperament   202
     Disability   207
     Gender   210
     Conclusion   211

**15 Attachment across the Lifecourse: Continuity
and Discontinuity, Stability and Change** **213**
Introduction 213
Childhood 216
Adoption and foster care 219
Adulthood 224
Conclusion 225

Epilogue **227**

Further Reading 229

Bibliography 231

Author Index 257

Subject Index 260

Preface

'In 1956 when this work was begun I had no conception of what I was undertaking.' This is the sentence with which John Bowlby (1907–1990), a child and family psychiatrist, begins the Preface to the first book in his famous *Attachment* trilogy (Bowlby 1969: xi). He continues: 'At the time my object appeared a limited one, namely, to discuss the theoretical implications of some observations of how young children respond to temporary loss of mother,' observations that he was happy to acknowledge had originally been made by his social work colleague, James Robertson.

Over 50 years later, attachment is one of psychology's busiest, and most productive areas of research and theorising. This is in no small part due to Mary Ainsworth's happy collaboration with Bowlby with whom she first worked as a research psychologist while living in London in the early 1950s. Born in Ohio, raised in Canada, and spending the bulk of her professional life at Johns Hopkins University, Baltimore and the University of Virginia, Ainsworth brought a keen researcher's eye and discipline to the study of attachment. Along with Bowlby's theoretical genius, Ainsworth's rigour was critical for attachment's eventual acceptance and success, not just in academic circles but also in the clinic and beyond into the worlds of policy and practice.

The time therefore felt right to produce a book that takes stock of modern attachment theory, written with the interested, but perhaps relatively new reader to the subject in mind. The hope, then, is that the book will appeal to psychology students, counsellors, psychotherapists, social workers, health visitors, child care workers, foster carers, health professionals, clinical psychologists, child protection workers, teachers, child and family lawyers, and indeed, the many lay readers who remain curious about human relationships and our psychological condition.

This short book aims to provide the reader with a brief introduction to what is now a vast, international subject of enquiry and investigation. Parts of it are based on ideas and sections first developed in Chapters 4 to 7 of an earlier book, co-written with my colleagues Marian Brandon, Diana Hinings and Gillian Schofield (Howe 1999). However, as the discipline has moved on apace over the intervening decade, the present intention is to appreciate how modern thinkers, though still able to trace a very strong line back to Bowlby's original trilogy, have elaborated and enriched the subject to such an extent that I doubt that the theory's founding father could have imagined where his 'limited' project would find itself today.

One of the hallmarks of attachment theory as currently fashioned is its interest in, and use of a wide range of biological, social and developmental sciences. This approach remains firmly in the spirit of Bowlby who throughout his life remained eclectic and open-minded in his approach to children's psychosocial development. So don't be surprised to meet in this book, albeit at an introductory level, many different disciplines, including psychology, animal biology, human physiology, neuroscience, evolutionary theory, genetics, systems theory, and social psychology. There are strong hints in this list that we are at the beginning of an exciting time in the developmental sciences. Powerful, and often unexpected links are being found between genes and environment, early brain development and the quality of care offered by parents, evolutionary theory and social psychology. Attachment is one of a number of theories that is providing a vehicle to explore these links, and in so doing it takes us into some cutting-edge thinking about human beings, their behaviour and development. So, although attachment theory itself is only part of the story, because it plays such an important role in the early years of life, it does influence many later life experiences as individuals set off down their own unique developmental pathway.

Thus, in one of those delicious philosophical insights, thinkers over many centuries have recognised that our very sense of being – of who we are and how we are – emerges out of our relationships with other human beings. To become self-aware *and* socially savvy, from life's outset we need to interact with other people. But it is also the case that the quality and character of our relationships with others affect the specifics of who we are and how we are. Of course, other factors play a part, including our genes, but even their expression is influenced by the environment in which they find themselves. So, there is something deeply important about the quality of our relationships – for our development, sense of self, ability to deal with others, and mental health. We shall see that attachment theory has much to say about these matters, not just in infancy, but across the lifecourse.

Consider Jamie, two and half years old, living at home with his mum and dad. His uncle Jack has to come to visit. Jamie finds him lots of fun. He makes a bee-line for him the moment he comes through the door. In no time the two of them are racing around the garden as Jamie demands to be chased or twirled round as he is held by the hands. There are lots of giggles and laughter until Jamie, not looking where he is going, trips up and grazes his knee. He cries, shouts 'Mummy', and hobbles back into the house, clutching his knee, needing mum's care and a cuddle. Uncle Jack is abandoned. No-one else but mum will do. There are no surprises in this scenario, but it does beg a number of questions. Why doesn't Jamie show his grazed knee to Uncle Jack, who, the moment before the accident, was the centre of Jamie's excited attention? Why does it have to be mum? Attachment theory delves deep into such apparently obvious questions.

Attachment theory also has many interesting things to say about our thoughts, feelings and behaviour in adult relationships. A scratched knee might not trigger too much distress, but loss of a job, death of close friend, diagnosis of a serious illness, or the threatened breakdown of a romantic relationship might. And with the anxiety and distress that such events provoke, we might also see adult versions of attachment behaviour as we seek out a supportive partner or a shoulder to cry on. However, as adults, we bring our complex emotional histories to bear on all our close relationships. Our attachment needs, and the responses of partners and close friends might not always be played in lines that are straight.

Ayesha and Raz have been married a couple of years. Ayesha knows that Raz wants children. She hasn't told him that she has been encouraged by her boss to apply for a key promotion in the law firm where she works as a solicitor. Ayesha has always studied hard and done well at school, university and work. She is fond of telling people how proud her parents are of her success. She jokes that she has always been a 'good girl', never complaining and just getting on with things. The promotion would be a feather in her cap and would certainly impress her parents. But Ayesha is nervous about discussing the prospect of the new job with Raz who more than once has said he's looking forward to being a father. As a couple, they have enjoyed material success and a good life style. Ayesha is feeling more and more tense. She is not used to sharing her feelings with others – 'I just put my head down, work hard, and get on with things.' She is afraid that Raz will not support her bid for promotion and that their relationship, which is important to Ayesha, will suffer. Although she would like to air her hopes and fears with Raz, she has never presented herself to him other than as a cool, competent, worldly woman who knows her own mind. She does what she always does when she feels vulnerable and anxious; she bottles up her feelings and gets remote and tetchy. So, we might wonder, why does Ayesha find it so difficult to show and share her worries? Why does she find it so difficult to turn to other people, particularly those to whom she feels most close, for help? Attachment theory is rather good at helping us think about how people's past relationship experiences affect the way they currently process strong feelings, particularly negative feelings in the context of close relationships.

Although originally the preserve of developmental psychologists and child welfare practitioners, attachment theory, true to Bowlby's early predictions, now has things to say about personality, behaviour and human relationships across the lifecourse. One of the biggest growth areas has been research into adult attachments. Under the gaze of social psychologists, the theory's horizons have expanded to look at romantic relationships, couple relationships, sexuality, lifestyle choices, health, and old age. Meanwhile, the developmentalists have also kept their eyes open and wide. They have shone ever brighter lights on children's biological, emotional and social development in the context of close relationships.

Clearly, within these few pages, only a sketch of the main ideas can be given. Brief examples and vignettes are provided throughout to illustrate the different attachment groups. They are derived from my own experience working with families, writing reports, and carrying out research. Names have been changed, and in some examples I have conflated cases, mainly to preserve anonymity. The book is organised into three main Parts.

Part I introduces the reader to the key conceptual components of modern attachment theory. These include attachment behaviour, caregiving, safe havens and secure bases, the regulation of the emotions, the internal working model, and the various adaptive strategies that we all use to increase our feelings of comfort and safety. These strategies give rise to various patterns of attachment that have been identified by attachment researchers. Inevitably, these early sections of the book take a particular interest in the parent–child relationship. This reflects Bowlby's initial fascination with children's development in the early years. However, he clearly anticipated the relevance of the theory to relationships and behaviour in adulthood. As the book progresses, increasing interest and attention will be paid to attachments in adulthood, and how many of the concepts, such as careseeking and caregiving, affect regulation and defensive behaviours, continue to have relevance through childhood, adulthood and on into old age.

In practice, most adult attachment research has looked at the relationship between couples, particularly those in romantic partnerships. Perhaps the major difference between attachment in childhood and adulthood is the role of the caregiver. Whereas in childhood it is the infant who seeks protection and comfort from the parent as attachment figure, in adulthood, each partner can both seek *and* provide care and comfort. Adult partners therefore display both careseeking and caregiving behaviours, depending on which partner happens to be in a state of need. These differences begin to be spelled out in Chapter 5.

Part II looks at the four main attachment patterns (secure, avoidant, ambivalent, and disorganised) that have been identified by attachment researchers. Each pattern is explored and examined as it plays out across the lifecourse beginning in infancy, moving on into the preschool years, then middle childhood, through adolescence and adulthood, before ending with a brief look at attachments in old age. The mental health, physical health and relationship issues associated with each pattern are also considered.

Part III takes a step back and acknowledges some of the unresolved questions and controversies that continue to stimulate the theory. Is each attachment pattern really the product of different types of parental nurture or is each pattern simply describing natural differences between children's sensitivity and temperamental make-up? Can children, or indeed adults, change their attachment style as they journey along the lifecourse or, having established an attachment style early in life, is it fixed for good? These questions focus on whether an individual's attachment organisation remains stable over time or not, whether there is continuity or discontinuity in attachment style across the lifecourse. These, and similar questions, will be raised and considered in the final chapters. By the end of the book, it will be apparent that attachment research and theory continues to be a busy and bubbling area of enquiry into the human experience, one that is happy to make links with all the other major developmental sciences that are beginning to piece together a wonderfully subtle but increasingly coherent picture of our psychosocial progress from infancy to old age.

So let's return to the beginning and rejoin Bowlby on his original journey as he set out 'to map the multitude of intricate pathways along which any one person may develop' (1998a: 419).

Acknowledgements

Once again, I am delighted to have the opportunity to thank Catherine Gray, Palgrave Macmillan's social science publisher and editor for her continued enthusiasm and support. It was March 2009 and I had just proof-read a previous book and was looking forward to a life of quiet contemplation. But publishers are made of stronger stuff. Catherine was of the view that the world needed a short introductory book on attachment theory and that as I seemed capable of only writing short introductory books these days, I was the person for the job. I think it was flattery. Anyway, I fell for it and had a splendid time both re-reading attachment classics and catching up with the latest research and writing on the subject. Catherine is a joy to work with and I remain grateful for her expertise, experience and thoroughness.

Catherine does not work alone. She is supported by equally excellent colleagues who have, with humour and forbearance, guided me through the many stages through which a book has to travel before it finally sees the light of day. So warm thanks too, to Kate Llewellyn and Katie Rauwerda. The typescript for the book was originally reviewed, anonymously, by four readers, all clearly very clued up and knowledgeable about attachment. All four reviewers gave keen advice and made helpful suggestions about how best to improve the book. Although I have tried to follow most of what they had to say, limitations of space meant that regrettably a number of very sensible ideas simply had to fall by the wayside. Part of the price for writing a book that is brief and introductory is that not everything can be said or done. Nevertheless, it is a pleasure to thank the reviewers for their informed advice and canny judgement.

My final thanks are to Guilford Press, New York, for granting me permission to reproduce Mario Mikulincer and Philip Shaver's adult attachment Figure 4.2 on page 89 of their book, *Attachment in Adulthood*, first published in 2007, and described here as Figure 5.1.

David Howe

PART I

Attachment Theory, Models and Measures

1
Attachment Behaviour

Evolutionary beginnings

About 150,000 years ago on the plains of north-east Africa in what we now call Ethiopia, small groups of primates, walking upright, might have been seen wandering the savannas. These primates would be immediately recognizable as members of the species *homo sapiens,* biologically no different from you and me; that is, modern men and women. They lived as hunter–gatherers in small co-operative family groups.

Although lacking great size, strength or speed, this new species was in possession of a relatively large and certainly complex brain. In fact, so large was the mature brain that in order to get through the birth canal during labour, a good deal of the brain's growth and development had to take place after the baby was born. This meant that the infant was highly dependent on the succour and protection of its parents and other close kin for many months, indeed, for many years after birth. During this time of vulnerability and dependence, the young of this, our own species, display a range of *careseeking* behaviours. In response, the adults provide a variety of *caregiving* behaviours. It is these careseeking and caregiving behaviours that enhance infants' chances of survival.

Ethology is the science of animal behaviour in the wild, in its natural habitat. Human behaviour can also be looked at in everyday settings, especially when it involves biologically basic activities such as caring for young children. From an ethological perspective, behaviour of any kind, including careseeking and caregiving, cannot be fully understood 'without some knowledge of the environment to which the species has become adapted through evolution' (Hinde 2005: 1).

In addition, evolutionary biology teaches us that the goal of all life is the replication of genes in future generations (Belsky 2005: 91). One of the major insights of the evolutionary sciences is the recognition that any attribute or behaviour that increases the chances of an organism's survival, however marginal, is likely to be selected, and therefore passed on to future generations. These attributes and behaviours represent genetic adaptations to the environment. They become part of that species' character and make-up. Inasmuch as a characteristic increases the odds of the individual surviving into adulthood and reproductive fitness, then that characteristic will be inherited by any offspring of that sexually mature individual. This, by definition, will include most of what makes up the animal, physiologically, behaviourally, and psychologically.

John Bowlby (1997: 47) termed the environment to which a species adapts (that is, its ecological niche), and in which it is currently surviving, the *environment of evolutionary adaptedness*. So, for example, the group living, social and co-operative behaviours shown by our species certainly allowed us to take advantage of the environment in ways that were not only adaptive but also flexible. The creative potential of these social behaviours witnessed increasing divisions of labour and individual specialization. Thus, although any one individual would only have a limited number of talents, large groups of individuals collectively would enjoy a great range and variety of skills and attributes. Some would be superb hunters, some good at leading the group and making decisions, while others would know where the ripest fruit might be found or how best to resolve disputes and conflict. The ability to communicate and co-operate therefore helped maximize the benefits of individuals and their talents, thus giving our species a tremendous advantage. In Darwinian terms, we might therefore conclude that the highly emotional and social nature of our species is the product of natural selection pressures.

Stepping back, for any species, genetic traits include all characteristics that are obviously adaptive and aid survival: the colour of an animal's fur, the possession of keen hearing, the ability to digest tough grasses, the presence of strong leg muscles for speedy running, or the attribute of being nervy and wary by nature. For each species, the list, of course, is potentially enormous as the evolutionist's compass ranges from what is going on within each cell to the function of major organs, from the shape of the animal's body to the specifics of mating behaviour. Thinking along these lines encouraged Bowlby to consider which behaviours and characteristics might enhance the survival of small, vulnerable and very dependent human infants. His enquiries eventually led to the identification and description of a number of innate behaviours that were present at birth and remained active throughout the early and later years of life. These are the careseeking behaviours of which we have spoken and which are displayed by all young children of our species.

Danger and staying safe

Returning to our origins 150,000 or so years ago, north-east Africa was a place of open woods and grassland. Jackals, wolves, and big cats, especially leopards, probably represented the biggest danger, particularly for babies and small children. Our social, co-operative, group-living nature certainly afforded some protection from predators. Many group-living species find safety in numbers. This being the case, to be outside the group, apart and alone, was a particularly dangerous, stressful place to be. Indeed, observed Bowlby (1997: 173), for weaker members of all ground-living primates, 'especially females and young, the old and sick, isolation often spells speedy death'. For infants, then, safety lies in staying close to the group in general, and principal caregivers in particular. In most cases, as we shall see, an infant's principal caregiver is destined to become his or her 'attachment figure'. This is how Main *et al.* summarize Bowlby's thinking on these matters:

> Bowlby further proposed that the infant primate's focus upon the attachment figure … has been rendered all the more emotional and insistent because – due to the fact that many primates are seminomadic – it is inevitably closely intertwined with fear. The substantial distances travelled by most primates means that they cannot establish a fixed location for protection of the young, such as a burrow or den. In contrast to those mammals for whom a special *place* provides the infant's haven of safety, then, for the primate infant *the attachment figure is the single location that must be sought under conditions of alarm.*
>
> (2005: 253, emphasis original)

Deep echoes of these ancient dangers are still very active in our physiological and psychological make-up, even today. When threatened or under stress, we often seek social support. We gravitate to those who seem to be sharing our plight, or turn to those to whom we feel most close. We are particularly sensitive to social rejection and abandonment. Anything that casts us outside the family, group, community, or tribe is likely to cause great anxiety. It unsettles us, even frightens us. And for babies and young children, feelings of fear are at their greatest when they suffer the loss of their primary sources of protection – their parents and other close kin. To emphasize this point, Bowlby (1998a: 52), quotes the great American psychologist William James who said that 'the great source of terror in infancy is solitude'. It is for this reason that we should never underestimate the long-term effects of neglect, abandonment, and prolonged separation.

The real dangers posed by the loss of a primary caregiver in the environment of evolutionary adaptedness suggested to Bowlby that vulnerable infants probably came equipped with a number of in-built behaviours that functioned to keep the baby safe and out of harm's way. At times of felt danger, these care and protection-oriented behaviours, which Bowlby termed attachment behaviours, propel young children towards places of safety. Such places include mothers as primary caregivers, but also fathers and other family group members.

Caregivers protect their offspring in two basic ways (Goldberg 2000: 135). They can respond proactively by removing hazards and anticipating danger. This means that infants don't encounter the risk and so their attachment behaviours don't get activated. Or, should infants feel in danger, caregivers can react to the signals of distress emitted by the infant. Here, it is important for the caregiver to see things from the child's point of view. The mother might know that there is no real danger but she can also appreciate that for a small child, the perception might be different. A mother will know that a friendly dog running enthusiastically towards you might well be frightening if you are small and have limited experience of dogs.

Similar dangers and the maternal responses they provoke can be observed in the behaviour of many species of young primates. Here is an example that Bowlby gives of a mother monkey's response to separation:

> Like all other primate infants, the baby chimpanzee spends the whole of its infancy in close proximity to its mother. During its

first four months it clings to her in the ventral position and only very occasionally is seen apart from her, and usually then is sitting beside her. Should it venture more than a couple of feet from her, she pulls it back; and should she observe a predator approach she hugs it more closely.

(Bowlby 1997: 190)

The origins of attachment theory

John Bowlby was medically and psychoanalytically trained. As a child psychiatrist, he retained a life-long commitment to object relations theory which describes how the self and mind develop as children relate to others, particularly the interactions they have with their primary caregivers (Bretherton 1998). After returning from the army medical service in 1945, he joined the Tavistock Clinic in London as Head of the Children's Department, promptly renaming it the Department for Children and Parents, reflecting his growing conviction that the quality of the parent–child relationship was profoundly important for development and mental health.

It was while thinking about the behavioural distress shown by children separated from their parents, particularly when separation also involved finding yourself in unfamiliar surroundings or in the presence of strangers, that Bowlby began to piece together his ideas about what we now refer to as attachment (Bowlby 1958). To make sense of the distress, upset and behaviours shown by young children at times of alarm, loss and separation, Bowlby wove together an extraordinary range of ideas drawn from many different sciences. As well as his clinical work, the animal behavioural, ethological and evolutionary sciences, along with developmental psychology, control and systems theory, and the cognitive sciences also provided him with many of his key concepts as he attempted to make sense of children's behaviour and development in the early years.

With a mind that was highly original, Bowlby fashioned his ideas in a series of groundbreaking books that made up his famous trilogy: *Attachment and Loss* (1969, 1973, 1980). But if Bowlby was the integrating force behind the theory of attachment, it was Mary Ainsworth who brought research rigour and her own conceptual wisdom to the enterprise. With a grounding in developmental psychology, she worked with Bowlby for a couple of years in the early 1950s before eventually, by way of Uganda, returning to the United States. Over several decades of innovative research, methodological advances and creative theorizing, Ainsworth helped develop and extend Bowlby's ideas (for example, see Ainsworth *et al.* 1978). As the founders of attachment theory, Bowlby and Ainsworth maintained a highly active and productive relationship until John Bowlby's death in 1990. Mary Ainsworth herself died a few years later in 1999.

The attachment system and attachment behaviour

Ethologists use the concept of behavioural systems to describe the various neural programmes, that is the in-built behavioural repertoires with which animals are biologically equipped to help them survive, negotiate, manage, and reproduce in their physical and social environment. Each behavioural system is automatically activated whenever the senses are stimulated by specific environmental cues – signs of danger, food, a potential mate. When the activated behavioural system has achieved its 'set goal' – a place of safety is found, a meal is eaten, a sexual partner met – the system terminates. In effect, then, the daily activities of any animal are being constantly guided by whole suites of behavioural systems being turned on and then being switched off. The bottom line of each behavioural system's presence and purpose is to maintain optimal functioning, that is, to ensure survival, continuity and reproduction.

Although each behavioural system in itself is relatively mechanical, organisms can and do learn from experience. Learning from experience allows the animal to develop a range of strategies that help it adapt to the particular characteristics of its environment. Each adaptive behavioural strategy represents a learned attempt by the organism to optimize its survival and reproductive potential. Using straightforward learning theory principles, behaviours that achieve their goal are likely to be experienced as pleasurable. These behaviours are therefore reinforced and will be repeated under similar environmental conditions. Behaviours that fail to achieve their goal are less likely to be repeated. For example, we shall see that children's attachment behaviours are shaped by, and adapt to the characteristics of the caregiving environment in which they happen to find themselves.

One of the most important and fundamental behavioural systems is the fear system. It helps to keep us alive. It is the fear system that alerts us to the presence of danger, or the possibility of danger. And as fear also activates the attachment system, fear and attachment work in synchrony (Kobak *et al.* 2005: 74). So, remembering the world and the very real dangers that it presented to our earliest infant ancestors, the *attachment system* is that behavioural system which gets activated whenever the individual feels threatened, alarmed, in danger, in distress, or in need. When activated, the attachment system sets in motion *attachment behaviours* whose *set goal* is to recover physical or psychological proximity to one or other of the child's caregivers where safety and protection lie. In the environment of evolutionary adaptedness, babies 'who are biologically predisposed to stay close to their mothers were less likely to be killed by predators, and it was for this reason that Bowlby referred to protection from predators as the "biological function" of attachment behavior' (Cassidy 2008: 5).

Once a child's attachment behaviours have achieved their set goal of recovering proximity to the caregiver, the child once again feels safe and the attachment system 'switches off' along with any displays of attachment behaviour. 'By utilizing the concept of feedback,' explains Bowlby (1997: 20), attachment theory 'gives as much attention to the conditions that terminate an act as to those that initiate one.' In other words, attachment theorists are as much interested in how parents help (or in some cases, fail to help) children feel safe and regulate their arousal as they are in the things that trigger attachment behaviours in the first place.

Attachment behaviour, being about seeking protection from danger, means that young children routinely monitor their environment for two classes of experience:

Is danger or stress present? This can be experienced as either external dangers (the presence of a stranger, a loud noise, the rapid approach of a large animal, darkness), or internal discomfort (feeling hungry, tired, or ill).

Where, and how accessible is my attachment figure? Children, even when happily playing, repeatedly make eye contact with their attachment figure, point to something new or unknown whilst looking at the parent, or toddle back to show mum a toy. Uncertainties about the whereabouts and availability of the caregiver activate the attachment system. Separation, abandonment, being alone for too long, rejection, neglect and abuse can all lead to acute, and in many cases, chronic activation of the attachment system.

Many animals, and certainly most mammals show attachment behaviour. Take the example of a young lamb, busy eating grass, who wanders further and further away from its mother, the source of safety. For lambs, increasing distance from mother represents potential danger. Lambs separated from their mothers and the flock are easily picked off by wolves, big cats, and large eagles. The lamb's sudden sense that mother is too far away for safety activates its attachment system, triggering attachment behaviour, the set goal of which is to recover proximity with mother where safety and protection lie. While the attachment system is activated, the lamb is in an aroused, dysregulated, and temporarily stressed state. During this distressed state, the lamb is likely to alert its mother by bleating. Once visual contact is achieved, it will run quickly back to its mother. On its return the lamb might suckle, typically with some urgency. However, when the lamb's attachment behaviour achieves its goal of getting back to the protection of the ewe, its attachment system terminates. The lamb will then go back to what lambs do: eat grass.

It's the same for human babies, although there are differences. Infants need to experience their parent as both *available* and *sensitively responsive to their needs, signals and communications*. If you are unable to crawl or walk back to your mother, then the only alternative is to get your mother to come to you. Protest, crying, clinging, grasping, and other displays of need and distress are very effective attachment behaviours. These *fight* responses to the frustration of having your needs ignored or unmet draw you to your caregiver's attention. They are *signalling* behaviours. Most reasonably sensitive parents will attend quickly to their child when she protests or cries, particularly crying that indicates pain or severe distress (van IJzendoorn and Hubbard 2000: 388). This does not mean that parents fail to respond to other distress signals such as a hunger cry, but in these cases, the caregiving response is less urgent and more self-conscious. It reflects the understanding that a pain might require immediate action – it could, after all, be life-threatening. In contrast, a slight delay in feeding a hungry baby is unlikely to cause much harm and at worse will leave the baby feeling a bit more cross than either mother or child ideally would wish.

Vocalizing, cooing, burbling, sucking, smiling, visual tracking, eye contact, following, and raised arms (signalling 'I want to be picked up') can also act as attachment behaviours. They are good at keeping any besotted parent engaged; we're all suckers for a smiling, babbling baby. Mothers naturally seek eye contact with their babies and when it is achieved, parents become livelier, smile and vocalize more, and exaggerate their facial and vocal expressions. Babies are naturally 'tuned-in' to human faces as well as voices that are higher pitched, slowed down, musical and sing-songy.

As babies get older, they begin to smile more at the people they know best. They can play quite happily at a distance, but are likely to glance frequently in the direction of the caregiver and make eye contact. And once toddlers have learned to walk, then of course they can also run back to mum or dad at times of need. These are *approach* behaviours:

> In man's environment of evolutionary adaptedness it is clearly vital that the mother of a child under three or four years should know exactly where he is and what he is doing, and be ready to intervene should danger threaten; for him to keep advertizing his whereabouts and activities to her and continue doing so until she signals 'message received' is therefore adaptive.
>
> (Bowlby 1997: 247)

With maturation and improving ability to make sense of relationships and social situations (social cognition), the appraisal of caregiver availability becomes more sophisticated. The various cognitive-behavioural mechanisms allow more refined and nuanced monitoring and evaluation of the caregiving environment. This sees children using more complex, flexible and revisable (goal-corrected) behaviours and strategies in order to achieve their goals. Given that caregiving environments vary from warm, responsive and available to cool, insensitive and unpredictable, this helps explain why children in different parent–child relationships might well be using different attachment behavioural strategies. Each of the major attachment patterns describes the type of attachment strategy and cognitive appraisals being used by children under specific caregiving regimes (see Chapters 6, 8, 10 and 12).

Attachments and affectional bonds

Forming attachments is what young children do in the presence of familiar adults, even if those adults are harsh and abusive (see Chapter 12). Infants instinctively attach to their carers (Prior and Glaser 2006: 15). Only in extreme cases of severe institutional deprivation or environments in which carers are utterly indifferent and forever changing will children fail to form attachments. But for most children, during the course of healthy development, attachment leads gradually to the formation of *affectional bonds* with key adults, particularly primary caregivers. Thus, we might observe that 'whereas an attachment bond endures, the various forms of attachment behaviour that contribute to it are active only when required' (Bowlby 1998b: 40).

From birth, babies become more and more able to differentiate among the various people who populate their lives. They quickly begin to distinguish who is who in their environment showing clear preferences for their primary caregivers. Between six and nine months of age, most children develop clear-cut attachments with those adults with whom socially they most frequently interact, and who are most likely to soothe, comfort and protect them. These people are therefore referred to as the child's *attachment figures*. And with the formation of clear-cut attachments, young children become increasingly wary of unfamiliar adults and strangers.

By 12 months of age, attachment figures have become the centre of children's lives. Children can have more than one attachment figure. The possibility of multiple attachments echoes our hunter–gatherer, small group origins in which children would be looked after not just by their parents, but by the whole extended family. Hrdy (2005) calls this 'cooperative breeding'. Even in modern settings, those who regularly help protect and regulate children are destined to become attachment figures. Mothers, fathers, grandparents, and perhaps key day carers are most likely to earn this status. And although at times of need children can use their attachment figures quite flexibly, there tends to be an overall hierarchy, with mothers in most cases likely to be the principal, *primary* or *selective attachment figure*. So, for example, while a toddler might show little distress when his grandmother leaves, this would not be the case if he were to suffer a major separation from his mother in her role as principal attachment figure. This point is powerfully made by Bowlby when he considers the case of 4-year-old Wendy who is mourning the loss of her mother:

> [A]bout four weeks after mother had died, Wendy complained that no one loved her. In an attempt to reassure her, father names a long list of people who did (naming those who cared for her). On this Wendy commented aptly, 'But when my mommy wasn't dead I didn't need so many people – I needed only one.'
>
> (Bowlby 1998b: 280)

A number of other points need to be clarified. The strength of a child's attachment behaviour in a given circumstance does not indicate the 'strength' of the attachment bond. Some insecure children will routinely display very pronounced attachment behaviours, while many secure children find that there is no great need to engage in either intense or frequent shows of attachment behaviour. Children can also show attachment behaviour in the absence of their attachment figure. For example, a toddler frightened by a large animal is likely to run to and cling (attachment behaviours) to the nearest adult, whether or not he has an attachment bond with that person. Summarizing matters, Bowlby writes:

> To say of a child that he is attached to, or has an attachment to, someone means that he is strongly disposed to seek proximity to and contact with a specific figure and to do so in certain situations, notably when he is frightened, tired or ill. The disposition to behave in this way is an attribute of the child … Attachment behaviour, by contrast, refers to any of the various forms of behaviour that a child commonly engages in to attain and/or maintain a desired proximity.
>
> (Bowlby 1997: 371)

The parent as attachment figure develops affectional ties with the child in what we have learned to call a *caregiving bond*. It is worth reminding ourselves that as well as attachment and caregiving bonds, there are a variety of other affectional bonds that we can have with others – sibling bonds, friendship bonds, sexual pair bonds. Technically speaking, therefore, the term attachment is restricted to behaviour shown by the vulnerable towards the strong and protective, whether in childhood or adulthood. So, for example, parents, in this technical sense, are not attached to their children; rather they have a caregiving bond with their infants.

> Adopting this convention both parties can be said to be bonded. Attachment is then limited to behaviour normally directed towards someone conceived as better able to cope with the current situation; whilst caregiving specifies the complementary behaviour directed towards someone conceived as less able to do so.
>
> (Ibid.: 377)

In the case of young children, they will be attached to, and show attachment behaviour towards their parent as caregiver. In the case of adult couples, each partner can display attachment behaviours *and* offer caregiving responses depending who, in any particular circumstance, needs the other's care and protection, support and understanding.

Protest, despair and detachment

If attachment behaviours fail to achieve their set goal, the attachment system, along with the arousal and distress that go with it, remains activated. For example, a mother or father might be temporarily unavailable – she's in the bathroom, he's changing new baby brother's nappy, she's feeling ill.

More seriously, the loss and separation of an attachment figure can sometimes be prolonged or even permanent. Parents go into hospital, divorce, get depressed, or die. From the child's point of view, each of these major separations and losses is experienced as the breaking of an affectional bond. In these situations, there is significant protest and distress shown during the initial phase of the separation or loss, followed by intense clinging in those cases in which the attachment figure returns (Robertson 1953).

Bowlby (1997) observed that after seven months or more, babies begin to show a distinct sequence of behaviours whenever they experience prolonged separation or loss of a primary attachment figure. Bowlby felt that 'loss of maternal care at this highly dependent, highly vulnerable stage of development' was extremely significant (ibid.: xiii). Of course, the presence of other familiar people and objects can mitigate the intensity of the separation distress. But in the absence of such comforts, the baby's initial reaction when he or she finds himself or herself in a strange place without the support of familiar people or unable to recover proximity with the primary caregiver, is one of *protest* – loud crying, anger and attempts to follow or find the attachment figure. Angry crying and active searching for the caregiver make sense as the child attempts to recover the lost parent. Anger of course, can assist in overcoming obstacles that might get in the way of recovering proximity with the caregiver, and it can also discourage the 'loved person from going away again' (Bowlby 1998a: 286). 'So long as anger continues, it seems, loss is not being accepted as permanent and hope is still lingering on' (Bowlby 1998b: 91).

If the loss or separation is prolonged, babies enter a phase of *despair*. Their preoccupation with the attachment figure continues and they are vigilant for her return, but they begin to lose faith (Robertson 1953). This is a time of grief and mourning, characteristic of major loss at any stage during the lifecourse. There is increasing apathy and withdrawal. There is a loss of appetite. Sleep patterns are disturbed. In evolutionary terms, this second stage is also adaptive. If there is no attachment figure, and if predators are not to be attracted and energy is to be saved, then being quiet and inactive is the best thing to do.

However, continuation of the loss eventually leads to a defensive stage of apparent *detachment*. If the period of separation is not too long, upon return of the mother, children begin to recover their attachment. Nevertheless, observes Bowlby (1998a: 47), 'thenceforward, for days or weeks, and sometimes much longer' children will insist on staying close to their mother, showing acute anxiety if there is any suspicion that she may disappear again. He reports the response of a miner's wife when she was asked if her daughter ever wanted a cuddle:

> Ever since I left her that time I had to go into hospital (two periods, 17 days each, child aged 2 years), she doesn't trust me any more. I can't go anywhere – over to the neighbours or in the shops – I've always got to take her. She wouldn't leave me. She went down to the school gates at dinner time today. She ran like mad home. She said, 'Oh, Mum, I thought you was gone!' She can't forget it. She's still around me all the time.
>
> (Ibid.: 248)

We shall be looking at some of the effects of lost, broken and disturbed affectional bonds in later chapters. We might also note that as anger with the attachment figure is one of the stronger feelings expressed whenever issues of separation, loss, rejection or abandonment are present, it is worth emphasizing that in cases where such experiences are all too frequent, feelings of anger, aggression and anxiety are likely to continue troubling relationships throughout childhood and into adulthood. For example, some of the most aggressive and angry behaviours, particularly towards parents, can be shown by adolescents who have suffered abandonment and the repeated threat of abandonment by caregivers who might talk of walking out on the family, sending the child away, or committing suicide (ibid.: 289).

Caregiving

Attachment behaviours are telling the parent that something does not feel quite right for the baby or toddler. Attachment behaviours, certainly before children acquire language and can discuss their concerns, are a form of communication. Babies cry for a reason, not just for the sake of it. They certainly don't cry deliberately to annoy parents, as stressed and abusive mothers or fathers sometimes claim.

Faced with a distressed or crying baby, a sensitive, protective parent will try to work out what is the matter. This, of course, is often easier said than done. It's not always obvious, particularly with very young babies, what is wrong. Is it hunger (but I've only just fed you)? Does your nappy need changing, again? Are you too hot? Are you feeling unwell? The parent might also feel tired and sleep-deprived after weeks of waking up several times each night to feed the newborn. Nevertheless, although not always at their best or most responsive, in principle, the majority of mothers and fathers are committed to their child's health and well-being. At some level, babies sense this love, warmth and interest, and their parents' protective instincts.

George (1996) calls this reciprocal response of mothers and fathers to the infant's attachment system the *caregiving system*, a biological urge to care for, comfort, and keep safe one's young. Protecting children and ensuring their survival increases the parent's reproductive fitness, that is, makes it more likely your genes will continue into the next generation. Mirroring and complementing the child's attachment system, the caregiving system is organized around the goal of protecting, regulating and responding to the child, just as the child's attachment system is organized around being protected, regulated and responded to. It is the regular and repeated responses of a reasonably sensitive, consistent and available caregiver that *reinforce* infant attachment behaviours as the kinds of behaviour to display when you feel in danger and seek safety, comfort and emotional regulation.

Being fundamentally to do with children's safety and protection, Cassidy (2008: 10), following Bowlby, argues that the chief behaviours of the caregiving system are therefore retrieval, reaching, calling, grasping, restraining, following, smiling, soothing, and rocking. The sensitive parent anticipates and so prevents their child getting into danger, thereby forestalling activation of the child's attachment system. She also rescues and protects the child when he or she has got into danger. When the child is safe, the parent's caregiving system terminates, and other parental behavioural systems – such as play, tuition, work, socializing with other adults – can resume.

Play and exploration

It is equally important to remind ourselves that when children's attachment systems are ticking quietly away on 'background mode' simply monitoring the environment for danger and threat, their energies and behaviours can be freed up to pursue the full range of developmental opportunities that they are programmed to follow. When children feel relaxed and secure, they can enjoy the pleasures and benefits of play, social interaction, discovering new things, learning, being busy and creative, and simply following their curiosity. They explore their environment. However, whenever danger threatens, uncertainty arises, anxiety is felt, or distress is experienced, the attachment system kicks back in. Play and exploration immediately stop. In fact, because fear and survival are so basic, activation of the attachment system generally means that other important behavioural systems – exploratory, affiliative, sociable, and in the case of adults, sexual – are deactivated. When in a state of anxiety or fear, we are unlikely to feel playful, chatty, or sexy.

The attachment system and *exploratory system* might therefore be seen as complementary, though mutually inhibiting. For most children, the attachment system is acutely activated many times a day, but with sensitive and responsive parenting, these episodes last for relatively brief periods. This leaves the majority of time for play and social interaction. So although attachment keeps you safe and ensures survival, in its own way, so does exploration. Play and exploration help children learn about and adapt to their physical and psychosocial environment. They promote social skills, self-reliance, and general competence. In these ways, children acquire the skills and knowledge that will help them survive at a practical level. As children mature, they spend more and more time in play with a corresponding reduction in the frequency of displays of attachment behaviour (Bowlby 1997: 197). We might note, however, that for children who suffer chronic activations of their attachment system – children who are neglected or abused or rejected – activation of their exploratory system is inevitably compromised. Their energy and attention are spent on survival, and there is less time for play, fun and relationships. Repeated suppression of exploratory and social behaviours is therefore bad for children's emotional, social and cognitive development.

A similar complementary relationship exists between the attachment figure's caregiving system and the child's attachment system. From the child's point of view, when his parent's caregiving system is activated, his attachment system can be deactivated. Responsibility for providing proximity, protection and the monitoring of danger is being provided by the caregiver. This allows children to explore without worry. This is why, in the presence of their caregivers, children are at their most relaxed and playful.

When early childhood is reviewed overall, we see that attachment behaviour is most readily activated between the ages of six months and five years. This makes sense as this is the time of greatest vulnerability and highest dependence.

Safe havens and secure bases

Pulling these various threads together, Bowlby and Ainsworth saw the attachment figure as both a *safe haven* and a *secure base*. Whenever children run into difficulty, they know that there is a safe haven to which to return for comfort and protection. And knowing that if things do go wrong there is that safe haven, children can also use the attachment figure as a secure base from which to explore (Ainsworth *et al.* 1978; Ainsworth and Wittig 1969; Belsky and Cassidy 1994: 375). The more confident and secure children feel in the availability of a responsive attachment figure to be there at times of need, the more independent and playful they can be. Caregivers who provide a secure base allow their children to be autonomous, curious and experimental. Secure children cope well with being alone. They are keen to try out new skills without always feeling the need to ask for help. However, if they do get into difficulty, they are happy to seek advice and support.

Children and adults who lack a secure base feel much more anxious about engaging with the world on their own. Uncertainty about whether or not your attachment figure will be available and responsive at times of need leads to feelings of insecurity. Individuals who don't feel they have a secure relationship base lack confidence. This has profound developmental consequences. Children and adults who lack a secure base find that their attachment needs keep over-riding their attempts to be independent, playful, and work-minded. Their social interactions are more fussy and agitated. Confidence is easily sapped and attempts to go it alone are quickly undermined.

Conclusion

Whenever young human infants feel anxious, in danger or need, their attachment systems are activated. This triggers attachment behaviour, the goal of which is to recover proximity to the caregiver where safety and comfort lie. This basic definition of attachment behaviour is wonderfully simple. It is in its implications and elaboration that the full richness of the concept unfolds. So far in this introduction to attachment and its functions, we have simply emphasized the instinctual, programmed nature of the behaviour and the bonds children have with their primary caregivers. In evolutionary terms, this makes sense. To leave the development of an attachment relationship and its protective functions to the caprices of individual learning, said Bowlby (1988: 5), 'would be the height of biological folly'. There simply is not enough time for human infants to learn these complex survival behaviours. They need them to be up and running from birth. But attachment behaviours are also accompanied by strong feelings. We now need to look at how caregivers respond to, and deal with the emotions that get aroused whenever attachment systems are activated.

2
Emotions and their Regulation

Born to be sociable

We noted at the beginning of this book that human beings are a very social, indeed sociable, species. We spend a great deal of our time in the company of others. Evolutionary ethnology teaches us that being a member of the group offers protection. The social group promotes survival, supplies resources (food, shelter, warmth), transmits knowledge, and provides opportunities (sexual partners, new skills). Becoming socially competent is therefore a key skill for survival, sexual reproduction, and mental health. But in order to be socially skilled, we also need to be psychologically smart. One of the defining characteristics of our species is the desire to make sense of both ourselves and other people, particularly at the psychological level. Whereas most other species respond only to behaviour, we also respond to minds and their intentions. Psychological sense-making allows us to communicate, interpret and collaborate so that we can 'work, love and play' (Fonagy *et al.* 2002: 6). We are rarely content simply observing behaviour. We want to know what triggered it and to answer this question, we need to be psychologically curious. This is the stuff of gossip, shared puzzlement, offender profiling, novels, and the answers that agony aunts and uncles give in their advice columns:

At the end of another difficult team meeting Mel and Royce looked at each other and sighed. Once again the office administrator had threatened to leave saying that no one, except the departmental head, valued what she did. The changes she wanted to make in the way the office was organized had taken up a vast amount of her time, including working at weekends, and she was upset that she was getting so much resistance from the practitioners. Not for the first time, she broke down in tears, obliging other people to offer her support, sympathy and a willingness to temper some of their misgivings about the proposed changes. 'She always does this,' said Royce. 'I feel emotionally manipulated every time. Why does she do it?' 'You're a man and you don't see the half of it,' said Mel. 'She flirts with you and Eli but slags us girls off behind our backs, I know she does. It's always all or nothing with her. Hugs, kisses and best mates one moment, sulks, threats and rejection the next. It does my head in. I think she's insecure.'

This great interest in other people – their behaviour, thoughts, feelings, plans, hopes, beliefs – is also shown by babies. At a deep evolutionary level, being accepted, becoming part of the group, and enjoying close relationships generally represents safety and survival. It is in our relationship with others that most of our strongest feelings occur. To be near, to approach and be reunited with an attachment figure generates feelings of love, comfort and joy. Prolonged separation causes anxiety and heartache, and sometimes anger. The permanent loss of an attachment figure leads to grief, sadness and despair. It hurts to be rejected. It is excruciatingly shaming to be ridiculed.

Human infants, then, are born prosocial. Almost immediately after birth, they begin to show a preferential interest in the human face and voice, and over time this refines further into a specific interest in the primary caregiver's face, voice, touch, and smell. Tactile stimulation that helps soothe distress – stroking, massaging, kissing, holding hands – can be particularly important in cementing close relationships. More generally, though, babies find social stimulation the most fascinating. Indeed, from a very young age, babies are able to influence their social environment by responding positively to some stimuli and aversively to others:

> By noting how he responds to different stimuli … it is possible to obtain valuable information about an infant's preferences. Thus, some sounds make him cry whereas others quieten him; to some things seen he pays much more attention and to others far less. Some tastes elicit sucking and a happy expression, others aversive movements and a disgusted expression. By means of these differential responses, it is evident that a child exerts a not inconsiderable influence over the sensory input he receives, greatly increasing some sorts and reducing others to zero. Again and

again, it is found, these inbuilt biases favour the development of social interaction.

(Bowlby 1997: 269)

Babies also appear to have a biological need to feel understood (Fonagy *et al.* 1995). All of these predispositions mean that from the outset young children have a particular interest in social relationships and what might be going on in the minds of other people. The interest shown by babies in responding to the social and psychological environment is sometimes referred to as 'purposeful intersubjectivity' (Trevarthen and Aitkin 2001). As development continues, children become increasingly interested in mental states, both their own and other people's. They are born psychologists, always wanting to know the psychological whys and wherefores of other people's behaviour. Babies are therefore not passive in their relationships with carers. They are active, they interpret, they respond. They can make their needs known, their intentions clear. From a very early age, they seek to control themselves and their environment as much as possible.

Parents who recognize that even very young babies appear to have a sophisticated interest in other people are more likely to interact with their infants as if they had a complex mind, a mind worth knowing. They believe that the more they can make sense of their child, particularly psychological sense, and the more their child can make sense of them, then the easier it will be to meet needs and deal with upset and distress.

The co-regulation of affect

Let's return to the moment when the distressed child's attachment behaviour has achieved its set goal of re-connecting with the caregiver. Contact and closeness provide safety and protection. However, the thing that caused the distress might still be present. Hunger, the pain of the injured knee, the barking dog, the memory of the bad dream, any of these might leave the child still feeling anxious and agitated.

The next task of the sensitive and responsive caregiver is to do something about the upset. The young child needs to be soothed, and her arousal, both physiological and emotional, needs to be regulated.

We might note that emotions are experienced both physically (I feel hot and bothered, I'm shivering with fear) and subjectively (I feel anxious, I feel sad). They are also expressed physically – on our faces, in our body language. The term *affect* is often used to cover all three components of an emotional experience – our physical feelings, psychological feelings, and facial expressions. Many attachment theorists talk of *attachment as a theory of affect regulation* in the context of close relationships, with each of the various attachment patterns representing a behavioural strategy for managing stress under different caregiving regimes. It is at this point that attachment theory gets especially interesting.

The ways in which parents regulate their children's physical and emotional arousal, or deal with their joy and distress, have profound implications for children's neurological, physiological and psychosocial development. This is why the quality of the parent–child relationship in which all this regulation takes place matters. It is this aspect of attachment that ties up with many other branches of the developmental sciences including stress regulation, early brain development, the growth of social understanding, the emergence of personality differences, and the acquisition of emotional intelligence.

It's not possible for very young babies to regulate emotions on their own. They need a relationship with an adult, a primary caregiver if they are going to be helped to deal with arousal. And here again, we find that blind evolution has arranged things rather beautifully. In order to understand how children gradually learn to self-regulate, develop social cognition, and slowly become competent players in the world of people and relationships, we have to bring together a number of ideas from very different disciplines. The attachment relationship provides a useful vehicle in which to explore these interests.

When parents try to deal with their child's pains and pleasures, they typically engage all of the child's senses. Babies are soothed by touch, cuddles, rocking, a calm voice, an attentive face, the familiar taste and smell of a mother's skin. Sensitive parents also tune into their infants' emotional states in ways that help children make sense of, and manage their own feelings. Sensitive parenting is therefore harmonious parenting. Babies' signals are recognized and read, responses are in tune with infant rhythms, and an environment is created in which young children derive a sense of the consequences of their own behaviour (Ainsworth and Wittig 1969; Bowlby 1997: 346).

Babies, too, are active in this relationship. Their behaviours indicate their needs and condition. They are aware of, and responsive to the caregiver's behaviour, voice, face, look, feelings, and body language. They can turn their heads, look away, and shift their bodies if the carer distresses them. They can monitor and track a parent whose behaviour might be experienced as unpredictable. Or they can make eye contact, smile and show excitement if the interaction feels good. A full understanding of attachment therefore requires recognition that interaction between caregivers and babies is two-way. Parent and child respond to each other on the basis that each can predict the other's behaviour, as well as his or her own behaviour during the interaction (Beebe *et al.*2010).

Children who are helped to regulate their arousal in the context of a sensitive and responsive caregiving relationship gradually learn to regulate themselves physiologically, emotionally, cognitively (Perry and Szalavitz 2006). They can think about and reflect on feeling. As a result, they become less reactive, less impulsive, more reflective, more thoughtful. Co-regulation appears to lie at the heart of attachment, the ability to self-regulate, and the gradual growth of social cognition, empathy and interpersonal skill.

There is a growing body of research on the *psychobiology* of attachment, both in childhood and adulthood (Diamond and Fagundes 2010). It explores how mind states and the neurological systems or brain structures that underpin them can affect the body, and vice versa. For example, sensitive care and soothing responses 'down-regulate' the baby's biological stress systems, including the important Hypothalamus–Pituitary–Adrenaline (HPA) axis involved in production of the stress hormone, cortisol. Well-regulated, securely attached children tend to have less reactive stress systems. Their daily production of cortisol follows the normal pattern of high in the morning followed by a gradual decrease throughout the rest of the day. The picture is not so good for children who have suffered abuse, neglect and trauma in their early years, children whose feelings and physiologies have been poorly regulated. They have abnormal patterns of cortisol release, with peaks and troughs occurring erratically throughout the day. Their nervous systems become hypersensitive. They are easily aroused and dysregulated even by low doses of stress. In considering the HPA axis, we see how brain and body, psyche and soma, are linked.

Equally important in terms of children's early emotional development is the caregiver's recognition and enhancement of the infant's positive emotional states. The joy of play, the deep bliss and contentment of shared eye gaze, the fun of singing songs together, the pleasure experienced by both parent and child when a new skill is learned give powerful boosts to the security of the infant's attachment. The positive emotions also help the brain deal with stress, and lay down rich neurological structures that enhance children's ability to think about feeling and regulate affect (Schore 2001).

In her discussion of Schore's work, Sable (2007) also suggests that the positive, joyful elements of early parent–child interactions promote security, increase resilience and allow children and adults to sustain good quality social relationships across the lifecourse.

> [These] early stable and positive affective experiences are built into the nervous system through the reciprocal interactions between caregiver and baby, typically with the release of endogenous opioids such as the endorphins which are responsible for feelings of safety, pleasure, and well-being. These opiates shape memory networks that will be invoked to deal with subsequent stress, and they also regulate attachment. Therefore, bonds that impart positive affect are crucial to ongoing neurological development.
>
> (Ibid.: 364)

Attachment theorists are as keen to accentuate the importance of parents promoting the positive emotions as they are to emphasize the need of good enough caregivers to regulate the negative.

The social brain

Parents who support children, via a secure attachment, in the management of the emotions also effect changes in the young child's brain organization, particularly in the area of the brain above the eyes known as the pre-frontal cortex. Modern research tells us that 'variations in the quality of maternal caregiving shape the neurological systems that regulate stress reactions' (Fox and Hane 2008: 229). In fact, according to Coan (2008), these broad links between caregiving and brain development add up to a new field of enquiry: *attachment neuroscience* (also see Schore 1999, 2003). Early close relationships have the power to sculpt the brain and develop our very sense of a psychological self. The more young children are thought about, treated and enjoyed as independent, complex psychological beings, the more they become independent, complex psychological beings.

The infant brain is programmed to make sense of experience but it needs exposure to experience before it can make sense of it. This means that over time the brain learns to understand the particular world in which it happens to find itself. Brains feed on experience. The brain can also be understood as a self-organizing development system. It organizes itself at the neurological level as it processes and seeks to make sense of experience. Experiential learning in this context can mean many things: acquiring language, learning to process visual stimuli in order to see, making sense of one's own and other people's emotions. As we interact with the world via our senses, the brain processes the incoming information, laying down more and more connections and building up vast, intricate neuronal networks dedicated to making sense of speech, seeing colour, interpreting facial expressions, understanding emotions, and so on. In these various ways, the brain becomes exquisitely organized, attuned and shaped to make sense of the very world in which it finds itself, and of which it needs to make sense.

We have already noted that babies are socially oriented. The same delicious developmental logic that helps the brain learn to see or acquire language also applies to making sense of psychological, emotional, and social experience. The more the child is exposed to these psychosocial experiences, the more he or she is able to make sense of them. Children need to make sense of themselves and others as complex psychosocial and intentional beings if they are to become socially skilled and emotionally literate. Children who fail to develop good quality psychosocial skills and the ability to self-regulate risk serious setbacks in their social development, behavioural competence and mental health.

The development of the psychological self

Secure caregivers are therefore those parents who are willing and able to interact with their young children as psychological partners. They relate with their infant as if the child had a mind and what goes on in that mind is worth knowing (Fonagy 2006). They also explain their own state of mind (thoughts, feelings, goals, plans, expectations) to their children as they discuss how the world of people, relationships and social behaviour works. 'Good enough' parents are happy to explain what is going on to young children in terms of their own and other people's psychological states, how feelings affect behaviour, and how someone else's behaviour affects other people's feelings. In short, good enough parents train their children to be psychologists. They help them become astute observers and interpreters of the social scene.

The self is therefore forged as the young brain purposefully engages with other minds where it begins to experience itself as a burgeoning, independent psychological entity. The 'development of the self,' say Fonagy *et al.* (2002: 40), 'is tantamount to the aggregation of experiences of the self in relationships.' The parent's capacity to observe the child's mind seems to facilitate the child's general understanding of minds, and so children find their minds in the minds of others who have them in mind (ibid.).

Thus, parents who value the emergence of mental states in their children act as a kind of mirror to the child, reflecting back the infant's internal world (Fonagy and Target 1997). This mirroring is particularly important when parents interact with their babies at the level of the emotions. In a process referred to as 'affect mirroring', Fonagy *et al.* (2002; also see Winnicott 1967) describe how carers typically mimic the emotion that they believe their child to be currently experiencing. A mother, her facial expression being one of joy and surprise, might say to her excited baby 'Who is this come to see you? Is it grandma? Is that why you're excited? You didn't know she was coming to see you, did you? That's a nice surprise, isn't it?' From the baby's point of view, this is a kind of 'psychofeedback' in which 'my carer shows me my feelings', my mind (Gerhardt 2004: 25).

The carer's exaggerated facial expressions and tone of voice give back to the child an idea of what he or she is feeling. Mirroring takes the infant's aroused condition and organizes it for him. It is the kind of sympathetic mirrored look that most of us adopt when we are acknowledging a friend's sadness or pleasure. In these ways, children begin to develop an understanding of their own emotional make-up and how they work at the level of feeling. They learn about their inner world. Parents who are not interested in their infant's mental states and fail to mirror their baby's affect, impair the child's psychosocial development. In these suboptimal caregiving relationships, it is more difficult for children to develop a coherent sense of their own and other people's psychological selves.

Mind-mindedness and mentalization

Elaborating these ideas on what kind of parenting helps children develop a coherent sense of self, good social understanding, and emotional intelligence, Meins (1997, 1999), in a series of studies, found that caregivers who are interested in what their children are thinking and feeling, and seek to share this understanding with their children, show what she calls *mind-mindedness*. When asked to describe their children, they focus on their children's mental attributes rather than just their physical and behavioural characteristics. Mind-minded parents are good at translating psychological experiences into an active, coherent dialogue with their children. They help children attend to their inner thoughts and feelings and how these affect mind and body. Children are helped to understand that they have an inner experience that is unique to them and different to those of other people. Such mind-related interactions facilitate emotional understanding and regulation. Thus, parents who focus on their children's subjective experiences help them understand their own and other people's psychological states, and how these are linked to actions and behaviour.

Children who have mind-minded parents typically have a secure attachment. In contrast, babies and toddlers of carers who are insensitive and incurious about their children's minds, thoughts and feelings – who lack mind-mindedness – do them a profound developmental disservice. As we shall see, children in these relationships are more likely to be insecurely attached.

The concept of *mentalization* is similar to mind-mindedness but it takes matters of psychological awareness even further (Fonagy *et al.* 2002). It is also a development of the idea that mentally healthy individuals have 'meta-cognition', that is, they are good at 'thinking about thinking'.

Mentalization is the capacity to understand how one's own and other people's mental states affect behaviour. It is a form of social cognition. It involves the capacity to 'think about feeling and to feel about thinking' (Mary Target, in a personal communication to Slade, cited in Slade 2005: 271). The ability to mentalize is therefore the ability to 'hold mind in mind' (Allen 2006). It also involves an appreciation of how my behaviour affects your thoughts and feelings, and how your behaviour affects my thoughts and feelings. I also recognize that as I am 'mentalizing' our interaction and modifying my behaviour accordingly, you are probably doing exactly the same. We are both the authors of our actions. Human beings are 'intentional beings' and so we understand each other to the extent that we see intentional, purposeful mental states behind our own and other people's actions and behaviours. In this sense, mentalization is more 'two-way' and dynamic than mind-mindedness. The mind-minded individual recognizes, acknowledges and responds to the other's interior mental experience. The individual who mentalizes and has high *reflective function* has the ability not only to think about their own and the other's mind but also how each is affecting and being read by the other, cognitively, emotionally and behaviourally.

Parents who recognize that their children have an interior world of thought and feeling that underpins their behaviour, and parents who engage with their children on this basis tend to have children who also develop the capacity to mentalize. 'Secure attachment history of the mother permits and enhances her capacity to explore her own mind and liberates and promotes a similar enquiring stance toward the mental state of the new human being who has just joined her social world' (Fonagy and Target 2005: 337). The parents of secure children therefore show good 'reflective functioning' (Grienenberger *et al.*2005). Having been held safely in mind by their parents, secure children feel that both their own and their parents' minds are known, knowable and safe. This safe experience is the basis of future intimacy and relationship competence. Children begin to see themselves and others as meaningful, understandable and more predictable.

Conclusion

Babies show great interest in the behaviour and intentions of other people. They are born to be sociable. In their relationships with other people, particularly their attachment figures, they learn to recognize and regulate their own, and in time, other people's feelings and arousal. The ability to make sense of yourself and other people as complex psychological beings, regulate your emotions, and relate with sensitivity and skill are major protective factors. Good mentalization, in parents and children, correlates with secure attachments, a coherent sense of self, successful relationships, resilience, and good mental health. With thoughts of this kind in mind, Bowlby (1998b: 442) concludes the third book of his groundbreaking trilogy with this rally:

> Intimate attachments to other human beings are the hub around which a person's life revolves, not only when he is an infant or a toddler or a schoolchild but throughout his adolescence and his years of maturity as well, and on into old age. From these intimate attachments a person draws his strength and enjoyment of life and, through what he contributes, he gives strength and enjoyment to others. These are matters about which current science and traditional wisdom are at one.

3

The Internal Working Model

Learning through experience and by association

So far the emphasis has been on attachment *behaviour* and the regulation of the *emotions* in attachment theory. This is right and proper because from an evolutionary point of view, the survival advantages conferred by attachment behaviour and affect regulation are fundamentally important. But children grow, mature and accumulate more and more experience of the world. They learn how it treats them and the part they play in it. As the brain develops, it seeks to make sense of these experiences. It finds patterns. It sees cause and apparent effect. It sees links between one behaviour and another. The world, and our passage through it, is not entirely arbitrary. Children begin to realize that, to an extent, the environment, particularly the social environment, is predictable. 'When I do this, she does that.' 'When he behaves in that way, I respond in this manner.' 'When she does that, it makes me feel this.' This early ability to make sense of the world at a more conscious, reflective level represents the beginning of *cognitive* understanding. And with cognition comes the possibility of intention, choice, and options.

Thus, if infants are to rise above a basic stimulus and response relationship with their environment, they need to develop ways of thinking about and representing the world around them. Having described what he understood by attachment behaviour and the regulation of emotion, Bowlby (1969) then went on to consider the cognitive implications of his theory.

Internal working models and mental representations

One of the key propositions of attachment theory is that experiences in earlier relationships influence how people behave in later relationships. This is achieved by the construction of mental models of how the world has worked in the past, and might work in the future. In any current situation, we receive information through our senses but give it meaning on the basis of what we have experienced, thought and felt in the past. The meaning we give the experience then influences what we do, say, think and feel.

Inspired by the work of Young (1964) and Craik (1943), Bowlby developed a key concept to explore this proposition: *the internal working model*. The basic thesis was that our brains construct cognitive models of our environment, including the world of other people. Brains do this in order to make sense of their world, to anticipate it, manage it, and negotiate it. Information coming in via our senses helps construct these models, or 'internal simulations'. New information also gets interpreted by existing models, and, if sufficiently discordant, helps modify the models. Sroufe *et al.* (1999: 5) believe the concept of the internal working model to be a profound idea. 'It means that children approach new situations with certain preconceptions, behavioural biases, and interpretive tendencies.'

For young children, attachment figures are a particularly important bit of their environment of which to make sense. Repeated experiences of interacting with attachment figures allow infants gradually to develop *mental representations* (that is, internal working models) of their own worthiness based on other people's availability, and their ability and willingness to provide care and protection (Ainsworth *et al.* 1978). In order to improve social competence and increase other people's availability, it is useful to be able to generate mental representations of the following three things:

The self.
Other people.
The relationship between self and others.

Young children begin to learn about the self and others as they relate with parents and family. The quality of these close relationships has a profound bearing on how the self, others and social interaction are viewed and understood, not just in childhood but also into adulthood. Indeed, the 'adult personality is seen as a product of an individual's interactions with key figures during all his years of immaturity, especially his interactions with attachment figures' (Bowlby 1998a: 242). In fact, one of Bowlby's original aims was 'to describe certain patterns of response that occur regularly in early childhood and, thence, to trace out how similar patterns of response are to be discerned in the later functioning of personality' (Bowlby 1998b). So for example, if an individual has enjoyed reliable, responsive caregiving, he or she is likely to approach the world with confidence and trust. In contrast, if the individual's experience of key relationships has been one of hurt and indifference, the world will be viewed as unpredictable, unreliable, not to be trusted, one in which there is little safety or comfort. In this sense, early attachment experiences help explain personality development and personality differences. The important thing to note is that different attachment strategies and the internal working models they sponsor are the product of actual, lived experiences, particularly those involving relationships with parents and other close family members.

Cognitive models of the environment influence what we remember, feel and see as we interact with the world. They contain the memories, thoughts and feelings associated with past relationships. It is these memories, thoughts and feelings and any defensive behaviours associated with them that are evoked in current relationships, particularly those that seem as if they have the same character and 'feel' of key, early attachment relationships. Internal working models therefore act as a cognitive bias when attachment-related situations are experienced and appraised. Based on learning from past experiences with, and expectations of the caregiver, these models promote more efficient behaviour when we have to deal with our current environment.

Bowlby (1969) emphasized that in order for behaviour to be varied, adaptive and appropriate and yet remain organized towards the achievement of the attachment system's set goal (proximity seeking and felt security) it must be guided at the level of these mental representations. That is, the child must have ideas and expectations about how the self is being viewed and understood by the attachment figure, and what is the likely interest and responsivity of the attachment figure at times of distress and anxiety.

Internal working models also tap into an overall state of mind. They harbour memories of past relationships, how they worked, what to expect, and the language that was used to evoke and define them. These organized mental representations of the self and others (as either positive or negative) are carried forward by individuals into later childhood and beyond into the adult years. They are used to guide our behaviour in subsequent relationships. The internal work-ing models formed with the most regular, familiar and important attachment figures (primary caregiver in childhood, romantic part-ner in adulthood) tend to be the ones that guide expectations and behaviour in most other relationships. Not surprisingly, primary attachment figures have been found to have the biggest influence on internal working models and attachment patterns (e.g. van IJzendoorn and Bakermans-Kranenburg 1996). The role of mothers tends to be critical, but actively involved fathers also appear to have long-term effects, for example, on children's positive feelings about their selves, and their competence with peers.

Key attachment figures, therefore, influence core personality char-acteristics. Quite how this is achieved is still not entirely understood. For example, if a child is looked after by two or more people and develops different attachment strategies with each, it is not clear how the different internal working models formed in each relationship become integrated into one prevailing set of mental representations (Cassidy 2008: 16). Suffice it to say, optimal development seems most assured if you have two secure, responsive parents, and least likely if relationships with both your primary caregivers are insecure (van IJzendoorn and Sagi-Schwartz 2008).

Drafts and revisions, beliefs and expectations

However, internal working models are also provisional. If an attach-ment figure persistently behaves and reacts in ways that do not match expectations, the internal working model has to be revised. 'Working' in this sense means that mental models are always draft, revisable representations of self, others and relationships. So, although inter-nal working models tend to be relatively stable over time, Bowlby called them 'working' models because they do remain open to change and correction at any time during the lifecourse, particularly in the context of close relationships.

Internal working models therefore contain *expectations* and *beliefs* about (1) one's own and other people's behaviour; (2) the lovability, worthiness and acceptability of the self; and (3) the emotional avail-ability and interest of others, and their ability to provide protection. Internal working models orchestrate and guide what we do, think and feel in close relationships:

For example, present cognitive and behavioural structures determine what is perceived and what ignored, how a new situation is construed, and what plan of action is likely to be constructed to deal with it. Current structures, moreover, determine what sorts of person or situation are sought after and what sorts are shunned. In this way, the individual comes to influence the selection of his own environment; and so the wheel comes full circle.

(Bowlby 1998a: 417)

Armed with these mental models of how others are likely to behave and how the self is likely to feel, individuals begin to *organize* their attachment behaviour at times of need in order to increase the availability, proximity and responsivity of carers in the case of children, and partners in the case of adults.

There is a tendency for internal working models to become self-fulfilling and self-confirming as others react to our expectations of how we think they will behave. This is one of the ways in which working models influence the way other people perceive and react to us. To an extent, new relationships are created and re-created in the light of previous relationship experiences that have helped build the current internal working model. Initially at least, new partners are treated in the same way and with the same assumptions as old attachment partners were treated (Brumbaugh and Fraley 2006). It would be difficult to approach each new encounter totally afresh. So, internal working models prefer to organize experience rather than be organized by it. In this sense, mental modelling produces continuity in the way we behave, relate, feel and respond. Our personality begins to acquire a regular, enduring quality. We begin to expect certain things of ourselves and of others, while others feel that we are becoming more familiar and predictable to them. For example, in the case of children, parents soon begin to know their child's 'ways'. And then it's only a matter of time before children, not necessarily consciously, begin to know how their parents will react to their needs, feelings and behaviour. For the child, the social world therefore begins to take shape. It is no longer experienced as random: 'Such dynamics allow working models to shape the kinds of interactions the person experiences and, in concert, help to maintain the individual on the pathway that is already being travelled' (Fraley and Brumbaugh 2004: 91).

At least in the case of secure attachments, internal working models give us more behavioural options in challenging social situations. Working models also employ rules that govern how emotions, attitudes and behaviours might be used to increase feelings of safety and regulate emotional distress. Based on the expectations and understandings built into the internal working model, individuals develop behavioural strategies to ensure that their various needs are optimally met. 'The functions of these models,' said Bowlby (1973: 203) 'is to simulate happenings in the real world, thereby enabling the individual to plan behaviour with all the advantages of insight and foresight.'

In contrast to the regular, warm and predictable parenting and partnering enjoyed by secure individuals, parents and partners who are insensitive, rejecting, interfering, or emotionally unavailable present their children and partners with a psychological problem. Individuals whose attachment systems have been activated enter the relationship in a state of high arousal. But they discover that there is no immediate or appropriate response from their attachment figure (whether parent or partner) which helps them recover emotional equilibrium. Psychologically, therefore, individuals in these 'sub-optimal' caregiving relationships need to develop behavioural strategies that get them into proximity and psychological engagement with their under-responsive and otherwise unavailable attachment figure. Proximity, after all, is the goal of attachment behaviour, no matter what kind of caregiving the individual experiences.

Attachment behavioural strategies

Thinking about childhood in particular, depending on the character of the parent's caregiving behaviour, the behavioural strategy developed over time will be different for each child. In effect, once an attachment has been formed, the different caregiving environments demand different attachment strategies, each based on 'the generation of rules for *if, when, where*, and *how much* attachment behaviour should be exhibited with relation to a specific attachment figure' (Main *et al.* 2005: 257, emphasis original). Each adaptive response therefore reflects the quality of the attachment relationship.

This results in the recognition of a number of distinct attachment behavioural patterns, each shaped by the particular character of the caregiving responses of the attachment figure (Ainsworth *et al.* 1978). Each pattern is associated with a particular type of internal working model whose characteristics have formed defensively in response to the attachment figure's caregiving behaviour which may be sensitive or insensitive, accepting or rejecting, available or unavailable, co-operative or intrusive, predictable or uncertain. If the caregiving remains consistent over time, whether it's sensitive or not, the internal working model generated by the child in that caregiving relationship is also likely to remain relatively unchanged even through into adulthood. These different patterns and their associated internal working models will be described in more detail in the next chapter.

Goal-corrected partnerships

The internal working model also allows the possibility of more mature and flexible approaches to the conduct of relationships. After the age of about two or three years, attachments evolve into a *goal-corrected partnership*. The goal-corrected partnership is one in which parents and children 'learn when and how to compromise and rearrange their individual plans for the sake of the relationship' (Lieberman 1992: 562). Children gradually begin to recognize that attachment figures have their own needs, views, plans and intentions which have to be taken into account if the relationship, and its availability, are to run smoothly. If the needs of each partner are to be met, both parent and child will have to negotiate, compromise, empathize and understand:

> In addition, the child now begins to rely more on mental representations of attachment than the actual presence of the attachment figure ... the goal-corrected partnership that emerges during the preschool years sets the stage for attachment across the life span. As the child grows towards adolescence and adulthood, internal working models of attachment are expected to reflect an increasing understanding of the parent's own motivations, feelings, plans, and developmental goals resulting in a relationship of mutual trust and understanding.
>
> (George 1996: 413)

Goal-corrected partnerships allow children to contemplate, negotiate, manage and tolerate the increasing number of separations that they begin to experience as they play with friends, stay with grandmother, or go to nursery. They also set up the potential for conflict:

> Once his attachment behaviour has become organized mainly on a goal-corrected basis, the relationship developing between a child and his mother becomes much more complex. Whilst true collaboration between the two then becomes possible, so also does intractable conflict ... Since each partner has his own personal set-goals to attain, collaboration between them is possible only so long as one is prepared, when necessary, to relinquish, or at least adjust his own set-goals to suit the other's.
>
> (Bowlby 1969: 354–5)

Conclusion

Relationship experiences in infancy and early childhood influence how people behave in later relationships. The construction of mental or internal working models of how the world has worked in the past helps us anticipate how it might work in the future. The meaning that we have given to past experiences then colours what we see, say, do, think and feel in our current relationships.

Depending on the quality and character of children's relationships with their attachment figures, the quality and character of their internal working models will vary. The internal working model of the self and others gives rise to different patterns of attachment behaviour with primary caregivers. Each attachment behavioural pattern represents an unconsciously played out strategy for survival in the context of the environment in which children find themselves (Belsky 2005). In relatively benign environments where food is plentiful and dangers few, the secure strategy makes most sense. Adults can be approached and trusted. Affectional bonds last. It is worth investing heavily in your own children as they are likely to survive. This in turn encourages having fewer children. When environments are harsher and attachment figures less reliable, other attachment behavioural strategies are likely to develop. So, although caregiving can range from poor to good, in practice, four basic patterns of attachment have been identified. Each is associated with a particular internal working model. The next chapter explores the behavioural logic underpinning each of these four attachment types.

4

Patterns of Attachment

Introduction

The idea of an internal working model provides a way of thinking about how the quality of external relationships gradually becomes part of the child's mental inside to form his or her psychological self. As attachment relationships become psychologically internalized, the quality of a child's social experiences becomes a mental property of that child. In turn, the mental inside influences the child's view of the self and others. The concept of the internal working model explains why close relationships matter, and how their qualities influence psychological experience, cognitive modelling, interpersonal behaviour and relationship styles.

One simple way of mapping the different types of mental representation and the expectations associated with them is to see whether the child's self in relationship to his or her attachment figure is experienced as one worthy of care or not, worthy of protection or not, lovable or not, likeable or not, valued or not, the subject of interest or not, socially effective or not, competent or not. In short, is the self experienced positively or negatively?

Caregivers will have their own attachment organizations and dispositional representations of self, others and relationships, including the relationships they have with their own children. This means that different caregivers will perceive, understand, process, interpret and respond differently to their children's needs, signals and attachment behaviours. Children will therefore experience their attachment figure as loving or not, sensitive or not, emotionally available or not, responsive or not, interested or not, attuned or not, rejecting or not, hostile or not, intrusive or not. In short, other people will be viewed either positively or negatively.

These different perceptions and expectations of the self and others suggest that children's attachments might vary depending on the type of caregiving environment in which they find themselves.

Defensive strategies, adaptive strategies and internal working models

It must be emphasized that the perceptions and behaviours that each internal working model sponsors, at least for the organized infant patterns, are *adaptive responses*. Babies need to adapt to the behaviours of their mother, father and other attachment figures. We have to look at infants' attachment behaviours and strategies, says Crittenden (2008: 16), as their best attempts to 'thrive and survive' in the context of their particular family. The attachment behaviours make sense in terms of how children can best maintain some kind of proximity to their care-givers at times of need, no matter how unpredictable or insensitive or cold the parenting. The pattern of attachment behaviours developed by a child represents a particular *defensive strategy* adopted to help them cope with feelings of distress and anxiety triggered in situations of perceived need, danger and threat. Whatever the quality of the parent–child relationship, the set goal of any attachment behaviour is to bring the child into proximity with his or her attachment figure where, ostensibly, safety and protection lie. In the case of warm, responsive parenting, attachment behaviour also leads to comfort and understanding. This produces feelings of security. In contrast, if the routes to proximity and security are blocked, rough or unpromising, children have to develop psychological strategies that attempt to ward off their anxiety. This can also involve children finding alternative ways of achieving psychologically proximity to the attachment figure.

> Four year old Teshi's mum, Lewa, was a lone parent with three children. Money was tight. Teshi's father had left the family and there was no contact with him. As a teenager Lewa had harboured ambitions to be a nurse but she now felt that life had dealt her a mean hand. Her temper was short and her parenting abrupt. Teshi knew better than to make a fuss when she was ill or complain if she couldn't twist the lid off a fresh jar of peanut butter. Instead she had learned to be helpful, to anticipate her mother's needs, to sense when it was wise to keep quiet. Although never likely to get too many hugs from mum, Teshi did occasionally earn her mother's grudging respect. 'Teshi is OK, I guess,' the little girl overheard her mother say to her aunt one day. 'I don't seem to have no energy to love them they way they deserve but I know how hard Teshi tries.'

Both secure and insecure attachment strategies therefore represent efforts by children to *organize* their behaviour to achieve proximity with the caregiver and with it a 'felt security'. Each pattern of attachment represents a behavioural strategy to elicit and maximize care and protection. All attachment behaviours make some kind of sense in the context of a particular parent–child relationship. Even insecure attachment behavioural strategies function to increase children's feelings of safety and decrease their feelings of anxiety. However, in contrast to securely attached children, insecure children learn that there are 'conditions' attached to their gaining proximity to their caregiver.

Reworking these experiences and the cognitive representations they sponsor, it is possible to generate four combinations of the way the self and others are being experienced and mentally modelled within the parent–child relationship. These give us avoidant, secure, ambivalent, and disorganized patterns of attachment, also referred to as the A (avoidant), B (secure), C (ambivalent), and D (disorganized) types. Each pattern of attachment behaviour illustrates a different adaptive strategy adopted under different parenting regimes. Each strategy represents a behavioural attempt by children to stay close and connected to their attachment figure at times of intense negative arousal no matter what type of caregiving they receive. Individual patterns also reflect a behavioural strategy for accessing the caregiver in order to reduce stress.

Secure patterns of attachment (Type B)

Securely attached children approach their carers directly and positively, knowing that their distress and upset will be recognized and responded to *unconditionally* with comfort and understanding. Secure babies happily play and explore but are confident to access their caregiver should the need arise. A sense of trust in others and a recognition of the value of cooperative behaviour soon become established. Caregiving which is responsive and reliable means that children develop an internal working model of the *self* that feels loved, lovable, and loving. The child feels effective, autonomous and competent. *Other people* are experienced as attuned, loving, available, co-operative, predictable and dependable. Overall, the caregiving comes across as *consistently responsive*. The child is able to express his or her need for protection and comfort freely, directly and without distortion.

Avoidant patterns of attachment (Type A)

When parents rebuff overtures of need and attachment behaviour, children are likely to develop attachment strategies that are *avoidant*. From the children's point of view, the caregiving feels rejecting and controlling. If children display distress, it seems to annoy or agitate their caregiver. Displays of attachment behaviour result in rebuke and dismissal, or irritable attempts to control, deny or dismiss the infant's need or anxiety. In these cases, explicit attachment behaviours (distress, crying, clinging, following, demanding) fail to increase either the responsivity or availability of the caregiver. The best defensive strategy therefore seems to be to *minimize overt shows of attachment behaviour and displays of negative affect*. On the face of it, and seeming somewhat perverse, proximity to the attachment figure is best achieved or maintained by avoiding displays of need and overt attachment behaviour. Children can be tolerated by otherwise rejecting caregivers so long as they do not make too many demands. As a result, children learn to contain their feelings. Their *affect is over-regulated*. A high threshold of arousal is required before attachment behaviour is elicited in avoidant children. Thus, 'infants who adopt a Type A response may mislead their parents into thinking they are OK – when they are actually uncomfortable' (Crittenden 2008: 24).

Avoidant children, although in a state of arousal and anxiety, therefore either deny or do not communicate their distress. They don't indicate vulnerability. Negative feelings are defensively excluded; emotions are contained. Upset is downplayed. There is a *flight* from the explicit display of attachment behaviours. Play and being occupied are acceptable to rejecting caregivers, although play is often carried out in a rather perfunctory manner. These defensive strategies help children contain their need and mask their distress. This allows them to remain reasonably close to, or accepted by attachment figures who might otherwise reject them.

Children classified as avoidant have an internal working model in which the *self* is represented as unloved and unlovable, although it is seen as self-reliant. *Other people* are cognitively represented as rejecting, unloving, and intrusive, and predictably unavailable at times of need. Overall the caregiving is therefore experienced as *consistently unresponsive*.

Ambivalent patterns of attachment (Type C)

In order for children to gain proximity and attention from carers who are *insensitive, unreliable,* and *inconsistently responsive,* children using an *ambivalent* strategy *maximize displays of attachment behaviour.* By exaggerating and overplaying their needs and distress, they increase the chances of getting a response from an otherwise under-responsive carer. As a result, their *emotions are under-regulated.* Their threshold of arousal is low. It doesn't take much stress to produce intense displays of protest, demand and upset. The attachment behaviours of ambivalent children are therefore those of an angry approach. They are prone to whine, cling, fret, and shout. These attention-seeking strategies might be defined as *fighting* for attention, pleading for protection. These behaviours are most pronounced at times of separation, parental insensitivity, or emotional unavailability. Children begin to doubt that they are worthy of interest. Thus, 'infants who adopt a Type C strategy may mislead their parent into thinking they are very distressed or exaggerating their distress in order to control the parent – when, in fact, they are somewhat distressed' (Crittenden 2008: 24).

As a result of these caregiving experiences, the ambivalent child's internal working model represents the *self* as of low worth, ineffective and dependent. *Other people* are experienced as insensitive, depriving, neglecting, unpredictable and unreliable.

Organized attachments (Types A, B and C)

Secure, avoidant and ambivalent attachments are all said to be 'organized'. This means that young children behaviourally adapt to the characteristics of the caregiving environment. In effect, attachment behaviours are variously being shaped, reinforced, punished or extinguished by the quality and character of the caregivers' responses to those attachment behaviours. Each attachment pattern represents the best way of organizing your attachment behaviour in order to achieve the set goal required of any attachment behaviour, that is to increase and maintain proximity to the attachment figure at times of need, danger and threat. Thus, says George (1996: 414):

> Whether guided by primary or secondary strategies, secure, avoidant and ambivalent infants have developed a set of coherent

and organized rules based on experience that predict and guide their future behaviour. Bowlby ... stressed that as long as the representational system is *organized*, individuals are capable of maintaining functional relationships with others. The important point to be made here is that despite their anxiety, avoidant and ambivalent infants have been able to adapt to their parents and select, evaluate and modify their behaviour in a manner that allows them to achieve proximity and contact when needed.

After Ainsworth *et al.* (1978), it is possible to present these three organized subgroups, A, B, C, with their finer divisions, along a continuum from suppression to high expression of attachment behaviours under conditions of stress (Table 4.1).

Infants classified A1 are described as extremely avoidant, showing no distress on being left completely alone and displaying no proximity-seeking on reunion with their caregiver. A2 children are only moderately avoidant. B1 infants, though essentially secure, show some avoidant tendencies. They tend not to show too much distress on separation and are happy to smile and babble happily when their caregiver returns without actually needing to have physical contact. B2 infants show some avoidance initially but with increasing stress show strong proximity-seeking behaviours with their caregiver. B3 infants are defined as being very secure. Those classified as B4 do

Table 4.1 *Attachment subgroups along a continuum of deactivated →
balanced → hyperactivated attachment behaviours*

Deactivated attachments		Balanced				Hyperactivated attachments	
A1	A2	B1	B2	B3	B4	C1	C2
Avoidant		*Secure (Balanced)*				*Ambivalent*	
Expressions of need and distress kept low, contained or hidden. Play and exploration maintained at the expense of attachment		Needs and distress expressed appropriately. Distress quickly soothed in contact with caregiver. Infants play with confidence when the attachment system is not active				Expressions of need and distress tend to be exaggerated and prolonged. Infants not readily soothed by their caregivers	

show more distress at separation and are keen to make physical contact when they are reunited, taking a little longer to soothe than B3 children. All infants classified ambivalent or C show strong, somewhat exaggerated distress on separation, intense proximity-seeking behaviour on reunion, and a failure to be soothed easily when their caregiver returns. C1 children are described as *angry* or *resistant*. They both demand contact but then might push the parent away. They remain distressed and resist returning to play even in the presence of the caregiver. C3 infants are highly distressed on separation but behave in a *passive*, helpless manner when their caregiver returns, failing to settle or return to play.

However, there are some caregiving environments in which young children find it difficult to organize any attachment strategy that results in either increased caregiver availability or increased responsivity. Children's attachments in these environments are described as disorganized.

Disorganized (Type D) attachments

Children who find it difficult to organize an attachment strategy that achieves proximity with the caregiver also find it difficult to terminate the activation of their aroused attachment systems. Relationships with caregivers are experienced as stressful. This is most often the case when the attachment figure is actually the cause of the child's initial fear and distress. Parents who are confusing and dangerous (abusive) or emotionally unavailable (psychotic, depressed, heavy drug or alcohol abusers), or who fail to offer protection at times of danger (neglect) not only frighten their children, but having frightened them, they also fail to recognize or do anything about their children's fearful state. Children's attachment systems therefore remain chronically activated and their arousal goes unregulated. Whatever behavioural strategy the children use, it fails to bring proximity, care or comfort. As a result, their attachment behaviour appears to lack a strategy, direction or focus. Sometimes it is incomplete, contradictory, or odd. A child might slowly approach his attachment figure, only to turn away a moment later, whimpering. In such cases, children's attachment behaviour becomes increasingly *incoherent* and *disorganized*, showing confused, alternating mixes of avoidance, angry approach responses, behavioural disorientation,

apprehension, or inertia. In cases where the fear escalates to traumatic levels, children might *freeze*, physically and psychologically.

In the internal working models of children classified as disorganized, the *self* feels frightened, alone, ignored, dangerous and even bad.
Other people are represented as unavailable and unpredictable, confusing and contradictory, frightening and frightened, hostile and helpless, dangerous and unreliable. In short, a disorganized attachment
indicates an undermining and a disorganization of the mental self,
and the lowest level of reflective function and mentalization (Fonagy
and Target 2005: 336)

However, when stress levels are lowered, otherwise disorganized
children can, and do show some organization in their attachment
behaviour such that their strategies might be recognized as either
avoidant, ambivalent, or even secure. Thus, children might be classified as disorganized-secure, disorganized-avoidant, disorganized-
ambivalent, or more generally disorganized-secure (D-Secure) or
disorganized-insecure (D-insecure) (for example, see Lyons-Ruth *et
al.* 2004). The overall model in which these four types of attachment
are recognized is therefore referred to as the ABC+D model with each
model indicating the meaning and organization of the infant's goal of
seeking parental protection under stress (Figure 4.1).

The ABC+D model has been very influential in the development
and theorization of attachment. But in Chapter 12 we shall also be
meeting another powerful, alternative model of the various attachment patterns known as the Dynamic Maturation Model (DMM) of
attachment and adaptation (Crittenden 2008; Farnfield *et al.* 2010).
The DMM does not recognize the disorganized attachment type,
preferring instead to see self-protective organization and adaptation
even under conditions of great fear and danger.

Measuring attachment in infancy and childhood

It was Mary Ainsworth who first developed a way of measuring children's attachment in infancy. The procedure she developed in known
as the Strange Situation. It is an experimental procedure that looks at
the level of security experienced by infants, typically aged between 12
and 18 months, in relationship with their main caregiver (Ainsworth
et al. 1978). The procedure examines the representational or internal
working model which children have of their relationship with their

Insecure-Avoidant (A)	Secure (B)	Insecure-Ambivalent (C)
Self (unloved but self-reliant); other people (rejecting and intrusive)	Self (loved, effective, autonomous and competent); other people (available, co-operative and dependable)	Self (low value, ineffective and dependent); other people (insensitive, inconsistent, unpredictable and unreliable)

Disorganised (D)
Self (unloved, alone and frightened), other people (frightening, rejecting and unavailable).

Figure 4.1 *ABC+D model in terms of the representation of self and others*

attachment figure. It provides opportunities to observe children at play and under conditions of mild distress. The low levels of stress experienced by infants are sufficient to activate their attachment behavioural system. The stresses experienced by the infant are caused by (1) the 'strange' room; (2) the periodic presence of a 'stranger'; and (3) brief separations from the attachment figure (mother or father). These stresses were chosen as relatively common, non-traumatic occurrences. In the case of mothers, for example, the procedure runs as follows:

Mother and infant together. Child has the opportunity to explore and play with toys. Mother watches.
A stranger then enters the room. After a short while, the stranger attempts to play with the child.
Mother leaves the room. The stranger remains and plays with the child.
Mother returns after a short while (say, 30 seconds) or as soon as the infant begins to show heightened distress (First Reunion). Mother settles the child. The stranger leaves the room.
Mother exits the room and leaves the infant on his or her own.
Stranger then enters and attempts to play with and comfort the infant.

Mother returns after a short while or as soon as the child begins to show heightened distress (Second Reunion). Mother settles the child. Stranger leaves.

The whole procedure takes about 20 minutes. When mothers leave the room, most children stop playing. They show separation anxiety which normally triggers attachment behaviour. Infants protest by crying and attempt to follow the mother when she exits. This illustrates that when attachment behaviour is activated, exploratory or play behaviour ceases. However, more important for making a classification of the infant's attachment type is the infant's behaviour upon reunion with the caregiver: how well can the attachment figure recognize, acknowledge, tune into and regulate the child's distress? 'The infant's behavior must be evaluated in relation to the set-goal of the attachment behavioral system: parental protection' (George 1996: 414). The procedure is filmed and the child's attachment type is classified using a complex scoring system that assesses the behaviours observed.

Since Ainsworth's pioneering work, many other instruments and ways of measuring children's attachments after infancy have been developed. These include 'Attachment Q-sorts' in which, for example, 90 items designed to assess security versus insecurity in children aged between one and five years are completed by a parent or trained observer (after watching the child for a few hours in the home setting). This generates a Q-sort profile for the child which gives him or her a security score (Waters 1994). Narrative Story Stem techniques are also used for children aged between three and eight years old (for example, Bretherton *et al.* 1990). These techniques take advantage of children's growing ability to mentally represent attachment relationships. Children are shown pictures or given the beginnings of a number of attachment-related stories (narrative stems) and asked to say (using puppets or dolls) what happened next. A typical 'story stem' might begin 'Sally falls off the high rock and hurts her knee.' Or 'Mummy and daddy go away for the night and granny comes to look after Carlos.' The assessor then says 'Show me and tell me what happens next.' Reviews of these, and other similar measures crop up from time to time in books and journals, two excellent examples of which can be found in Part Two of Prior and Glaser's *Understanding Attachment and Attachment Disorders* (2006), and Chapter 18 in the *Handbook of Attachment* written by Solomon and George (2008). To support her Dynamic-Maturational Model of attachment and adaptation, Crittenden has also developed a number of widely used assessments for children ranging from the CARE-Index for infants and toddlers, The Pre-School Assessment of Attachment (PAA), and the School-aged Assessment of Attachment (SAA) (see Crittenden 2008: 278–9, and Farnfield *et al.* 2010, for a review and references).

Culture, class and attachment

Almost from the outset, researchers wondered whether culture and socio-economic status (SES) made any difference to the distribution of attachment groups. Challenges were also made to the very concept of attachment suggesting that it was merely a white, Western construct forgetting, perhaps, that Mary Ainsworth's very first studies of maternal sensitivity and parent–child interaction were carried out in Uganda with young mothers from the Ganda tribe (Ainsworth 1967). Since then there have been many studies that have looked at caregiving and attachment in countries and cultures across the world. Helpful reviews of this literature have been provided by Prior and Glaser (2006), van IJzendoorn and Sagi-Schwartz (2008), and van IJzendoorn and Bakermans-Kranenburg (2010).

The first main conclusion of the analysis of the cross-cultural studies is that attachment behaviour itself is a universal phenomenon. Given its evolutionary character, this ought not to surprise us. Furthermore, in all cultures, the secure pattern predominates, typically occurring at rates of 55–60 per cent. It is generally associated with the most sensitive parenting. It has also been observed that 'the three basic attachment patterns – avoidant, secure and ambivalent – can be found in every culture in which attachment studies have been conducted thus far' (van IJzendoorn and Sagi-Schwartz 2008: 900). The proportion and distribution of the two insecure patterns – avoidant and ambivalent – do vary between cultures, but again this makes sense insofar as each attachment organization represents a strategy and adaptation to the particular relationship context in which the infant finds himself or herself. Here, we do pick up cultural differences in social and interpersonal expectations. Children adapt to these. Again, this reminds us of attachment's evolutionary and ethological character – that in order to maximize safety, children will develop those attachment behavioural strategies that best allow them to maintain proximity to their attachment figure at times of need and danger. Attachment theory predicts that the overall distribution of the three basic attachment patterns will show subtle variations as the cultural context changes, and indeed this seems to be the case.

It is acknowledged that more cross-cultural studies are needed, but as van IJzendoorn and Sagi-Schwartz (2008: 901) conclude, given what we know so far, it seems reasonable to claim that attachment theory has cross-cultural validity.

Within particular countries and cultures, differences between the proportion and distribution of attachment patterns do occur between classes and socio-economic groups. In general, the greater the poverty and the harsher the life, the more insecure patterns we see (Belsky and Fearon 2008). This seems entirely understandable. Parents whose lives are blighted by poverty and environmental deprivation will experience more stress. All of us under stress tend to be less sensitive. Less sensitive parenting increases the likelihood of an insecure attachment. Also consistent with this analysis is the over-representation of avoidant and dismissing patterns in low SES populations (van IJzendoorn and Bakermans-Kranenburg 2010). When life is hard, issues of survival dominate. There is a dismissive attitude towards signs of weakness, need and fussiness which would correlate with more children being classified as avoidant.

In countries where particular disadvantaged ethnic groups experience greater poverty, we do find higher rates of attachment insecurity among their children. But it is important to note that it is not the ethnicity itself that is determining insecurity but the poverty associated with low SES. When people's lives materially improve, stress reduces, and more children are classified as secure. This offers a powerful argument for the value of poverty reduction programmes. However, we also need to remind ourselves that even in very harsh environments, some parents continue to show resilience and high reflective function. This is why when researchers do study disadvantaged populations, they still find surprisingly high numbers of secure children relative to the conditions. This is testimony to the strength of character and resourcefulness that some parents maintain even under the toughest circumstances.

Conclusion

As good evolutionists, having recognized the four patterns of attachment, we need to ask ourselves why we see such variations. It is certainly the case that secure children and adults are most likely to enjoy optimal psychosocial development and good mental health. Nevertheless, it must always be remembered that attachment behaviour at heart is to do with safety and survival. Bearing this in mind, even insecure attachments represent behavioural strategies that are attempting to increase caregiver proximity at times of need, so improving the chances of survival. Survival is always the ultimate evolutionary driver.

If we consider the case of children raised in environments in which adults are less reliable, food less certain, and dangers greater, we realize that they are more likely to survive if they adopt, say, an avoidant strategy in response to their less responsive, more stressed caregiving. By downplaying their demands on struggling, hard-pressed parents, the risk of abandonment is diminished. Your own chances of survival increase when you learn that independence and opportunism are the best strategies to have in a harsh world. So, wonders Belsky, might insecure attachments represent an evolved psychological mechanism, responsive to caregiving conditions, 'that conveys to the child the developing understanding that others cannot be trusted; that close, affectional bonds are unlikely to be enduring; and that it makes more sense to participate in opportunistic, self-serving relationships rather than mutually beneficial ones' (2005: 91)?

On this analysis, the different attachment patterns and the individual behavioural and personality differences they sponsor are simply the product of prevailing rearing conditions and the qualities of the physical environment. Insecure patterns actually make more adaptive sense in environments that are less predictable, or more dangerous, harsher, more deprived.

Evolutionists do not deny that secure attachments promote good quality mental health. It is just that survival, and the strategies that increase it, have to outbid the secondary benefits of sound mental health. It is no good enjoying psychological well-being if you're dead. Secure children who trust others, expect fair play and co-operation, and delay finding a mate are unlikely to do well as orphaned street children, survive in a war zone, or cope in places of long-term drought. When all the normal rules have broken down, when parents might die at any moment, and where everyone is desperate, those most likely to survive, reach maturity, and have children of their own are the more self-seeking, socially deceptive, interpersonally aggressive, and sexually active individuals. Therefore, conclude Lyons-Ruth and Jacobvitz (2008: 690),

> In very-low-resource environments, child disorganized/controlling strategies may be adaptive both for the individual and family unit as a whole from an evolutionary perspective, even though they are costly to the child in terms of physiological regulation of stressful arousal and integration of mental states.

'What this suggests,' concludes Belsky (2005: 92–4), 'is that it may be useful to move beyond a mental health orientation toward attachment to one that focuses upon reproductive functioning (i.e., mating and parenting).'

Even so, counsel Grossmann *et al.* (2005: 131), we must not forget that in relatively safe, resource-rich environments, secure attachments do represent the most optimal organization of emotions and behaviour. In safe worlds, secure attachments optimize survival, reproductive potential, and material success. In good quality environments, those best able to co-operate, negotiate, adapt, be open, be flexible, trust and be trusted are likely to thrive, as well as enjoy the best mental health. The hope and ambition are that most children of the world might be raised in environments of love and plenty, in which case, secure attachments and good mental health are the developmental ideal.

5

Attachment in Adulthood

Cradle to grave

Attachment and development in the early years dominated the original research agenda. However, over the past twenty or so years, spurred on by some very creative social and personality psychologists, the study of attachment in adulthood has added a new impetus to the subject. Beginning as a theory of child development, Bowlby's (1979: 129) hope that attachment's potential as a lifecourse theory of human behaviour and relationships began to be realized. 'To dub attachment behaviour in adult life regressive is indeed to overlook the vital role that it plays in the life of man from the cradle to the grave' (Bowlby 1997: 208).

Attachment in adulthood has interesting things to say about many key life experiences. Romantic relationships, sexual behaviour, parenthood, behaviour in the workplace, physical health, and mental well-being have all been the subject of detailed enquiry. Threats that can activate the adult's attachment system include both physical and psychological events: a wife threatens to leave her husband, a woman is diagnosed with a serious illness, a man out walking becomes lost in a menacing neighbourhood, an employee is made redundant. When faced with these various threats, secure people tend to draw on the positive elements of their internal working model. They believe that at times of need, others will be there to offer protection, help, comfort, support and advice. Having been protected, comforted and loved in the past, they perceive themselves to be of value and worth in the present. The high self-esteem they enjoy confers further resilience helping them to cope with life's stresses and strains.

In contrast, in situations of threat and challenge, when insecure people's attachment systems are activated, negative memories flood their thoughts and feelings. A feared sense of helplessness re-surfaces. A past hurt or rejection is prodded back into life. Not only are challenging situations experienced as dangerous and stressful but there is also the added fear of being left on your own to deal with them. Other people cannot be relied on to offer support, comfort or protection at times of need.

Adolescence through to adulthood sees a gradual shift in the choice of principal attachment figures, away from parents to close friends, lovers and spouses. These are the people to whom we increasingly turn for comfort and support, recognition and encouragement. But our attachment hierarchies can extend to include siblings, work colleagues, teachers, and therapists. Of course, parents continue to be available, particularly at important times such as graduation, being pregnant, the birth of a baby, the care of a child, or the unfaithfulness of a spouse but on a day-to-day basis, partners and close friends begin to assume more importance.

Adult attachment styles

As in childhood, a range of adult attachment types has been recognized. Each adult attachment style affects the way people conduct emotionally significant relationships, whether with partners, parents, friends, children or colleagues. As hinted in the beginning of this chapter, the research and theory-building around adult attachments have been generated by people working in two related but often separate traditions.

One tradition is associated with the developmentalists who have taken a particular interest in caregiving, children's attachments and parenting. The *Adult Attachment Interview* (AAI) was devised to help developmentally-based researchers explore adults' representations of attachment, taking a particular interest in their childhood experiences, memories and representations.

The other tradition is that of social psychology and the study of personality and individual differences. *Self-report measures* administered by questionnaire are commonly used by this group to assess adult attachment orientations in present relationships.

Each tradition – developmental psychology and social psychology – has tended to stay with its preferred approach to research design, assessment and analysis. There is therefore something of a split between the developmentalists who write mainly about caregiving, parenting and attachments in childhood, and the social psychologists who report mainly on attachment in adulthood.

Debate continues about the relative merits of the AAI and self-report measures (see Jacobvitz *et al.* 2002; Mikulincer and Shaver 2007, Chapter 4). Other assessment interviews and instruments have also been developed in attempts either to produce more practitioner-friendly interviews, or more sensitive self-report measures. Bifulco's Attachment Style Interview (ASI) is a good example of an interview-based method that is less specialist than the AAI, but relatively easy to use for clinicians and practitioners who value the importance of the ongoing relationship with parents, family and external supports (for example, Bifulco *et al.* 2008). It is still the case that developmental and clinical child psychologists prefer to use the AAI and similar narrative and interview-based assessment techniques, while personality and social psychologists remain largely committed to the use of self-report assessments for measuring adult attachments.

Although there is no immediate sign of a full-blown marriage between the two approaches, there is much overlap and common ground, and regular attempts are made at rapprochement and integration. This book, being brief and introductory, although acknowledging the virtues of both camps, will blur many of the distinctions. In Chapters 7, 9, 11 and 13 on attachments in adulthood, a blended view will be presented. The risk, of course, is that purists will be upset as I commit a number of conceptual solecisms. However, as the intention is to interest the reader who wants a broad introduction and overview of attachment, I hope these intellectual sins might be forgiven.

The Adult Attachment Interview (AAI)

The Adult Attachment Interview (AAI) and its many variants constitute the measure of choice preferred by developmental psychologists. It is an interview-based measure of adult attachments and was originally developed by Mary Main and colleagues in the 1980s (George *et al.* 1984; see Hesse 2008, for a good description). It is not the adult equivalent of the infant Strange Situation which considers infant attachment *behaviour*. Rather, the AAI looks at *states of mind regarding attachment*, that is, the overarching, consolidated, single internal working model that influences perception, expectations, memories, behaviour, and attachment style, particularly in the context of close relationships. In fact, Allen and Miga argue that the AAI does not even directly assess the individual's internal working model of attachment. Rather, what is actually 'being measured with the AAI is emotion regulation in the context of discussions about attachment relationships' (2010: 187).

The AAI is an hour-long semi-structured interview that explores people's descriptions of their attachment relationships in childhood, memories which either support or contradict the general descriptions, and descriptions of current relationships with parents and children (if they have any). Particular attention is paid to the following three experiences: (1) loss, separation and rejection; (2) emotional upsets, hurts and sickness; and (3) love and acceptance, with each caregiver. The adult is asked to talk about his or her early childhood attachment-related memories and to evaluate them from their current adult perspective.

The coding of the interview transcripts depends less on the literal content of what is said, but more on the way the story is told and holds together, or not – that is, how coherent are the accounts and reflections (Main *et al.* 2008). The questions about childhood attachment experiences take the adult by surprise, slightly raising levels of anxiety and stress. As the interviewee responds and reflects, he or she suddenly has to cope with emotionally laden thoughts and memories about key attachment relationships, both in the past and the present. In their attempts to regulate their emotions, adults use different strategies or rules to access, process and express attachment related material. The AAI therefore provokes a discourse of attachment-related memories.

The AAI recognizes four adult attachment organizations that correspond to, although they might not necessarily follow on directly from, the four childhood patterns (Hesse 2008; Main *et al.* 2008; van IJzendoorn and Bakermans-Kranenburg 1996).

A *Secure-autonomous* or *Free to Evaluate* (F) state of mind, yet one which also values attachment (compare infant Secure B patterns). Interview responses are internally consistent. Answers are clear, relevant and succinct. Adults are able to reflect on and realistically evaluate their emotional experiences. Autonomous individuals value attachment relationships and experiences but they are also objective about their quality and character. As they are answering questions and reflecting on those answers, they indicate that they are actively thinking about and appraising what they saying in a fresh, considered, objective manner. In normal, non-clinical populations between 55 and 60 per cent might be classified as secure autonomous (Bakermans-Kranenburg and van IJzendoorn 2009). Although the proportions of other attachment groups vary a little across different cultures, this figure of around 60 per cent for secure attachments seems to be consistent from one country and culture to another (Prior and Glaser 2006; van IJzendoorn and Bakermans-Kranenburg 2010).

Dismissing (Ds) states of mind with respect to attachment (compare infant Avoidant A pattern). For adults in this group, attachment-related and emotionally-charged memories are quickly glossed over. Any notion that early relationship experiences might have affected their personality is dismissed. The need for comfort and support is downplayed. Individuals tend to make broadly positive, even ideal-ized statements about parents and the care they received. However, these global claims are not supported by specific examples. Sometimes they are actually contradicted elsewhere in the interview with strong indications that at least one parent was being experi-enced as rejecting. It is also the case that some adults in this group, rather than defensively idealize their parents and childhood, are more likely to be dismissive, contemptuous and derogatory about their caregivers and childhood experiences. And yet others might idealize one parent while disparaging the other. There is a general tendency by adults who are dismissing to present the self as strong, a self unaf-fected by negative experiences. Interviews often tend to be on the short side. In normative populations between 15 and 23 per cent might be classified as dismissing.

Preoccupied-entangled (E) states of mind with respect to attachment (compare infant Ambivalent C patterns). Attachment-related events, including discussions of parents and their parenting, are talked about in a confused, enmeshed, rambling or angry manner. There is a preoccupation with relationships, particularly with who was loved and not loved, who was available and who was not, who coped and who did not, who gave and who deprived. Stories are often inconsis-tent and confusing. Interviews often tend to be on the long side. In normal populations between 10 and 15 per cent of people might be classified as preoccupied, although the figure rises a little in more 'collectivist' societies typical of many Far Eastern cultures, Israel and some African countries (van IJzendoorn and Bakermans-Kranenburg 2010).

Unresolved-disorganized (U) states of mind with respect to attachment (compare infant Disorganized D patterns). During their answers, adults may lose the thread of what they are saying as they become absorbed by past losses, hurts and traumatic memories. During such moments, it seems as if the individual is momentarily back in the past, swept up, disoriented or disturbed by old, troubling, painful memories. The individual fails to understand what happened in the past, and the past's ability to disturb the present, which is to say, 'recall of such past experiences can irrationally motivate behavior in the present' (Crittenden 2008: 35). Nor are they able to regulate the strong feelings aroused when painful, unresolved memories are triggered by current stimuli. In normal populations between 10 and 15 per cent might be classified as unresolved, usually in association with either autonomous, dismissing or preoccupied states of mind. These more organized states of mind with respect to attachment are recovered when stress levels are low. Thus, as with the disorganized pattern in infancy, adults with unresolved states of mind are also given a secondary classification as either autonomous, dismissing, or preoccupied. In clinical populations, the number of people classified as 'unresolved' can rise to 40 per cent or more (Bakermans-Kranenburg and van IJzendoorn 1993, 2009).

A number of refinements and variations have been added to these adult classifications including one of *cannot classify* (in which dismissing and preoccupied discourses co-occur), and one of *helpless-hostile* (H/H) (Hesse 2008; Lyons-Ruth *et al.* 2005). The H/H classification is often allocated to people whose own childhood histories are disfigured by abuse and neglect.

Each adult attachment type has some power to predict the attachment classification of any child of that adult as parent (Main *et al.* 1985; Steele and Steele 2005b). For example, Fonagy *et al.* (1991) administering the AAI on first-time pregnant mothers were able in 75 per cent cases to predict from the mother's classification whether the infant would be classified as either securely or insecurely attached when measured at 12 months. The infants of 'secure/autonomous' mothers were highly likely to be classified as securely attached. Similarly, the majority of the babies of 'insecure dismissing or preoccupied' mothers were classified as insecure.

Self-report measures

Self-report measures, as well as interviews, have also been used to determine people's attachment styles. A wide variety of self-report measures now exist in which respondents complete a questionnaire or carry out an attachment-related exercise (see Mikulincer and Shaver 2007, Chapter 4, for a good review of these measures). They have the advantage of being relatively easy and quick to use, and most are well validated and achieve good levels of reliability. Typically they require respondents to say how strongly they agree or disagree (on a Likert scale) with a whole series of propositions and statements that explore beliefs about the self and partners in various types of relationship. For example, three of the propositions on the Adult Attachment Questionnaire (AAQ) with which a respondent is asked to agree or disagree include 'I find it relatively easy to get close to others', 'I find it difficult to trust others completely', and 'I usually want more closeness and intimacy than others do.' The Experiences in Close Relationships Scales (ECR and ECR-R) employ similar items but many more of them. For example, 'I tell my partner just about everything' and 'My romantic partner makes me doubt myself'.

Using these measures, individuals classified as secure retain positive expectations of themselves and others. However, 'insecure people have learned through many painful experiences with unavailable or unresponsive attachment figures that the primary attachment strategy (proximity seeking) often fails to accomplish its emotion regulation goal, making it necessary to consider alternative secondary strategies' (Mikulincer and Shaver 2008: 508). Doubting the reliability of other people's emotional availability at times of need, insecure individuals develop other ways, described as secondary attachment strategies, of trying to regulate their own arousal and increase their partner's availability. To these ends, they either hyperactivate or deactivate their attachment system.

It has gradually become apparent that two dimensions of insecurity underlie adult self-report measures: avoidance and anxiety. Self-report measures can therefore be used to generate a simple 2 by 2 grid, with one dimension ranging from low to high on *avoidance*, and the other from low to high on *anxiety* (Bartholomew 1990; Brennan *et al.* 1998) (see Figure 5.1).

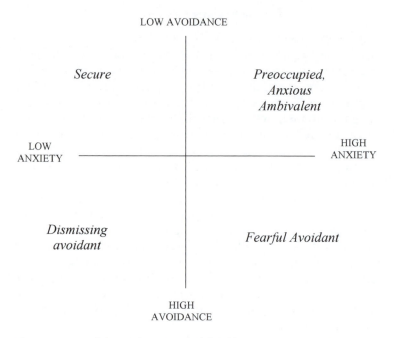

LOW AVOIDANCE

Secure

Preoccupied,
Anxious
Ambivalent

LOW
ANXIETY

HIGH
ANXIETY

Dismissing
avoidant

Fearful Avoidant

HIGH
AVOIDANCE

Figure 5.1   *Adult attachment types defined by anxiety and avoidance*

Source: Adapted from Bartholomew (1990), Mikulincer and Shaver (2007: 89)

Attachment *avoidance* indicates the level of discomfort the individual feels with psychological intimacy and dependency. Adults assessed as high on avoidance value independence and autonomy. They tend to be compulsively self-reliant, even detached. They prefer emotional distance, try to limit emotional expression and intimacy, and rely on *deactivating* their attachment system to manage arousal. They don't seek support, relying mainly on themselves to deal with feelings of vulnerability, upset and need. By keeping their attachment system turned down, they avoid activating anxieties about what happens when you make emotional demands on others, get rejected, or suffer hurt.

Individuals scoring high on attachment *anxiety* remain preoccupied with relationships and the need to feel loved and close. They also have a corresponding fear of separation, abandonment, and not being loved. However, these needs are suffused with uncertainty about whether other people do care or really are that interested. The strong desire for closeness is matched by intense worries about whether or not the other is aware, interested, and available. Anxious individuals therefore rely heavily on the approval of others for a sense of well-being. They get distressed when they feel the other's recognition and valuation lacks sincerity or feels insufficiently intense. At times of need and stress, their attachment systems are therefore prone to *hyperactivation*. Dangers are exaggerated, anxiety emphasized, and over-dependence increased. Emotions get intensified and heightened. Anxious adults maximize signals of distress, and present themselves as helpless and vulnerable to hurt, disinterest and abandonment.

The grid presented in Figure 5.1 defines the characteristics of the four basic attachment types recognized by social psychologists using self-report measures: secure, avoidant, anxious preoccupied, and fearful avoidant (Bartholomew 1990). The character of each of the four types broadly coincides with those described by the AAI, with the fearful avoidant type, though not strictly equivalent, nevertheless having many features typically found in those classified as unresolved, controlling, coercive, hostile-helpless, and cannot-classify using the AAI and its variants. The following descriptions for each type are offered by Bartholomew (1990) and Bartholomew and Horowitz (1991).

Adults classified as *secure* are comfortable with both intimacy and autonomy. Intimacy is defined as closeness to another person and openness in sharing thoughts and feelings. Secure adults agree with statements such as 'It is easy for me to become emotionally close to others. I am comfortable depending on them and having them depend on me. I don't worry about being alone or having others not accept me.' Self-esteem, confidence, feelings of competence, and a willingness to trust and co-operate with others in order to achieve goals are high.

Dismissing avoidant types value autonomy but they are uncomfortable with intimacy and defensively prone to dismiss its importance. They identify with statements such as 'I am comfortable without close emotional relationships. It is very important for me to feel independent and self-sufficient, and I prefer not to depend on others or have others depend on me.' They value self-reliance. Esteem is more easily achieved through success at work, sport or task accomplishment than in close relationships.

Preoccupied and anxious types seek intimacy and are preoccupied, to the point of clinginess, with close relationships. Autonomy and independence make them feel anxious. They recognize themselves in the following statements: 'I want to be completely emotionally intimate with others, but I often find that others are reluctant to get as close as I would like. I am uncomfortable being without close relationships, but I sometimes worry that others don't value me as much as I value them.' Individuals have major self-doubts about their own lovability, self-esteem and competence.

The fourth group, the *fearful avoidant*, fear both intimacy and abandonment. They score high on both anxiety and avoidance.

> Like dismissing avoidants, they often cope by withdrawing and distancing themselves from relationship partners, but unlike dismissing individuals they continue to experience anxiety and neediness concerning their partner's love, reliability and trustworthiness. In this sense, they are likely at times to seem 'disorganized', like babies classified D (disorganized/disoriented).
>
> (Shaver and Mikulincer 2003: 248)

Fearful avoidant individuals therefore often appear socially withdrawn and untrusting. They endorse statements such as 'I am uncomfortable getting close to others. I want emotionally close relationships, but I find it difficult to trust others completely, or to depend on them, I worry that I will be hurt if I allow myself to become too close to others.' They feel unlovable. Self-esteem is low. Although they seek intimacy and have a desperate need for comfort, there is a fear that as they get close to others, they risk being hurt and rejected. This produces troubled, conflicted behaviours in the context of close relationships as approach is followed by avoidance in repeated cycles of need, fear, anger, and escape.

Conclusion: attachment across the lifecourse

There is now a robust and thriving interest in attachments in adulthood. Two study groups have emerged, each with their own preferred measures of assessment and models of attachment types.

Developmental psychologists' research into adulthood is derived from their interest in parents as caregivers. The attention that social and personality psychologists have given adult attachments came via studies into couple and romantic relationships.

So far, in these opening five chapters, attachment's basic ideas and concepts have been roughly sketched. We now need to consider each attachment pattern and style in more detail, across the lifecourse, from infancy to old age. Although differences in outlook and understanding do occur between attachment theorists, particularly when they appeal to different research traditions, of necessity we need to ride a little roughshod over these debates in order to present a reasonably concise and coherent picture. The next eight chapters consider each of the four basic attachment groups – secure, avoidant, ambivalent and disorganized – as they play out, first in childhood and then in adulthood.

PART II

Attachment Patterns, Types and Styles

6
Secure Attachments in Childhood

Introduction

When caregivers are available and responsive at times of need, when they have their child in mind, children are able to use them as a safe haven and a secure base from which to explore and play. Parents who have made sense of their own early childhood experiences, whatever their quality, who can mentalize, are likely to have securely attached children. Securely attached children are the most likely to develop emotional intelligence, good social skills, and robust mental health.

Infancy

Parents of secure children are good at reading their babies' signals, most of the time. There is synchrony and a sense of harmony between carer and infant. When parents play with their children, they co-operate. They are also happy to be led by their child as well as provide gentle encouragement to get them to try new things if they feel their baby is ready. Babies who feel understood and in tune with their parents feel safe and relaxed. 'Put in attachment terms,' says Crittenden (1992a: 580), 'when mothers are sensitively responsive, infants are freed from the disorganizing effects of intense emotional arousal and are able to explore their world.'

Strong and potentially overwhelming feelings are both regulated and kept to a minimum by responsive caregivers. It is in the context of a secure relationship that emotional conflict and contradictory feelings can be managed and understood (Steele and Steele 2005b). Such relationships create a 'tolerant atmosphere in which self-control can grow' (Bowlby 1979: 12). This gives the clear message to the child that difficult feelings can be understood, contained and managed. By sharing emotions with a safe other, children learn that feelings are tolerable. Not only is it safe to have strong feelings, they actually provide you with useful information about you and your relationship with the environment. For example, yes, you will feel angry when your toddler friend plays with your toy, but there are other toys to play with, you will get your turn, and it might even be fun to play together. These are hard lessons for little minds to learn, but when they are appreciated, they help lay down valuable social understandings, useful social skills, and strong resiliences.

Along similar lines, it is also worth noting that these attuned reciprocal interactions only have to be 'good enough' for a child to feel secure. Babies appear very good at ignoring much parental insensitivity so long as they know that, in principle, the caregiver does care and that even though he or she isn't responding there and then, the 'safe haven' hasn't gone away and will return, eventually. So long as the parent doesn't routinely frighten the child, show hostility, or interfere with the child's attempts to achieve control, make sense, play, and self-regulate, all should be well. Even sensitive caregivers get it right only about 50 per cent of the time. Their communications are either out of synch, or mismatched. There are times when parents feel tired or distracted. The telephone rings or there is breakfast to prepare. In other words, attuned interactions rupture quite frequently. But the hallmark of a sensitive caregiver is that these ruptures are managed and repaired. There is acknowledgement that the baby has been ignored. Or a cross infant is eventually picked up, but not before the mother has said 'Who's a cross little boy? But you'd be even crosser if mummy didn't get your tea ready, wouldn't you? Come on, give us a cuddle and let's get you fed.' These episodes help children internalize ways of coping, building up their ability to contain, understand and self-regulate (Beebe 2004). A little frustration, coupled with sensitive repair, is good for development.

More generally, play, whether with parents or friends, provides children with extremely important experiences of give and take, how to deal with upset and conflict, have fun, show persistence, concentrate and stick with a task, relate with others, and see the world from their point of view.

It is in such loving and predictable environments that children begin to work out the consequences of their own and other people's actions and behaviours. This represents the beginnings of self-understanding and social skill. In short, secure children trust the communicative value of their own and other people's emotional states. And because their social world is reasonably reliable and predictable, they begin to trust their ideas about how the interpersonal world works. They begin to realize that there are connections between what they think, feel and do, and what other people think, feel and do. This helps secure children develop good reflective, mentalizing abilities. They become socially smart and psychologically literate.

It will be apparent that parents who are available at times of need, who respond with sensitivity and understanding, and who recognize and appreciate their child as a separate, complex, wonderfully interesting, endlessly fascinating little psychological being, are generating a rich psychosocial environment in which the child, her brain and her mind can grow to their full potential. Children who can make sense of their own and other people's mental states, particularly at the level of the emotions, experience less stress. When they do get agitated, aroused and emotionally upset, having been regulated by the caregiver, they gradually develop skills to regulate themselves. Having enjoyed parental interest, love and concern, they know how to use their attachment figure as a safe haven and a secure base.

Secure children's behavioural strategies are often described as *balanced*. The need for intimacy at some times, but autonomy at others are both equally important. The caregiver is approached at moments of danger and need (safe haven), but happily left in order to re-engage with life. Secure children are comfortable in relationships, but they are also quite happy to play independently and pursue their own interests as they explore the world of friends, school, and learning. They know that their attachment figures are there for them should the need arise. Knowing that comfort, support and protection are available if life gets tricky, secure children tackle life with confidence and enthusiasm.

Perhaps more surprising, secure children are not only more collaborative, friendly and self-confident but also more assertive, even to the point of risking conflict with their parents. This is all part of growing up and establishing independence. 'Although we generally assume that it is "good" for children to comply with parental suggestions and requests, it has often been suggested that there are appropriate times and ways for children to assert their independence' (Goldberg 2000: 174). In fact, parents might take heart from the findings of Kuczynski and colleagues (1987) who describe non-compliance as an important feature of developing autonomy that follows a clear progression. Goldberg (2000: 174) summarizes matters rather nicely: 'Very young children simply ignore parental requests. This later gives way to a confrontational refusal ("No!") and eventually the ability to negotiate ("Just a minute," "Can I finish this tower first?").

Resilience

It is not surprising to learn that children who have been on the receiving end of good quality relationships are not only secure, but also enjoy subjective well-being and high self-esteem. Self-esteem is a resilience factor. Resilience might be defined as the successful negotiation of challenges or risks. In other words, you can't show resilience or be resilient until you meet an adverse situation that makes demands of you. If you adapt well to the adverse situation and if you continue to cope well under pressure and still feel in control, then you are showing resilience. You have functioned well under that stress. Certain characteristics, experiences and attributes may help you cope well with a particular risk, but that same trait may not always confer a benefit when a different kind of risk is met. This approach to resilience sees it as a dynamic 'person–environment interaction', a process in which the individual achieves positive adjustment in the face of an adversity (Schoon 2006: 17).

Many factors have been associated with resilience. Some are innate such as enjoying a cheerful and optimistic temperament, possessing a good IQ, or having practical intelligence. Others are acquired as a result of environmental experience. These include higher socio-economic status; absence of early loss and trauma; positive social supports; good educational experience; good social understanding; empathy; the ability to plan; and a good sense of humour (Fonagy *et al.* 1994: 232). Secure attachments predict the presence of many of these experientially acquired resiliences allowing Fonagy *et al.* (1994: 235) to conclude that securely attached children are, indeed, more likely to be resilient.

Although it's true that secure children tend to meet less stress and tend not to generate much conflict, when they do encounter setbacks they generally cope well. Of course, it isn't always the secure attachment itself that confers resilience. Rather, securely attached children are able to take advantage of the opportunities that play, peer friendship groups, school and autonomy offer. Viewing development as a series of transactions between children and their ever expanding environment, each developmental phase builds upon all preceding phases. Development is a function of the interaction of both early and continuing experiences. The process is therefore dynamic, not linear (Sroufe *et al.* 2005a: 53; 2005b).

> [T]he environment itself is influenced by the individual; it does not simply wash over the person as an independent force. Individuals interpret, select, and influence the people and circumstances surrounding them to confirm existing beliefs and adaptational pathways.
>
> (Weinfield *et al.* 2008: 93)

This being the case, secure children tend to 'create' benign and responsive environments, which is yet another way of saying that they are resilient – that life generally throws fewer curveballs their way.

If we step further back, we see that it is the social understanding and skills which the opportunities of playing with peers and going to school provide that promote many of the resiliences mentioned above, particularly good social cognition and the capacity for empathy. These are attractive skills and qualities to have. It is expected, therefore, that secure children are more likely than insecure children to socialize, be popular with their peers, be collaborative, and take advantage of, and build on the opportunities that life presents. For example, Sroufe *et al.* (2005a: 58) have observed that when children classified as secure in infancy reach the age of 9, they are more likely to get on well with their peers than children classified as insecure when babies.

Social skills and emotional intelligence

Although all resilience factors have value, attachment theorists believe that one of the most important predictors of resilience is the possession of strong mentalizing abilities. We have seen how sensitive and attuned parents help their children develop self-reflective, mentalizing abilities, and how these in turn promote good social understanding. The open communications that secure children enjoy with their parents mean that their internal working models are constantly being revised and elaborated. Parents who help children recognize, name and reflect on feeling states are providing them with both the vocabulary and the understanding to handle their own and other people's emotions and behaviour.

Pursuing this line of thought, Fonagy *et al.* (1994) pose the idea that the individual's ability to mentally represent both the self and others without defensive distortion might be a major factor in understanding many aspects of resilience. Emotional intelligence and the ability to reflect on the mental state of both the self and others involve a recognition that much of human behaviour can only make sense in terms of what goes on in people's heads. Mentalization allows children and adults to step back, reflect and ponder. It also helps them *think through* situations, plan effectively and learn from past experiences. Rather than behave impulsively, it gives people options. These self-reflective and reflexive abilities clearly advantage children and adults in social situations.

In tests, secure pre-school children are particularly good at recognizing whether other people's facial expressions indicate anger or fear, sadness or joy. Secure children are also better at understanding emotions than non-secure children (de Rosnay and Harris 2002; Liebowitz *et al.* 2002). Mothers of secure children and their families tend to use a lot of words and make a lot of observations about other people's mental states. 'Don't tease your brother, he's tired.' 'Your sister's sad because her pet hamster has died.' 'That's nice; you're sharing your toys with Emma. Look, she's smiling because you've made her happy.' This helps children to talk about feelings, and talking about feelings helps them understand and manage their own and other people's emotional states (Walden and Garber 1994). Broader still, parents of secure children affirm the child's perspective on emotionally salient issues. Parents don't impose their own views. They are interested in what the child thinks and feels about the situation. The result is that children's thoughts and reflections are validated (Raikes and Thompson 2008b) and they develop a rich language about the emotions. Many of these features of emotionally intelligent family life are particularly pronounced when there is satisfaction by both parents with their marriage, and if children experience their parents as content with each other and their relationship. In these families, the stage is set for optimal and relatively trouble-free development. Indeed, in terms of what kind of attachment a child develops, the quality of the relationship *between parents* might matter as much as the quality of the relationship between children and their parents (George 2009; Millings and Walsh 2009).

Growing independence

Evolutionary biologists point out that as children age, mothers are likely to reduce the amount of time and energy they invest in their older offspring, particularly if they have new, younger, more vulnerable siblings to look after (Hinde 2005; Trivers 1974). Certainly by age 3 or 4 it seems to be the case that securely attached children play with increasing independence. Their play also becomes more complex and symbolic. By now they can walk, talk, think and plan. They reflect on their own and their caregiver's thoughts, feelings and point of view. This allows them to negotiate access and independence, intimacy and autonomy with their caregivers in what Bowlby called a 'goal-corrected partnership'. They develop an internal working model that represents their parents as emotionally available at times of need. They therefore become less concerned about their carers' actual physical presence. This allows them to play on their own or with peers for longer and longer periods without seeking parental involvement.

Play with friends becomes more interactive, reciprocal, and co-operative. Problem-solving skills improve. Pre-school children begin to talk with each other about what they're thinking, feeling and planning to do. Pretend play, which requires an ability to imagine what it must be like and feel like to be someone or something else, becomes well established. A sense of humour, and the ability to tease and deceive, all require a sophisticated understanding of both one's own and other people's minds. Children are more inclined to support and offer comfort to each other when distressed. However, these advanced social skills and awarenesses also mean that children begin to experience new emotions such as shame and guilt, feelings that can further inhibit behaviour that is socially unacceptable.

Middle childhood

Middle childhood spans the years 7–12. It is a time of expanding social horizons and skills. Conceptual abilities become more sophisticated. Moreover, having had a rich social life in terms of a shared family interest in feelings as a way of explaining behaviour, secure children continue to be good at recognizing and understanding emotional states in themselves and others (Steele *et al.* 1999). Their emotional range increases.

Secure children cope reasonably well with stress. They don't distort or defend against their own or other people's feelings. This open-mindedness provides them with maximum information with which to analyse relationship problems. The value of this non-defensive state of mind allows them to think flexibly and choose the best behavioural option when faced with a difficult social situation. Secure children therefore have the confidence to acknowledge, and the ability to understand and handle difficult and anxiety-provoking emotions. Children who can acknowledge, accept and conceptualize the potentially dysregulating emotions of fear and anger, rather than avoid, deny, defensively split, or misunderstand them, are better placed to manage and regulate their arousal. All of this helps secure children to continue learning from experience. Their internal working models are constantly being revised and updated.

More and more time is spent with friends. The secure base and growing emotional intelligence of securely attached children mean that they are likely to be both interested in peer relationships and rather good at them. There is evidence that secure children make more friends and interact with them more competently than those judged insecure (e.g. Elicker *et al.* 1992; Raikes and Thompson 2008a). Secure children know how to share, negotiate, co-operate, compromise, and, if appropriate, be assertive. They are able to recognize and keep to group norms. Social, sporting and hobby activities grow.

Children who are securely attached to fathers as well as mothers are least likely to be aggressive (Booth-LaForce *et al.* 2006). Perhaps even more important than social competence with peers is the secure child's ability to make and keep friends (Booth-LaForce *et al.* 2005). The trust and intimacy experienced with parents extend to relationships with school mates. Children who enjoy high-quality friendships tend to have good self-esteem. They are less likely to be bullied, and more likely to enjoy better mental health. These benefits often continue into adulthood.

Even so, although it is true that friends occupy an increasingly large part of children's lives, at times of need or confusion, setback or distress, decision-making or new experiences, parents as attachment figures still play a key role. The set goal of the attachment system for older children, however, is psychological availability rather than physical proximity. Children can tolerate increasingly longer periods of separation knowing that their parents have them in mind. Thus, whereas a few minutes separation in the Strange Situation is distressing for a 1-year-old baby, a child aged 10 might happily cope with a week away from mum and dad. And of course, text messages, phone calls, Skype, and emails are all good ways of keeping in touch with home. These contacts are effective and quick ways of terminating any mild activation of the attachment system. This helps parents feel increasingly relaxed as responsibility for safety and exploration shift more and more to the child, a change that is also reflected in fewer and less intense displays of attachment behaviour.

In their early school years, children begin to develop affectional bonds with an ever wider range of people – grandparents, aunts, uncles, friends. They also begin to use these people as additional 'secure bases' from which to explore. The presence of a teacher or close friend, for example, might allow the child to feel more confident to try out a new skill. Worries might be shared with a best friend. Or a problem might be discussed with a worldly-wise grandparent.

Along with home and family, school is the other major environment in which children have to learn to operate. The social skills and personal capacities of secure children mean that they are likely to enjoy and cope well with school. On the whole, they are well behaved, and more likely to follow school rules, and be cooperative. For example, Bradley *et al*. (1988) found that children whose parents played with them in the pre-school years handled school life with relative skill when they were 10 years old. As well as enjoying school and approach it positively, secure children often perform better academically and scholastically than their insecure peers (e.g. Aviezer *et al*. 2002).

Throughout middle childhood, children's attachment relationships become increasingly elaborate and complex. Even so, the majority of children say that their biological mother remains their primary attachment figure, although by this stage a growing number, possibly over 20 per cent, begin to identify other people, including their father and other close relatives as their principal figure (Kobak *et al*. 2005: 82). This widening range of relationships does not mean that attachments and affectional bonds with parents disappear. Rather, they settle and become a comfortable part of the relationship land-scape, even though friends, and later on, romantic partners might feature more frequently as everyday attachment figures. This slow, gradual shift of emotional investment from parents to peers and eventual sexual mates makes evolutionary sense in terms of safety and reproductive potential (Mayseless 2005: 16).

Conclusion

Sensitively responsive parents who can tune into, and see the world from their child's point of view are likely to have securely attached children. Securely attached children are able to use their attachment figures as a safe haven at times of need and a secure base from which to explore and play. Security gives children a good start in life. The psychological skills they develop help them to navigate the social world with skill and competence.

It has been suggested that as children mature, their 'attachment security or insecurity becomes increasingly an attribute of the person rather than of a specific relationship' (Mayseless 2005: 6, citing the work of Thompson and Raikes 2003). Features that defined the initial attachment relationship gradually become incorporated into the young personality, and it is these more internalized attrib-utes that begin to influence the maturing child's conduct in close rela-tionships. Indeed, Steele and Steele (2005a: 139) conceive that attachment in middle childhood is, in fact, 'an emerging property of the individual child'. The social outside, via the attachment relation-ship and the internal working model, therefore gradually permeates and forms the child's mental inside. If the environment of close rela-tionships remains relatively warm, loving and stable, secure children are very likely to grow up into secure adults.

7
Secure Attachments in Adulthood

Introduction

Many of the social and psychological benefits associated with secure attachments in childhood continue to be present in adults who are classified as secure. The internal working model of the secure adult is one in which there is a positive view of self, others and relationships. Individuals are happy with their own company but equally comfortable with closeness and intimacy. Secure people approach others at times of need. A worry about a hospital appointment or setback at work might prompt proximity seeking with a partner with the expectation of emotional support and understanding. When two secure people relate, care and reassurance, advice and encouragement are likely to flow happily in both directions.

The general approach of secure adults to relationships, tasks and challenges suggests confidence and optimism. Just like their infant counterparts, they feel positive about 'exploration', showing a willingness to take advantage of new opportunities. Their curiosity remains alive and their minds open to new experiences. All of this translates well into the work setting. Secure individuals are well motivated. Careers are generally enjoyed. Secure adults concentrate when necessary and more often than not they feel satisfied with their achievements. They are good team players.

Secure individuals value and can handle honest feedback in close relationships, seeing it as a way of improving self-awareness and understanding and developing a more accurate, non-deluded self-image. In short, having an active, positive, constructive, flexible, adaptive approach to life, secure adults are more likely to generate positive, rewarding environments.

Adolescence

Adolescence marks the beginnings of true independence. There is less acknowledgement of attachment-related needs and issues (Scharf *et al.* 2004). Whereas infants use attachment figures for both protection and affect regulation, adolescents tend to use them mainly for the regulation of their emotions. Throughout the teenage years there is a gradual displacement of parents as primary attachment figures to more secondary ones, or 'attachment figures in reserve' as Weiss (1982) called them. The speculation is that this weakening of emotional investment in parents possibly serves the evolutionary purpose of promoting self-reliance, individuation, independence, and sexuality, achievements likely to aid survival and reproduction (Scharf and Mayseless 2007: 3). However, even though friends, including boyfriends and girlfriends, increasingly provide relationships in which issues of care and attachment are managed, at times of need and stress, parents still feature high up in the adolescent's attachment hierarchy.

In adolescence, friends begin to be used as reciprocal attachment figures, providing relationships in which emotions can be explored and regulated (Allen and Manning 2007: 28). Close friends and dating partners provide opportunities to experiment with the skills required for forming adult-pair and attachment bonds (Kobak *et al.* 2007: 61). But unlike attachments with parents in the early years, adolescent attachments are liable to chop and change. There is relationship experimentation and social exploration. Attachments can be transient, and their loss is rarely mourned. There is a growing interest in intimate relationships. Self-disclosure with friends increases along with a growing awareness of emotional vulnerability. More profoundly, there is a marked improvement in social understanding and reflective functioning, defined as the capacity to recognize one's own and other people's mental states. Other people's behaviour is seen as meaningful, and their feelings and points of view are taken into consideration more and more. Of course, the growing struggle for increased independence can bring adolescents into conflict with parents, but at least in the case of those who are securely attached, this can be discussed and negotiated.

Nevertheless, the legacies of early attachments are still at work. For example, Sagi-Schwartz and Aviezer (2005) found that the social competence of adolescents in their late teens with their friends and romantic partners, and their ability to cope with life stressors was associated with their infant attachment status. A secure attachment history with parents predicts peer competence. If the tenor of our relationships with parents, family and friends remains largely unchanged, our internal working models will also continue largely unaltered, guiding our expectations and performance in close relationships.

Secure adolescents continue to show the resiliences that were present in their younger years. They are confident and independent. They enjoy high self-esteem and self-efficacy. And when they get into run-of-the-mill difficulties, whether in relationships or life more generally, their coping skills allow them to resolve matters in a constructive manner.

Autonomous adults

Secure adolescents and adults are sometimes described as *autonomous* in the sense that they can reflect, without too much distortion, on their own thoughts, feelings and behaviour. In general, they behave non-defensively. Mary Main says that they are 'free-to-evaluate' how they affect other people and how other people affect them, how their own behaviour and other people's behaviour are the product of what they think and feel. When they self-reflect, secure individuals tend to be honest and insightful. They are therefore good at monitoring what they say, even as they are saying it, so that they come across as 'fresh' in their speech and open in their attempts to be genuine and true. They continue to believe that in spite of occasionally behaving poorly or making social mistakes, they remain loved and accepted, though not necessarily condoned. Here is Laura talking about her relationship with her mother when she was a teenager:

> I was terrible in my early teens. I gave my mum a hard time. My dad had left us and I felt fat and angry and cross with everything and everybody. I was a bit of mess! I knew really it wasn't my mum's fault, but I kind of took it out on her. I said it was because she was so boring that my dad left her for another woman. That was a terrible thing to say. She's not boring! She's a lovely, funny woman. Looking back I can see that she was deeply hurt by dad's leaving, just as I was, and that she had a real struggle looking after me and my sister, but she kept the family together. She knew why I was so angry and awful, but never retaliated. We talk about it now and we get on great, but I wasn't a nice person back then.

Secure adults remember and acknowledge the good and the bad. They can see how past experiences affect, and may continue to affect them, perhaps leaving them vulnerable and fragile in certain areas. The key thing is not that secure people are without weaknesses or fault-lines in their personality, rather, they know that these fragilities are there and they understand how they can still affect behaviour. Imperfections in the self and others are acknowledged and tolerated. They appreciate that under stress and strain, they can sometimes behave unreasonably, but realizing this, they can recover, make amends, and repair any damage or rupture caused to the relationship.

This is a reminder that even people who have suffered childhood abuse and neglect can achieve a secure status if they can recognize and understand why a parent might have maltreated them ('my mother was rejected when she was a little girl and got heavily into drugs and simply couldn't do the parent-thing'), how the abuse has affected and continues to affect them, and what they think has helped overcome some of these early, tough experiences (usually a good relationship with someone who is secure, safe, available and attuned).

Secure individuals see others as a resource. Adult children continue to seek support from parents at times of stress. Parents might be turned to when you have your first baby, suffer a divorce, lose your job. Their sense of trust is also high. For example, several studies have shown that secure gay and lesbian individuals disclose their sexual orientation to others at earlier stages in the relationship than more insecure people (e.g. Mohr and Fassinger 2003).

Looked at in the round, secure adults live a life that is healthily balanced between intimacy and independence, relatedness and autonomy. They recognize and value *interdependence*. For most of us, there is desire to relate and engage with others but coupled with the need to feel independent, competent and in control of our own experience and destiny. Secure people enjoy being open in intimate relationships, and there is much self-disclosure and talk about personal experiences. They know how and when to get close to people for love, support, guidance, and fun. They are equally happy to be on the receiving end of other people's worries and need for understanding and comfort. That is, they can give as well as receive. Close relationships are therefore characterized by give and take, negotiation and compromise, reflective and empathic listening, co-operation and shared problem-solving (Feeney *et al.* 1995).

But people who are secure also value their own time and space. Although they enjoy company, they also feel comfortable on their own. When there are things to be done, they get on and do them. And when the work is done, they also know how to relax – friends, a chat, a cuddle, a run, a beer.

The characteristics possessed by people who are secure do not mean that they don't experience stress. But when they do face setbacks, their resilience, particularly their ability to appraise and mentalize, keeps them positively oriented for longer. Under threat or challenge, secure individuals can think and act flexibly. They remain relatively calm and constructive. Very often, rather than deal solely with the negative emotions that have been aroused, secure people also try and do something about the thing, person or situation that has brought about the unsettled state. Unlike their insecure counterparts who get helplessly caught up with their negative feelings, secure people adopt a problem-solving stance in an attempt to regulate emotional upset. And if they do seek help, say, from a friend, partner, colleague or counsellor, they are more likely to be helped than more insecure people. Therapists, for example, are more able to engage with secure people's ability to reflect on their own and other people's mental states. Dozier (1990) found that secure clients were more compliant with, and responsive to treatment. There was less rejection of therapists, more openness and greater self-disclosure.

Just in case this portrait of the secure individual implies a paragon of perfection, we must remind ourselves that there is a range of attachment styles even within the secure grouping (Crittenden 1997). Some secure people are more 'reserved'. They have mild avoidant and dismissing tendencies (see Chapter 9). Others might be more socially and emotionally 'reactive'. Their attachment behaviour shades towards ambivalence and preoccupation (see Chapter 11). But wherever the secure individual is placed along the autonomous continuum, he or she approaches life with an open and interested mind.

Loss

Loss was one of the great themes of Bowlby's thinking about the importance of relationships, both in the early years and later. The loss of an attachment figure, in childhood or adulthood, is the cause of great pain and despair. Grief tends to be intense. In many ways, the response to loss experienced in adulthood, is similar to the loss and separation experiences seen in childhood (Parkes 2006). Shock, protest, followed by pain, despair and sadness, before a final reorganization and adjustment to living with the loss is the general order of the 'loss-mourning' sequence. Loss is therefore best understood as a process, not an event. In the case of the death of a loved one, for many people, although by no means everyone, even though the loss is acknowledged and understood, a kind of continuing bond, perfectly normal and healthy, often exists with the deceased for months, even years.

The grief cycle is played out in its own unique way for each individual and their particular loss. There is no 'right' order or right way to grieve, although in some cases the mourning might be seen as disordered and problematic. The death of a close partner might lead to distress, a yearning ache and sleepless nights in one. Feelings of bewilderment, profound sadness and disbelief cause distress in another. While in a third, feelings of relief might prevail now that it is no longer necessary to provide the constant care for a chronically ill spouse. Similar reactions to loss might be experienced by those undergoing divorce or separation. To illustrate the complex feelings that loss can engender, Shaver and Fraley (2008: 64) quote the author C. S. Lewis writing about the loss of his wife who died:

> There are moments ... when something inside me tries to assure me that I don't really mind so much ... Love is not the whole of a man's life. I was happy before I ever met H. I've plenty of what are called 'resources.' People get over these things. Come, I shan't do so badly. One is ashamed to listen to this voice but it seems to be making out a good case. *Then comes a sudden jab of red-hot memory and all this 'commonsense' vanishes like an ant in the mouth of a furnace.*
> (Lewis 1961: 5-6, emphasis added)

Many factors affect the grieving process, including gender, the type and quality of the relationship with the deceased, including the attachment status of the survivor (Stroebe *et al.* 2006). With time, though, most people adjust. This doesn't mean they forget or that they don't still have moments of sadness as a memory comes unbeckoned into the mind of the present. Secure individuals are also more likely to reminisce about their loved ones, with fondness, some sadness, but without distortion (Waskowic and Chartier 2003). Only a few people get stuck or run into difficulty. This is more likely for those whose attachments are insecure. Individuals with anxious attachments, for example, might be more prone to chronic mourning. Their emotions are likely to be extreme, intense and dramatic (see Chapter 11). In contrast, more avoidant individuals might claim to experience fewer reactions in the face of a loss as they defend against feelings of distress, sadness, or anger (see Chapter 9). But for most, life resumes and energies slowly return.

Romantic and couple relationships

Many of the most intense emotions arise during the formation, maintenance, the disruption and the renewal of attachment relationships. The formation of a bond is described as falling in love, maintaining a bond as loving someone, and losing a partner as grieving over someone.

(Bowlby 1998b: 40)

Just as it takes time for the caregiver to become the infant's attachment figure, so forming an attachment bond with a romantic partner in adulthood is also a gradual process (Zeifman and Hazan 2008). In adult romantic attachments, unlike the asymmetry of the parent–child relationship in which at times of need the child seeks care and protection from the parent and the parent provides the care and protection, the adult *pair-bond* is symmetric. Adult romantic attachments are defined in terms of an emotional bond between two individuals based on the expectation that each member will provide both care and protection for the other (Goldberg 2000: 134; Mohr 2008) Sensitive partners will provide comfort and support at times of need and distress. They offer a safe haven and an emotional sanctuary. They also provide a secure base from which the partner is able to explore – their feelings, goals, work, ambitions, hopes, career, interests, skills, personal growth. When both partners provide each other with a safe haven and a secure base, when each is sensitive and responds to the other's signals, we can predict relationship security, stability, satisfaction, good health and well-being (Collins *et al.* 2006). Paradoxically, the more we can rely on partners to be available, responsive and supportive at times of need, the more independently we can behave.

Attachment behaviour has close links with other behavioural systems including those associated with courtship, mating and the formation of romantic relationships. So, during the conduct of romantic relationships, we see a number of behavioural systems coming together and being simultaneously activated. Romantic relationships therefore witness complex behaviours between partners in which attachment, caregiving, sex, reproduction, sociability, work, and play interact in fluid, shifting, sometimes confusing ways, although attachment security generally enhances the performance of most of the other systems. Romantic love, of course, involves liking and respect, but in most cases it also involves sex. Liking and respect may be 'subject to sweet reason', but 'desire is the joker in the pack, the dark force that renders everything volatile, complex, and unstable' (Foley 2010: 193). The ability to reflect and mentalize, even when in the throes of passion, help us to keep our bearings as love, friendship and sex swirl around us.

Sex, of course, can lead to children. A further evolutionary benefit of adult pair bonding is the growing psychological and physiological interdependence between partners. Cementing relationships in this way increases both partners' commitment to the protection and survival of any joint offspring of the pairing (Zeifman and Hazan 2008).

But let's stop for a moment and begin at the beginning. What happens after the eyes first meet and a frisson of something passes between a couple? There are certainly interesting parallels between falling in love and the formation of affectional bonds between mothers and their babies. Just as babies progress through a number of stages in the formation of their attachments, so adults who become intimate develop their attachments through a number of recognizable steps (Zeifman and Hazan 1997).

Early interest in possible sexual partners tends initially to be playful, flirtatious, arousing, and to an extent indiscriminate. Before the potential partner is known better, there is bound to be some anxiety during the initial phase of flirting. Lack of interest or rejection remains a distinct possibility. This uncertainty will activate the attachment system, and with it one's internal working model. Secure individuals are likely to handle this anxiety constructively which has the knock-on effect of making the potential partner feel more relaxed, happy, and interested. Secure people score well on matters of commitment, intimacy and a willingness to forgive. Possessed of good self-esteem, secure adults are more likely to let down their defences in the context of a close relationship. Being less defensive increases emotional attunement and being understood. There is less anxiety at the prospect of having sex in the context of a loving relationship. These qualities also predict greater likelihood of feeling satisfied with the partnership.

Not surprisingly, therefore, it is generally the case that secure people are particularly attractive to others (e.g. Klohen and Luo 2003). They engender feelings of safety and pleasure. To be recognized, understood and liked by another is always an attractive prospect.

However, once the sexually charged interest is established as mutual, the attachment becomes both selective and discriminating. We talk about 'falling in love.' Touch, gazing into each other's eyes, cuddling, touching, kissing, caressing and crying look remarkably similar to what happens in well-established mother–baby relationships (Bowlby 1997: 233). The absence of the other can be experienced as painful. Separation leads to 'heartache'. Reunion is sheer joy.

However, just as it takes time for a full-blown attachment to form in infancy, it takes anything up to two years for a couple to use each other as a safe haven and secure base (Hazan and Zeifman 1994). If the relationship is working well, further developmental benefits accrue. We all have the capacity to grow, mature and improve our mental well-being in the context of a close relationship in which we appraise the other as available and responsive.

> When the appraisal is positive, it contributes to what we call a broaden-and-build cycle of attachment security … this cycle includes positive emotions (comfort, relief, love, pride), promotes positive perceptions of both self and others, and encourages comfortable, confident engagement in intimate relationships and growth-oriented activities (e.g. exploration, education, helping others). In other words, this cycle helps to explain the documented benefits of interacting with available and responsive attachment figures: healthy personality development, satisfying close relationships, and good personal and social adjustment.
>
> (Mikulincer and Shaver 2007: 6–1)

Once the relationship becomes established and secure, the intensity of the need for physical contact and the pain felt at separation ease off. Partners begin to turn to each for support and understanding, particularly at times of anxiety and need, setback and stress. These are times, or course, when the attachment system is activated and when we expect to see attachment behaviour being directed towards our partners – our safe havens and secure bases. Indeed, when we feel under stress or even in pain, the mere presence of an attachment figure, such as a romantic partner, can help us feel safe and more relaxed. And although partners can still be experienced as stimulating, indeed arousing, they become increasingly important as providers of care, calm and comfort as the relationship settles down into one of secure and safe familiarity. Relationships that make us feel safe and validate our worth lower our anxiety and raise our confidence so that we might set about life in ways that help us realize our potential, embrace opportunities, grow emotionally, and improve our self-image (Collins *et al.* 2006). Throughout the life course, secure attachments continue to promote and enhance our personal development.

Hazan and Shaver (1987) were among the first to take a detailed look at romantic relationships using an attachment perspective. Their work actually grew out of Ainsworth's empirical studies rather than Bowlby's theoretical ideas (Hazan *et al.* 2006: 48). In order to examine adult attachments, Hazan and Zeifman (1994) constructed measures that paralleled the kind of observations that had been developed for young children. To establish whether an adult relationship was attachment-based, they asked questions such as 'Who do you most want to be close to and spend time with?' (proximity maintenance), 'Who do you turn to when upset or feeling down?' (safe haven), 'Who do you miss and hate being apart from when you're away?' (separation distress), and 'Who do you count on being there to provide help and support at times of need? (secure base). Not surprisingly, intimate partners are frequently and most often named in answer to such questions. Nevertheless, even in later adulthood, many parents continue to be available as providers of support, emotional as well as material. This suggests that early childhood attachments are enduring even though adult partners clearly begin to replace parents as the primary attachment figure.

Conflict and disagreement are inevitable in all close relationships, although secure couples tend to experience fewer upsets than inse-cure partners. When the relationship is one based on reciprocal attachment and caregiving, conflict activates both partners' attach-ment systems, leading to protest, anxiety, or careseeking behaviours. Secure couples are generally good at acknowledging the conflict and its source. In principle, they are also prepared to do something about the disagreement, by voicing their own feelings but also attending to those of their partner. Stable relationships tend to be characterized by both partners' willingness to repair the damage caused by their differ-ences.

The origins of these conflict-resolution skills lie in childhood. Parents who are prepared to explain, encourage perspective-taking, and promote harmony help children to develop constructive strate-gies to resolve relationship difficulties. Similarly, adult attempts to resolve conflict and consider the goals of the other offer 'an opportu-nity to enhance intimacy and communication because partners learn about each other's goals and feelings and because they may engage in collaborative strategies to try to resolve the conflict' (Pietromonaco *et al.* 2004: 269). In general, secure couples and their attachment bonds are not too threatened by conflict. All of these skills predict that rela-tionships should be reasonably satisfying and long-lasting. So, towards the end of their review of close relationships and exploration in adulthood, Feeney and Van Vleet summarize this happy state of affairs, declaring that:

> When adults have, in their relationship partner, a secure base that supports their exploration by being available, encouraging, and non-intrusive, they are able to explore their environment and reap the benefits of such exploration in terms of enjoyment, successful performance, learning/discovery, self-efficacy, and self-esteem.
>
> (2010: 232)

Parenthood and caregiving

Having been on the receiving end of good enough caregiving, secure children who grow up to be secure and autonomous adults can parent their children as they were parented as children. To a signifi-cant extent, attachment patterns, whether secure or insecure, remain fairly stable from infancy to adulthood.

However, as we shall see in Chapter 15, this does not mean that secure children are automatically destined to become secure parents, nor indeed does it mean that insecure children are inevitably going to become anxious or uncertain parents. Attachment patterns and the defensive strategies that underpin them can change at any time during the lifecourse. Such shifts are most likely to occur in the context of major changes in the quality and character of a close relationship, for better or worse. This is a reminder that although we have a stable core to our personality make-up, we do remain sensitive and responsive to our social environment. Even so, most secure children, possibly up to 70 per cent, will enjoy care that remains good enough, most of the time, throughout their childhood and into adulthood. Continuity in the provision of sensitive and attuned care predicts that when secure children become parents, they are more than likely to parent in a sensitive and responsive manner.

Caregiving also needs to be viewed in its social context, that is, from a social ecological perspective. As well as the caregiver's own attachment history and organization, other ecological factors affect the quality of care provided. The more social support that parents receive from partners, family, friends and the local community, and the more stress-free they feel materially, the more responsive becomes their parenting (Belsky and Jaffee 2006). Children are much more likely to be secure and enjoy good psychosocial development when they grow up in happy families in which couples have good relationships with each other. Parents who are mutually secure in their attachments create families in which communications are open and emotions acknowledged. It is in these families that children are more likely to be secure (for example, see the special issue of the journal *Attachment and Human Development* 2009, Volume 11(1) on couple relationships and children's attachments).

As parents, secure adults are good at co-operating with their children to achieve both the parents' and the child's goals. As well as being protectors and providers of comfort, parents also act as 'playmates, disciplinarians, teachers, role models or sources of stimulation' (Goldberg 2000: 250). Secure and autonomous parents' descriptions of themselves and their children are realistic. They acknowledge behaviours that are both good and bad, with an overall bias towards the positive.

Secure adults encourage their children to be independent. They are proud of their achievements, burgeoning talents, and growing individuality. Secure parents feel less anxious about their teenage children growing more distant. Paradoxically, of course, this parental understanding of the need for independence and willingness to let go decreases conflict and helps adolescent children maintain feelings of attachment and security (Hock *et al.* 2001). Such confident and sympathetic parenting also predicts better adolescent peer relationships and social skills. Again, secure parenting doesn't mean that everything runs smoothly all of the time. But when there is conflict and disagreement, both children and parents have the strength, skill and resources to get themselves out of the potential impasse. The inevitable tension that all parents experience between security and discipline, socialization and individuality, exploration and safety, separation and comfort is negotiated with some success. These are the parents who know when to give and take, concede or confront, reason or put their foot down, negotiate or suggest. These are the techniques that help children improve their ability (and willingness) to control their impulses, comply, and be independent. These are *authoritative* parents, ones who are fun, fair and firm.

Physical health

One of the more intriguing findings of health psychologists is that happy people tend to enjoy better health and live longer. The usual explanation is that people who are happy are more relaxed, less stressed, feel in control, experience high self-esteem, and benefit from good quality close relationships. For example, Gump *et al.* (2001) found that close social supports increase feelings of security. People with good quality social contact and support experience less stress, and are less prone to emotional extremes. We tend to feel emotionally more relaxed, supported and competent when we are with partners and friends. All of this is reflected in better physical health. For example, we find that blood pressure is lower when people interact with romantic partners than with others.

In contrast, high stress and anxiety tax the immune system. Therefore stressed, anxious and unhappy people are more likely to get ill with colds and influenza, fall prey to disease, recover less well from illness, eat less well, smoke and drink more, and generally lead poorer quality life styles (Sapolsky 1998).

It follows, then, that if secure people are more likely to set about life positively, have good quality relationships, and be happy, their health prospects will be good (see Diamond and Hicks 2004, for a review). Secure people tend to appraise situations reasonably accurately without too much distortion and so respond constructively. Secure adults do tend to lead healthier life styles. They seek health advice earlier than those classified insecure, and are more likely to follow medical prescriptions. They manage their stress and emotions better, including using other people to acknowledge, discuss, think about and regulate any worries and upsets they might have.

It is generally admitted that the links between secure attachments and good health, and insecure attachment and poor health, are still tentative, but it is acknowledged that it is a topic worthy of further study. The most promising insights are likely to come from a better understanding of how early infant–caregiver relationships help children regulate both body and mind, emotion and feeling, particularly at the level of the central nervous system. The relatively new sciences of epigenetics (the study of how genes get switched on or off depending on the character of the environment, including the caregiving environment) and psychoneuroimmunology (the study of how psychology, the brain, the nervous system, and the immune system are all interconnected) have the potential to link attachment, emotional states and their regulation with the immune system and its functioning, and ultimately people's physical health.

Mental health

Over recent years, our understanding of development, including psychopathology, has taken into account the complex and dynamic interactions between nature and nurture. Throughout life, particularly in the early years, development takes place as a series of elaborate transactions between individuals' genetic make-up, their caregiving experiences, and their encounters with the environment, some of which will pose risks while others offer opportunities (Sroufe *et al.* 2005b). When the elements stack up positively, the transactions are likely to result in developmentally enhancing experiences. A child with a cheerful temperament raised by responsive parents is likely not only to cope well with peers, but also to gain new skills and social insights from the experience of coping well with peers. This way good mental health lies. However, when elements of vulnerability enter the mix, including insecure attachments, our ability to manage life's stressors decreases (Kobak *et al.* 2006). The chances of sound mental health reduce and the risks of psychopathology increase.

Secure individuals tend not to generate or experience too many major stresses in their lives. Their relationships with other people are usually positive. Because they have high 'reflective function' and can 'mentalize' the complexities of psychosocial events, secure individuals buffer themselves against the dysregulating effects of feeling lost, helpless and out of control. Both internal and external levels of 'felt security' are high. When they are faced with a new situation, they approach it with confidence and optimism. And if they do feel under stress and are faced with negative emotions, they tend to cope better with them. Secure adults also enjoy good social support which acts as a further buffer against stress. As a result, levels of the stress hormone cortisol are generally normal. Low stress, normal cortisol production, high reflective function, and good quality relationships equate with the increased chance of enjoying good mental health.

Old age

Finally, in old age, when attachment behaviour can no longer be directed towards members of an older generation, or even the same generation, it may come instead to be directed towards members of a younger one.

(Bowlby 1997: 207)

There is a small, but growing literature on attachment in later life. However, it is still limited and at the moment, it is difficult to draw a clear picture (Bradley and Cafferty 2001). The help-seeking behaviour of older people, notes Magai (2008: 543), remains grossly understudied.

Old age increases the chances of becoming physically, socially and emotionally dependent on others. The death of partners, friends and siblings becomes all too common. And one's own death looms ever closer. These changes and losses have major implications for the attachment systems of older people. In spite of increasing physical fragility, many old people fight hard to maintain self-care and independence. A lifetime of experience can stand you in good stead when it comes to solving problems and remaining in control. Wensauer and Grossman (1995, cited in Bradley and Cafferty 2001: 213) found that secure old people tended to enjoy better social integration, life satisfaction and physical health than those classified as insecure. Nevertheless, there may come a point when help and support are needed, and attachment issues of dependency and interdependency once more return to the frame.

In their close relationships, most adults act as both careseekers and caregivers. Their close relationships are symmetrical. However, with advancing old age and physical vulnerability, the balance can shift to one of increasing dependency. 'Stronger' and in some respects 'wiser' children (that is, they know the ways of the modern world) are turned to for care and guidance, safety and protection (Antonucci *et al.* 2004). Adult children's attachment figures become support seekers. Sons and daughters become safe havens and care providers for their physically fragile parents.

Secure adults with dependent parents reciprocate the style of empathic, joyful care which they themselves enjoyed as children (Cicirelli 1995; Steele *et al.* 2004). Affectional bonds between the generations remain strong. Emotional support from close family members in which respect for the elderly relative's autonomy is maintained. But their need for comfort, care and intimacy is also recognized. Getting the balance right between care and independence appears to be particularly important for well-being. Middle-aged children accept, understand and tolerate their parents' growing vulnerability. Having been cared for, they are willing to care.

Nurses or staff in residential homes can also become attachment figures (Antonucci *et al.* 2004). For those who do not have children, siblings and close friends might become safe havens and secure bases. Doctors, clergy and careworkers can provide comfort and emotional support. Pets, too, often provide companionship. And for many in their later years who have lost close friends and relatives and who are approaching their own death, God and other religious figures increasingly serve attachment functions (Cicirelli 2004). Being a sociable species, we continue to need a degree of intimacy and relatedness in our lives, and even if we cannot find it immediately in the form of partners or family, a range of other people can happily fall into our attachment orbit.

Interestingly, the return of pronounced attachment behaviours is often seen in the early stages of dementia. The sense of growing fragility, vulnerability and confusion seems to activate the attachment system resulting in increasing displays of proximity-seeking behaviours towards adult children, siblings, and residential care staff (Miesen 1992). And as the dementia advances, some elderly people begin talk about their own parents and may act as if they are still alive.

We often leave this world as we entered it, vulnerable, possibly frightened, and physically dependent on others, but also comforted by the bonds of love.

Conclusion

Adults classified as secure continue to be comfortable with being emotionally close with partners, parents and friends, but also happily independent when situations require it. They are relaxed about seeking help should the need arise and good at providing comfort and support for others when approached.

In most stable, responsive environments, including those generated by families, we should expect the secure pattern and autonomous states of mind to prevail. Autonomous states of mind confer a range of mental, emotional and social benefits. But like all attachments, they represent an adaptation to the social context in which individuals find themselves. It is hard to resist the obvious conclusion, therefore, that the world would be a better place if all environments were benign and all attachments secure. Perhaps implicit in much social policy, positive psychology, and the growth of social capital is an argument for promoting the security of attachments, from cradle to grave. But because attachment patterns represent strategies of survival and adaptation, and because humankind continues to throw up a range of a difficult and challenging environments in which the young attempt to cope and stay safe, not all attachments will be secure.

8

Avoidant Attachments in Childhood

Introduction

When those who are most important to us seem cool, maybe a little uncomfortable with too much emotional display, or even rejecting of our need of them, it is likely that we will learn to contain our eagerness to be close and hide any hint that it hurts to be rebuffed and denied. Avoidance, in this sense, isn't necessarily a physical avoidance of closeness, but rather an avoidance of showing too much dependency and too much emotion in case one is rejected and suffers hurt. As a consequence, avoidant people feel anxious whenever their feelings become strongly aroused. They fear rejection or ridicule. Intimacy is desired, even pursued, but it increases anxiety and hesitation. So, emotions can't be trusted as a guide to action. Thinking is safer than feeling. Being rational and in control is better than letting your emotions run away with you. Each attachment pattern represents a behavioural strategy that helps the individual adapt as best they can to the quality and character of the close relationship environment in which they find themselves. Insecure attachments make sense under the circumstances.

Infancy

Young babies can only communicate their needs and states of distress through their behaviour. However, the insistent demands of a distressed baby whose attachment behaviour is operating at full strength cause some parents to feel not only distress but also irritation and anger, and in extreme cases hostility. Defensively, others may emotionally disengage as their child's attachment behaviour increases. In some cases, mothers of babies destined to become avoidant actually report seeing less arousal, need and distress in their children (Goldberg 2000: 145).

In general, it seems that attachment behaviour in children classified avoidant raises anxiety in parents who are very likely themselves to be classified as insecure, avoidant and dismissing. Displays of need and vulnerability create feelings of anxiety in parents who, when they were children, learned to contain and suppress their arousal and attachment behaviour knowing that if they made demands on others, rejection was likely. Thus, by rejecting their children's attachment behaviour, it helps caregivers keep their own anxiety in check and their own fears of rejection at bay.

George and Solomon (2008) see caregiving by parents of avoidant children as a form of defensive exclusion, a defence that allows them to organize their caregiving, albeit at some cost. This defence protects them from breaking down under the stress of parenting. Deactivation of the caregiving system is a way of keeping distress out of conscious awareness, and thus avoids too much arousal of the caregiving system. This leads to caregiving that Solomon and George (1996) describe as 'distanced protection':

> Mothers in this group express disdain for clingy children and do not enjoy caregiving closeness; they describe caregiving strategies that emphasize overseeing their children from afar or assigning care to someone else. Psychological distance is maintained through emphasizing negative portrayals of self and child (e.g., that the mother is not doing a good job, or that the child is manipulative and requires authoritarian discipline).
>
> (George and Solomon 2008: 845)

From the child's point of view, attachment behaviour appears to cause the parent to become more distant, more rigid, more rejecting. It is as if the parent is saying 'Your distress does not matter to me; do not bother me; I am not interested.' These are parents who give the message that caregiving is a chore. They don't seem to enjoy being a parent and they are unlikely to have fun, or be fun. The parent's availability actually appears greatest when the baby is least aroused or distressed.

Most parents have moments when their baby makes them feel helpless and even angry, but they recover, take stock and remember that babies can't communicate any other way than through their behaviour. They take a deep breath, tune in, and once again see the world from their baby's point of view, responding as best they can. In contrast, parents whose own childhood care was experienced as practical and hard-nosed rather than warm and loving, feel uncomfortable when other people make emotional demands of them. This includes everyday overtures made by their own children. The parents' own implicit memories are ones in which emotions, and displays of affection or distress were either ignored or dismissed. Their own parenting therefore often appears impatient and resentful. At some unconscious level, it's as if the parent is saying to the child 'No-one ever loved me just for myself, so don't expect me to be at your beck and call whenever you feel like it.' Emotions are not trusted. Attachment behaviour and displays of need and vulnerability are seen as weak. There is contempt for those who show tears and emotional upset.

So how might a needy baby, whose attachment system is fully activated, behave in such a relationship? Initially, activation of the attachment system will lead to any one or more behaviours out of the child's attachment repertoire. The goal of attachment behaviour is to recover proximity with the caregiver. However, avoidant infants soon sense that displays of emotion, particularly negative ones, do not appear to increase caregiver availability or comfort. On the contrary, need and arousal all too often cause the caregiver to back off or dismiss the child's need for attention as unworthy and inappropriate.

So the behavioural problem for the child in these kinds of parent–child relationship is how to achieve proximity and closeness to the parent without courting the rejection that any strong display of emotional need seems to induce in the attachment figure. What the baby experiences at the behavioural level is that *deactivating* the attachment system and suppressing attachment behaviours that signal distress increases the number of opportunities to stay close to the caregiver. In contrast, excessive shows of need, distress or conflict increase parental rejection. Rejection is painful, hurtful and definitely to be avoided. 'Inhibition of affective signals,' observes Crittenden (1995: 370), 'both has the predictable effect of reducing maternal rejection and anger and also teaches infants that expression of affect is counterproductive'. The young child learns, at least at the behavioural level, to *over-regulate their arousal*.

Deactivating strategies are a 'flight' reaction to an attachment figure's unavailability, which seem to develop in relationships with figures who disapprove of and punish closeness and expressions of need or vulnerability ... In such cases, a person learns to expect better outcomes if signs of need and vulnerability are hidden or suppressed, proximity-seeking efforts are weakened or blocked, the attachment system is deactivated despite a sense of security not being achieved, and the person attempts to deal with threats and dangers alone.

(Mikulincer and Shaver 2007: 22)

None of this means that the aroused and upset states that any baby is bound to feel during the course of any normal day actually go away. Rather, they are contained. The lid is kept on the more negative emotions. At the physiological level, children classified as avoidant typically experience high levels of arousal and stress in the context of close relationships – but they simply don't show it at the behavioural level.

Avoidant children also begin to falsify their feelings, perhaps appearing more positively cheerful than they actually feel, knowing that positive emotions are likely to be better received than negative ones. The caregiver offers love and acceptance but on his or her terms. Love and regard are conditional on the young child making minimal emotional demands of the carer, and behaving as the carer expects a 'good' child to behave. The child therefore begins to look to caregivers for what is expected of them and how to get it right.

Another feature of caregiving that is rejecting of infant need, dependency and vulnerability involves parents defining and making sense of their children's experience *for them* in terms that suit the parents' dismissing state of mind. Parents might attempt to define how their baby 'ought' to feel rather than acknowledge and confirm how the baby is actually feeling. Or a parent might talk about what any 'reasonable' child should experience in a given situation in a way that suits the parent rather than the child.

For example, a crying baby may be told that he is not really distressed and that there is nothing to be upset about, even if the child really is hurt, hungry or needs changing. A toddler might be told repeatedly 'Don't be a baby; stop crying for heaven's sake' or 'Grow up and don't be pathetic and forever whinging' or 'Oh, for goodness sake, it's only a bee sting, not the end of the world. You're not really hurt, so stop yelling' or 'Don't be a cry baby – I won't love you if you cry.' The implicit message here is that if you're not hurt, there is no need to cry and therefore I won't have to get irritated and reject you. If you are rejected, it is your own fault. You have only your self to blame if the world doesn't love you. Be as I say and then, only then, will I love you.

It has also been observed that some carers of avoidant children often 'correct' their child's feelings and memories, particularly if parents feel threatened or distressed by their child's mental representations. This 'intrusion' undermines children's confidence in their own memories and perceptions. It also instils the idea into the young mind that there is only one right view of events, the caregiver's view. 'No, we didn't get cross with you. You're imagining it. You're always getting things wrong. We all had a lovely time.'

In summary, avoidance, as a secondary attachment strategy, is attachment behaviour that is *organized* in relation to the set goal of seeking some kind of psychological proximity to the carer. It is also seen as *insecure* inasmuch as the child cannot assume that their own needs will be unconditionally met, or their caregiver is unconditionally available. Nevertheless, in spite of their anxiety, children learn to adapt their behaviour to the type of caregiving environment provided by their parents. These adaptive, albeit defensive strategies ensure maximum parental availability and acceptance under the caregiving circumstances in which the child finds himself or herself. So although young children classified as avoidant often remain self-contained and self-sufficient, they achieve a kind of interpersonal competence.

However, the avoidant strategy does come at some developmental cost. Avoidant children who feel uncomfortable with strong feelings, whether the feelings are experienced by them or other people, may not have had the opportunity to reflect on and make sense of feeling states. Having cut themselves off from some of their stronger feelings, emotions represent that part of their psychological make-up that is not fully understood. To have missed out on opportunities to experience and reflect on the nature and value of feelings, avoidant children often find themselves at a disadvantage when it comes to the skilled conduct of close relationships. Indeed, believes Main (1991), the failure to display emotion may constrain the actual experience of emotion. And according to Crittenden (1995), avoidant infants learn to organize their behaviour without being able to interpret or use affective signals. Individuals who block strong feelings can appear reserved, detached, a little distant, and perhaps inclined to be rather private. Only when the defences break down do we see the sudden release of strong emotions with anger and aggression being the most likely to erupt (McElwain *et al.* 2003).

This outline of the behaviours, strategies and characteristics of children who develop avoidant attachments acts as a template for avoidant attachments across the lifecourse. Defence against affect, deactivation of the attachment system, dismissal of the importance of emotions in the self and others, and anxiety when relationships become more intimate (because of the fear of rejection) can all be seen in avoidant children, adults and parents. In general, what we see are defensive moves to avoid being rejected and getting hurt in the context of close relationships.

Middle childhood

Maturation allows pre-school children to handle matters more symbolically. This means that avoidant children can replace behavioural avoidance with *psychological inhibition of emotional need*. Avoidant children aged 3 or 4 are less likely to seek emotional support from their carers, at least in a direct and overt way. They have learned that caregiver acceptance is conditional on 'good' behaviour which means being self-sufficient and grown-up about things. Children recognize that their carers feel more comfortable with behaviours that are low in emotional tone and high in independence. They therefore become 'defended' against displays of their own affect with the result that they downplay emotional involvement (Crittenden 1992b). The following case, admittedly rather extreme, is a distressing example of how far some children can take an avoidant strategy:

Before Tim was born, his mother was a beautician. She had a difficult pregnancy and Tim was born by Caesarean section. He was kept immaculately clean as a baby. Not being able to stand mess, his mother was forever wiping his face and changing his clothes. Dirty nappies, drools, and sloppy food getting everywhere made her very tense. Aged 4, Tim's behaviour had become odd and it brought him to the attention of the health visitor. His mother admitted that she was finding it very difficult to like Tim. Even touching him could make her shiver. She would spend as much time as she could in a different room, expecting him to play on his own. When the health visitor first observed Tim she saw a little boy who was dressed fashionably and neatly. But he seemed to behave like a robot – stiff, unsmiling, mechanical in his actions. He walked like an automaton, rarely speaking. He would follow his mother from room to room in a way that she said 'freaked' her out. It was almost as if he had decided that because robots don't have feelings, then this was the safest state in which to be. If he had no emotions then he could neither be rejected on the grounds of showing need nor be hurt because he was without feeling.

Some avoidant children can become good readers of other people's emotional states (though not their own). It makes sense to gauge the other person's expectations of you if you are anxious about being rejected if you get things wrong, but accepted when you get them right. Being seen as competent and successful by other people feels safer than being intimate and open. Although parents might reject and devalue children's attachment needs, they notice and praise their intellectual, practical and physical successes. Parental interest, approval and positive regard are granted when children achieve independence, task-competence, physical prowess, or academic success. Learning to dress yourself, being toilet-trained, and playing quietly are likely to be viewed with considerable favour by dismissing parents.

Competence in thought and deed brings about an inner sense of control (self-efficacy) and a feeling of positive self-regard. Positive self-regard is therefore conditional on the self being able to contain emotion, and the self seeing itself (and believing itself to be seen by others) as competent and in control. The first hints of an achievement-oriented personality emerge in these early years. And over time, at least in some cases, the trait might lead to perfectionist tendencies, workaholism, and the drive for material success (Mayseless 1996: 217). Thus, on the surface, avoidant children show cooperation and compliance but not a great deal of intimacy. The emotion most likely to erupt is anger because anger serves to keep others at bay, remembering that closeness is associated with potential rejection and hurt and is therefore best avoided (Booth-LaForce *et al.* 2006; Mayseless 1996: 209).

More generally, there is evidence that avoidant attachments do predict an increased risk of behaviour problems (Aguilar *et al.* 2000). Of particular interest is the finding that many insecure children aged 11 and showing 'behavioural perturbance' and experiencing poor peer relationships (e.g. Steele and Steele 2005b: 155) had fathers who many years earlier had been coded as insecure. The long-term influence of both mother and father insecurity as it affects parent–child interaction appears to be quite marked.

Avoidant school-aged children relate with others somewhat defensively, always anxious that the self, if viewed too closely, isn't going to be seen as likeable or good enough, a self that might therefore be rejected. There is some evidence that children are more likely to select friends with similar attachment organizations to their own (Hodges *et al.* 1999), including avoidant children choosing other avoidant children as playmates. Perhaps not surprisingly, therefore, even though avoidant children sometimes claim to have many friends, they find it difficult to actually name them.

There is a desire for closeness, but an anxiety about its implications. For example, with parents or teachers, children might be keen to talk about their achievements, and about things and objects, knowing from past experience that prowess and accomplishments are most likely to lead to acceptance. Often in these exchanges, parents take the conversational lead, asking factual-type questions which receive a factual-type response (Main 1995). There might even be a rather formal quality to talk between parents and children: 'How well did you do in the class test today? Were you the top?' 'I tried my best, mother. I hope the results will please you when they're out.' 'Well, let's hope so. You know how disappointed it makes me feel when you don't do well.'

A focus on tasks and achievements is an impersonal, non-emotionally based way of getting close to people. In similar vein, avoidant children tend to play more 'literally' without the free-flowing use of pretence and imagination that characterizes the play of secure children.

Some of these play features are captured in studies by Solomon *et al.* (1995). Using dolls to help them, 6 year old children were invited to develop stories with an attachment-related theme. Some stories offered to the children involved monsters, while others began with the children being looked after for the night by a babysitter. In developing their stories, avoidant children did not fully activate their attachment systems. In their play, children avoided developing storylines that got their dolls into any kind of danger or difficulty, situations in which need and emotion might have to be displayed. As a result, their stories were rather bland. The dolls simply watched television or ate meals. 'Their stories' says George in another study, 'suggest that they "immobilize" the attachment system by systematically scanning, sorting, and excluding fear, pain, and sadness from conscious awareness' (1996: 415).

Conclusion

Infants classified as avoidant have learned that overt displays of need, anxiety and fear do not bring protective or comforting responses from caregivers. Their attachment signals are rejected. The only way to maintain proximity – physically and psychologically – is to keep a tight lid on any expression of negative feelings and to be self-sufficient whenever possible. These strategies mean that avoidant young children make few demands of their parents. This allows them to avoid rejection and maintain some kind of relationship, albeit one in which shows of distress and dependency are not allowed.

By 6 or 7 years of age, we begin to see the classic components of the avoidant personality that appear throughout childhood and into adulthood. The internal working model is one in which others are not represented as available at times of need although the self is modelled as strong, in control and not easily upset or affected. The use of bright but false affect continues as a way of keeping others involved, positively disposed and therefore psychologically available. If the relationship does go wrong, children assume it is their fault. Shame and guilt ensue. To get on the right side of carers, children become increasingly skilled at understanding what their parents would like to see, and so avoidant children behave accordingly. They try to do 'the right thing'. What the outside world sees is the child's 'false' self and rarely their 'true' self. The true self – full of feeling, needs, flaws, anxieties and vulnerabilities – is the one that the avoidant personality fears will be rejected and so it is kept well under control, if at all possible.

One result of keeping strong feelings, particularly negative feelings, contained and under control is that the avoidant individual is less able to explore their own emotional make-up. Not thinking too much about their own feeling states means that emotion and cognition are not fully integrated in the psychological self. Thoughts are trusted; feelings are not. The avoidant child's feelings in emotionally charged situations are not read well. Remembering that avoidant children have learned that shows of feeling increase the risk of rejection, then any breach of the defence of emotional denial, in the self or others, causes distress. The result can be an exaggerated, though often short-lived loss of control, leading to anger, irritation and impatience with their own or other people's needy behaviour.

All in all, the avoidant strategy, involving as it does suppression of the emotions, is a stressful one. In cases where the parenting continues unchanged and rejecting, then we might expect to see the defences associated with avoidance still being employed in adolescence and beyond into adulthood.

9
Avoidant and Dismissing Attachments in Adulthood

Introduction

For those classified as avoidant as children, parental availability was most likely when they were doing things well and without a fuss. This conditional acceptance means that the avoidant personality has a moderate need for approval. So, although the self has to be seen as independent and strong, it appears that the avoidant adult's 'attempts to maintain distance in their personal relationships might be, at least in part, anxiety driven' (Feeney *et al.* 1995: 142). Psychological independence therefore feels more comfortable than emotional closeness. There is some recognition of this by avoidant people themselves. Although they generally present as able and competent, there is a willingness to admit that they find close relationships and intimacy more difficult. This is then followed by the qualification that feelings and relationships are not that important to them anyway. Feedback by partners, for example, is not always welcome and often dismissed.

Adolescence

Avoidant adolescents begin defensively to exclude attachment-relevant information by not engaging with issues of emotional need, anxiety and dependency. They talk generally, somewhat vaguely, and often in idealized terms about relationships with attachment figures. Or in some cases, if they do choose to acknowledge attachment-based relationships, they discuss them in dismissive, even derogatory terms, claiming that both the relationship and the person were of no interest or importance to them. These defences are employed to avoid thinking about difficult memories, ones perhaps in which the self felt rejected or unloved.

Mild forms of avoidance might come across as nothing more than a reserved personality. More extreme forms appear as compulsive self-reliance. These personality features begin to take clearer shape during adolescence. Many avoidant adolescents do experience levels of distress and poor self-image on a par with ambivalent teenagers, but, unlike them, they engage in less risky behaviours, perhaps with the exception of sex where for some there is a tendency to have more frequent and less committed sexual relationships (Cooper *et al.* 2004).

Although there is a general rise in externalizing and conduct disorders during the teenage years for all adolescents, this risk is even greater for those assessed as avoidant. The abuse of alcohol and drugs can also be relatively high, in part to be less emotionally inhibited, and in part to dampen down some of the more troublesome worries about one's own unlovability and the hurt this causes.

One of the defining features of being avoidant is the difficulty individuals have in appearing vulnerable and needing help. This becomes all too apparent in adolescence. Avoidant teenagers are not good at asking friends for support, finding shoulders to cry on, or approaching teachers for advice and guidance (Scharf *et al.* 2004). And for those who leave school and go on to college, there is a tendency to withdraw from peers as they approach the day of transition. Adolescence, with its complex demands of independence, sexual maturation, and expectations that peers become increasingly used as sources of support, can be a confusing, somewhat uncomfortable time for those whose style is avoidant. In many cases, this results in social withdrawal, shyness, lack of social acceptance by peers, and aggression.

Adulthood

For adults classified as avoidant, the tendency to downplay the importance of attachments and the anxiety felt in the context of close relationships remains characteristic. The attachment system is generally kept in a relatively deactivated state. In their behaviour and talk they direct attention away from anything that might threaten or distress them emotionally, including conflict. Vulnerability, emotional need, and feelings of anxiety are downplayed for fear that thinking about such matters might activate the attachment system, triggering reminders of past rejections.

Avoidant adults do not score highly on extraversion. The defences employed by avoidant people represent attempts to inhibit any experience of strong feelings, particularly those of anxiety, fear, anger, shame, and sadness but also too much joy, exuberance and excitement, particularly if they are likely to lead to uncontrolled intimacy or appearing in the public spotlight.

Given these anxieties about becoming too bogged down in relationships, avoidant individuals need to keep a defensive eye on the possibility of situations becoming too emotionally demanding. They need to anticipate such possibilities and forestall them by distancing themselves either physically, emotionally or socially. This means that dismissing individuals are particularly vigilant in monitoring other people's facial expressions and body language for any potential sign of attachment-relevant cues, particularly negative ones (Maier *et al.* 2005). There is even evidence that dismissing adults show greater discomfort than secure and preoccupied individuals when they feel that other people are physically too close (Kaitz *et al.* 2004).

In some cases, there is a tendency to hide behind a façade, presenting the self in rather inflated, grandiose terms and always strong (Shaver and Mikulincer 2004: 26). Talents, successes and achievements are exaggerated, probably as a form of defensive self-enhancement. Family and friends are not seen as a source of great social support. The internal working model of those classified avoidant represents the self as independent, indifferent, and untroubled by feeling, and other people as unavailable and potentially hurtful.

Many of these features are explored by Bartholomew and Horowitz (1991). Using self-report measures of avoidant attachment behaviour, they define the avoidant person's internal working model as one in which the self is seen as strong and positive, while others are viewed as unavailable and potentially rejecting. The willingness to disclose or admit personal need and vulnerability is low. Dismissing adults are unlikely to seek social feedback (for fear of what they might learn, for fear of rejection). Rather than depend on other people in times of difficulty, illness or setback, the avoidant personality either tries to deny that they are in a state of need or they go it alone.

During the course of a close relationship, avoidant individuals tend to over-regulate their own emotional arousal. For most people, experiences that have a heightened emotional charge are more likely to be remembered. But if the individual defensively suppresses the more emotional aspects of close relationships, then fewer relation-ship-based memories will be laid down for future recollection. As a result avoidant individuals are rather poor at recalling the details and incidents of past relationships (Miller 2001). But even if difficult experiences are recalled, any distress caused at the time is either minimized or not acknowledged. Nor does the memory appear to provoke much emotion during conversation, or indeed during an attachment-based research interview.

The adult equivalent of avoidant is therefore sometimes described as *Dismissing* (Ds) (Main *et al.* 2008). 'Yes, well, she did leave me in the end. To be honest, I think she was getting rather hysterical, and it was probably for the best. It did give me more space and I certainly managed to get on top of things at work again, so it worked out well. I'm not someone who generally lets things get to him.' This was Simon's response to a question about how he felt after the break-down of his relationship with Zara after five years.

Memories and other experiences are cognitively acknowledged but lack emotional valence. Some memories of past relationships, particularly with attachment figures, are idealized. Childhood is mis-remembered as continuously happy and parents as endlessly loving. However, when pressed, the avoidant individual finds it hard to come up with any specific examples to illustrate this unqualified love and undiluted happiness. Odd contradictions might enter the narrative in which there is talk of harsh (but allegedly deserved) punishments, or 'loving' parents who were rarely present or involved. Further discrepancies might also be heard between what is being described (emotionally laden) and its alleged emotional impact (very little): 'I was six, I think, and was messing about and fell off a wall and broke my ankle. My mum was very cross. But I was all right because she took me to hospital.'

Defensively, then, it is safer to maintain a landscape of memory that is general, one without too much uncomfortable detail, a world that idealizes childhood and the parenting that went with it. Idealized pictures of childhood are better than the painful recall of parents who were distant, unloving and where emotional needs went unmet. In recounting the past, avoidant people keep it short.

Adults who have been on the receiving end of intrusive parenting will have been repeatedly told that only unworthy children disappoint their parents. They come to believe that it is not the parent's fault if the child disappoints, but the child's. This is painful territory. The young mind needs to defend itself against such hurts. The most efficient way to do this is to deactivate and switch off those bits of the psychological self that have experienced these implied rejections. Having suffered rejection and dismissal of their attachment behaviour in the past, any current relationship experience that might activate arousal, attachment behaviour and the uncomfortable memories that go with such feelings is defensively excluded from consciousness. The result is avoidant attachment behaviour, emotional detachment, and a general downplaying of dependence and weakness of any kind, in others as well as the self. Any yearning for love and intimacy is viewed as a weakness. This reduces the avoidant individual's ability to act with compassion, a deficit not only played out in close relationships but one that reduces the likelihood, say, of doing voluntary work with vulnerable groups, or pursuing a career that involves working directly with people who are highly dependent.

In more entrenched cases of avoidance, the individual will contemptuously dismiss anyone, including themselves, who shows emotional dependence or vulnerability or is too free with their feelings. They dismiss the importance of attachment (*derogation of attachment*) and the influence it has on them or should have on others. To be needy is to be weak, and to be weak is stupid. Anyone who shows emotional need will only get hurt. They don't deserve sympathy or respect.

Continuities from childhood can also be seen in the way adults viewed as avoidant engage with the world. Avoidant children are most likely to earn parental acceptance when they are occupied, independent and successful. Similarly, adults seek acceptance by being good at what they do. If, in the past, so the thinking goes, acceptance has been won by doing things right and being in control, then maybe recognition and intimacy will follow in the wake of what I do rather than how I feel.

The avoidant internal working model is that the self is only accepted when it is competently getting on doing things, a self that does not make too many emotional demands on others. Sticking to the task is how control is maintained and rejection avoided. Losing control is unsettling. Thus, anything that, or anyone who distracts the individual or frustrates what he or she is doing will make those classified avoidant feel anxious, agitated and cross. Flitting between tasks, dropping one thing to take up another is not a comfortable way to work. That old feeling that if things unravel and control is lost, ridicule and rejection will follow. So anyone who adds to the workload, demands a change of focus, threatens to fragment the task, or undermines control, is likely to be viewed with hostility.

Another way of avoiding failure is not to take on challenges or demanding tasks where there might be a risk of not succeeding. Excuses will be made about why this or that thing can't be tackled. Such reactions represent a self-protective strategy against the fear of being seen as incompetent. It is the prospect of shame, ridicule and rejection that makes for such anxiety and caution. In the workplace as well as in relationships, therefore, avoidant people take the safe route, the least risky strategy (Elliot and Reis 2003). They are not great novelty seekers (Carnelley and Ruscher 2000).

Although the lid is normally kept on too much emotional display, it is during moments when control is in danger of being lost that aggressive behaviour is most likely to surface. The normal defence of emotional exclusion breaks down. There is also an underlying anxiety that if I can't keep everything in its place, including my needs and emotions, then I will be rejected, and then how can I ever be loved, how can I be accepted, how can I get close?

Love and acceptance are therefore conditional. People who don't play the game should not be rewarded. There is an inclination to 'keep to the rules'. People who 'break the rules', particularly if they appear to be getting away with something, should be punished, or at least suffer the consequences. The idea of 'something for nothing' is not acceptable to those who play fair. Not surprisingly, some avoidant personality types have a heightened sense of right and wrong, good and bad. A certain rigidity creeps into their ideas about how relationships, social groups, and organizations should work. We should all go by the book. It is certainly tempting to speculate, albeit mischievously, that some jobs might suit avoidant types more than others – traffic warden, tax inspector, town hall bureaucrat?

Some avoidant adults are keen observers of other people's moods and desires. This harks back to childhood and the need for the child to be as they think the parent would like them be. Failure to get it right risks rejection. Crittenden (1992b; 1995) argues as follows. Some 'defended' individuals want to be liked and loved but they doubt their lovability. They remain unsure whether or not others like them. In their attempts to gain acceptance, approval and admiration, the individual monitors both his own and the other's behaviour to ensure that whatever is being said or done is meeting with the other's approval and expectations. People can therefore become socially astute observers of other people's behaviour. They become keenly sensitive about how others might be viewing them. If they feel that the other's perceptions and evaluations are negative, they will modify their own behaviour in an attempt to shift the other person towards a more positive view of the self. This strategy of monitoring and manipulating other people's reactions and perceptions also means that there is less insight into one's own emotional states – cognitive attention is directed outwards and not inwards.

All of this produces a 'chameleon-like' response to social situations as the avoidant personality tries to be as they believe the other person would like them to be. There is an anxiety to be accepted, not as one is, but as the individual thinks others would like them to be. This produces a 'false' self. The *anxiety* to be liked (and not rejected) means that the individual 'is' that which he or she thinks the other would perceive as most likeable. The net result is that individuals tend to respond to the needs of other people rather than their own attachment needs.

Romantic and couple relationships

People who score high on emotional suppression find it hard to make friends. Although there is a desire to be in relationship, anxiety is felt about getting too close and involved. Emotional closeness can be uncomfortable. The more intimate the relationship, the more awkward and gauche the behaviour. Don't expect too many declarations of love or soft words of endearment from an avoidant romantic partner. There is therefore a tendency by avoidant individuals to be emotionally controlling of both the self and the other. The self is presented as strong, partly as a defence against feeling exposed and vulnerable. Falling in love can be thought difficult, or even illusory. There is no great faith in the idea of true love and romance. The initial phase of flirtation is a tricky one for the avoidant individual. Fears of possible rejection lead to defensive detachment and increased inhibition, even awkwardness. This is how Pam's partner talked about their relationship:

It's difficult. We have lots in common and when we're doing the things we both like – you know, cycling, bowling, that kind of thing – it's great. But she doesn't seem comfortable getting any closer to me, emotionally, I mean. I know she had a tough childhood and all that, you know. She said her mother was totally engrossed in her business and her dad left when she was five or something. Pam said she never felt good enough, could never impress her mum, though she does claim her childhood certainly toughened her up, which she thinks is good for a woman. She won't take risks, particularly with her feelings, with me. She bottles everything up and I can feel her switching off and drifting away. I'm left feeling exposed and pretty stupid sometimes. She says she knows that it's all her fault, but then clams up again saying it's hard to be sure that other people are really genuine and can be trusted.

For some, these defensive inhibitions mean that close relationships are either difficult to achieve or if achieved, conducted with brevity and superficiality. This can lead to short-term relationships that might look like promiscuity. Sex is always a difficult area for those who are avoidant. It clearly involves physical intimacy. Three strategies present themselves to deal with the anxieties surrounding sex. One is not to do too much of it. The second is, if it can't be avoided, don't enjoy it (Cohen and Belsky 2008). And the third is to pursue it functionally as a physical need, but one in which no emotional investment is made. Again, this can lead to shallow relationships, and for some promiscuity. One time-honoured way to overcome feelings of anxiety and inhibition about becoming emotionally close and sexually active is to use alcohol or drugs, a recourse favoured by both avoidant and ambivalent types.

The caricature of the adult classified as avoidant or dismissing is therefore of someone who is emotionally defensive, stoical with a stiff upper lip, low on self-disclosure (to know me increases the risk of you rejecting me), and who lacks emotional empathy when other people behave in a distressed manner. To manage information about who one is and what one knows helps people feel in control. And although the avoidant person will rarely risk becoming emotionally dependent on their partner, by the same token, they will not want their partner to become dependent on them (Feeney and Collins

2001). It might just be that romantic relationships are, by their very nature, untidy and really rather bothersome.

> Isobel did not have a boyfriend until she was in her early twenties. She had done well both at school and university. Her job as a translator meant that she was able to work at home a great deal which she enjoyed. Not long after her thirtieth birthday she became romantically involved with James. He had returned from a post in Japan and once he felt that the relationship with Isobel was serious, he was quite keen to move in with her. After some persuasion, she agreed. But it didn't work out. It wasn't simply the upset to her home routines that bothered her, she said, it was the loss of control that she felt was beginning to upset her life. 'His mother was getting divorced from his dad. She was on the phone to him every day. James said she was falling apart and he needed to give her all the support he could. It was all getting very messy and it really wasn't anything to do with me. I did feel rather cross and it did affect our relationship. He took days off work and even asked his mother to stay with us – in *my* house. I couldn't work or keep on top of things. In the end, I decided to take up an offer to work in Germany for a few months, just to give everyone a break, doing translations for an IT company over there, and really, I guess, that marked the end of the relationship with James – and his mother. If I'm honest, although I did miss James at first, getting away helped, and I was a bit relieved when it was all over and could get my life, my routines back together again.'

Insecurely attached people, including those classified as avoidant, are less likely to feel comforted or soothed by the presence of their partner, particularly in stressful situations (Feeney and Kirkpatrick 1996; Mikulincer 1998). Neither are avoidant people much good at supporting their partner's need for reassurance. The message is 'Don't fuss. Do it yourself. Just get on with it. I would.' There is a reluctance, fear even, in getting drawn into other people's messy emotional needs. When other people express strong dependent feelings or show distress (feeling ill, being helpless), levels of anxiety and irritation increase. This might be dealt with by behaving in a variety of avoidant and dismissing ways including withdrawal, intrusive control, irritation, even contempt: 'You're always ill. I'm never ill.

What's the matter with you?' 'Don't fuss, it's only a cold.' 'Oh for heaven's sake, it's easy, a kid could do it – can't you do it yourself – or are you just useless?' These characteristics and others such as defensiveness, impatience, detachment, criticism, and particularly contempt are generally not good for the long-term success of a relationship (Gottman 1994).

Boredom, too, can sometimes be characteristic of the avoidant adult's response to a partner's need for emotional closeness. There is even evidence that avoidant individuals smile and laugh less often, gaze at faces less often, and are generally not very attentive to the emotional condition of others (Guerrero 1996). Describing Feeney and Collins's (2003) study of couples and their mutual caregiving, Collins *et al.* report that:

> Avoidant individuals tended to endorse aversive (avoidance) motives. Specifically, they often *failed* to provide care to their partners because they were uncomfortable with their partners' distress, perceived that helping would lead to negative consequences (e.g., that their partners would be difficult to interact with or would lack appreciation), and because their partners were too dependent on them.
>
> (2004: 205, emphasis original)

The defence of intellectualization is also a nice example of the avoidant mind at work when faced with strong feeling. As the emotional temperature rises, let's say in an argument with a lover, the avoidant personality feels nervous and threatened. Strong feelings lead to fears either of rejection and hurt, or a loss of control. It therefore feels better to fall back on reason and logic. The avoidant individual dismisses the other's point of view or argument as flawed because it is based on emotion, and emotion distorts logic: 'When you calm down and listen to me, you'll see I'm right. If you think about it logically rather than get all excited and indignant, you'll realize that I'm being perfectly rational, reasonable and fair. So, stop, concentrate and listen to me. OK? Unless, of course, you really are stupid.' Hearing this response from a partner as you are rowing about his apparent indifference to your needs will be like a red rag to a bull. The more one partner gets heated, the more the avoidant other claims to be occupying the rational high ground (for fear of becoming lost, frightened and plain wrong in the tangle of the emotional undergrowth). These exchanges rarely turn out well.

Johnson (2004) describes a couple in therapy who feel increasingly isolated and alone. The man has become more and more detached and depressed. The woman feels increasingly helpless and hurt. The husband's initial response is to deny that there are 'real' problems, but on further probing by the therapist, he says:

> There is no point in talking. If I try, we fight and suddenly the whole house is on fire. I can't do this closeness thing. I'm no good at it – never come up to the mark. So I just try to keep things calm. Then, when I can't, I kind of numb out.

> (ibid.: 376)

Those on the receiving end of an avoidant partner's responses feel a lack of understanding, support and warmth. Dismissing individuals either minimize the need to feel upset or they try to divert attention from the state of being distressed, partly as a result of the way they would try to deal with arousal in themselves and partly in an attempt to control and subdue the appearance of distress in others (Simpson *et al.* 1996: 900). Thus, 'because they are apt to provide support with reluctance or annoyance, they may deliver support in a manner that makes their partners feel weak or needy, inadequate or incompetent, or like a burden' (Collins *et al.* 2006: 166).

As might be expected, both avoidant adults and their partners often feel dissatisfied with their relationships. The relative lack of sensitivity means that partners feel misunderstood and emotionally neglected. Avoidant individuals experience briefer relationships and higher rates of divorce than those classified as secure (Birnbaum *et al.* 1997). Given what avoidant individuals are unable to do, and based on what secure, contented couples can and do do, couple therapists who use an attachment perspective aim to help dismissing partners communicate more thoughtfully and with greater sensitivity so that intimacy and connectedness might be increased (Johnson 2004).

Parenthood and caregiving

When adults become parents, the character of their caregiving derives from their internal working model of attachment (George

1996). Their representations guide the way they perceive, experience and interact with their children. Babies in particular can only convey their needs through behaviour and emotional arousal. We know that when levels of feeling are raised within a relationship, the individual's characteristic ways of regulating affect are triggered. Thus, babies are likely to activate the defensive strategies typically used by their carers at times of stress. When examined from an ecological perspective, when risks multiply in a parent's life, children are more likely to develop insecure attachments. It is the interaction of parental attachment insecurity with a range of other factors – poverty, unsupportive marriage, less positive infant temperament, poor mental health – that significantly increases insecure attachments in children (Belsky and Fearon 2008: 310).

Dismissing parents, says Main (1995), find that mental representations of the self (as strong and independent) and others (as rejecting and hostile) is easily upset by the emotional and proximity-seeking demands of their baby. The defensive response of the mother or father is to back off and withdraw from, or control the source of emotional need and dependence (the baby). The baby's distress and dependency needs evoke feelings of anxiety in the parent. Anxiety triggers attachment behaviour, which in the case of the dismissing adult is dealt with by 'de-activating' the attachment system and withdrawing emotional availability. This causes parents to cut themselves off from their own uncomfortable emotional experiences making it difficult for them to recognize and tune into their children's needs and emotions. The following is a quote from a mother talking about her baby in DeOliveira *et al.*'s study of mothers and their affective mindsets:

> I don't really know why he's sad. But I don't really deal with it … Like – I'll do the hugging and the 'It's OK' and all that other kind of stuff but I don't … I try not to feel anything for anything … unless I have to. That's usually how I deal with it.
>
> (2005: 106)

The baby experiences this as a behavioural 'punishment' for displaying arousal and attachment behaviour. So in the case of babies whose primary caregivers are dismissing and defended against affect, attachment behaviour, instead of leading to increased proximity to, and comfort from the attachment figure, actually leads to decreased proximity and raised anxiety.

As we saw in the previous chapter, the only way for the baby to deal with this is to decrease his or her own overt display of attachment behaviours by deactivating his or her attachment system. The baby learns that containment of need, downplay of distress, and avoidance of dependence are the best behavioural strategies if the carer is to be kept close and available, which is still the goal of attachment behaviour whether it is manifest or not. The children's attachment strategy allows the carer to retain proximity and maintain involvement in a way that he or she finds much more comfortable. Nevertheless, the caregiving style is essentially one of *rejection* of the child's attachment behaviour and emotional dependency. The parent's caregiving system remains relatively de-activated. For example, Simpson *et al.* (1996: 900) found that mothers who scored higher on avoidant behaviours, displayed less warmth and supportiveness toward their preschool children when teaching them new and difficult tasks compared to less avoidant mothers.

Some carers wonder whether they are really suited for parenthood, even going so far as to say that they wished that they'd never had children. They feel uncomfortable with the caregiving role. Some recognize themselves as strict, impatient or demanding but don't know how else to do it (George 1996: 418). They therefore might be described as *authoritarian* parents. When there is little joy felt in the business of being a mum or a dad, children might be described as a chore, a nuisance, manipulative, and unrewarding to parent.

However, milder forms of the avoidant personality can lead to a slightly different caregiving style. The lack of confidence with the emotional demands of being a parent create a self-imposed pressure to be super-competent at the practical side of being a carer. The right diet, the correct way to discipline, the best time to wean, the optimum amount of television to be watched, all suggest an anxious need to grasp the theoretical side of parenting. Although there may be a build-up of defences against the unavoidable anxieties of being a parent, there is a great deal of intellectual recognition given to the importance of being a good mother or father. This might show itself in 'knowing the theory' and having the right equipment, the best buggy, and the most educational toys. Shelves are typically full of books on 'how to bring up baby' or 'how to be a good mum'. There might even be a preference for baby rearing books that advocate strict routines to train babies into regular patterns of feeding, waking and sleeping, and in which babies are allowed to cry themselves to sleep, books that forget that crying is the only way babies can communicate their urgent needs. There is therefore the danger that although the parent–child relationship is intellectually grasped, it is emotionally mis-read. A certain amount of tension suffuses the parent–child relationship. The parent copes with this defensively by backing off from the more emotionally fraught aspects of caregiving, while the child experiences this as rejection of attachment behaviour (and the vulnerable, emotional self that drives it).

Once the child can talk, the avoidant parent can use language as a more subtle, insidious, and powerful way to control the more uncomfortable bits of caregiving. If the parent can get the child to recognize that good children are children who don't make a fuss or tax parents with unreasonable needs and demands, and furthermore, that only good children are loved and accepted, then the child not only learns to contain and over-regulate their affect, they feel responsible for whether they are loved or not (Crittenden 1992a). For example, a child who has seriously hurt himself and begins to cry might be told 'That's only a scratch. For heaven's sake, you've not really hurt yourself. Don't cry. Don't be such a baby.' The mother offers no emotional comfort unless the child 'stops being a baby and ceases crying'. Those who make a fuss and who are not in control of their needs lack value and worth in the eyes of 'loving' parents. Love is conditional. True feelings therefore have to be denied. As a guide to being loved and accepted, trust only what you are told, rely on what you know, ignore what you feel.

Physical health

Individuals with insecure attachment styles are at increased risk of poorer health, partly because their life style choices are not always wise (bad diet, smoking, drug and alcohol use), their social relationships are less supportive, their emotional regulation skills are weak, and their levels of negative affect and stress tend to be high (Diamond and Hicks 2004). Under stress, avoidant adults, just like avoidant infants, show little outward display of their upset emotional state even though they are aroused physiologically and their bodies are highly stressed. So, although they suppress emotionally laden issues, their bodies remain stressed. There is some evidence that under stress, avoidant types are more physiologically reactive. For some, there is the risk of raised blood pressure. In a study of stress and dating couples, Kim concluded that the findings 'suggest that individuals scoring high on the avoidance attachment dimension are vulnerable to hypertension and other cardiovascular diseases due to such dysfunctional physiological patterns when they face relationship conflicts' (Kim 2006: 111). They under-report feeling ill or unwell. They are reluctant to visit doctors or follow medical advice.

The defensive strategy of dismissing adults is to cut themselves off from thinking about their own negative feelings associated with fears of rejection and unlovability. The physiological feelings associated with the pain of emotional hurt don't go away, but the awareness of their nature and true origins lies outside conscious awareness. In some cases, this can mean that the physiological symptoms of stress are not recognized as emotionally based, but rather misinterpreted as signs of physical illness or disease.

During times of physical vulnerability, secure people intensify relationships with others, deepening their connections with the social world. By relating with others, they confirm their sense of being and continuity, even in the face of death. Secure people often use attachment relationships for support, regulation, and stress reduction. Avoidant individuals find such strategies difficult. They go against the grain. They therefore find it harder to use others to help them manage arousal, and so they remain physiologically stressed for longer. Worries about serious illness, including the prospect of death, increase feelings of fear and isolation and the stresses that go with them. The avoidant personality is therefore one which is not good at dealing with health worries.

Mental health

Children who have not been on the receiving end of attuned, mind-minded caregiving are at risk of developing minds that lack a certain degree of coherence, adaptability and flexibility, particularly when they have to deal with relationship-based stresses. If high reflective function and mentalization act as a buffer against stress as well as confer resilience, children who find mentalization hard will experience greater difficulty dealing competently with social situations and the emotions they trigger. If these insecure patterns continue into adulthood, individuals remain vulnerable and at increased risk of poor mental health.

However, it seems unlikely that attachment insecurity on its own is sufficient to cause psychopathology. It is just one element, albeit a significant one, which, if found in association with other vulnerability and risk factors, adds to the possibility of psychological disorder. Poverty, an accumulation of life stressors, trauma – particularly childhood relational trauma – negative temperamental traits, illness, divorce, and learning difficulties are some of the other factors which, if combined with an insecure personality, might increase the risk of impaired mental health.

In the case of avoidant adults, fears of rejection, the need to achieve in order to feel accepted, feeling anxious and uncomfortable with emotions and their arousal, and the lack of close supportive relationships increase the risks of loneliness, poor mental health and psychological disorder. Not being in touch with feelings makes it more likely that emotions will be bottled up. Although the outward self is desperately trying to maintain a show of composure, physiologically and psychologically levels of arousal and stress tend to be high. Relationships become tense and strained. The anxiety of trying to contain emotions and the worry that you are not in control can lead to behaviours that are angry, obsessive, and compulsive. Conduct, eating, and personality disorders are more common, particularly when insecure individuals have a history of loss and trauma and an unresolved state of mind with respect to attachment (for example, see Barone and Guiducci 2009, on eating disorders). These internal pressures can also manifest themselves in a range of somatic symptoms and sleeping problems.

Avoidant, dismissing types often do not cope in a healthy way with loss. The pain and confusion around, say, the death of a parent, or abandonment by a partner is put to the back of the mind. Any upset is either denied or downplayed (see Dallos and Vetere 2009, Chapter 7, for a good discussion of this subject). This means that the grieving process does not get started, or that the thoughts and feelings associated with the lost other remain suppressed and inhibited. In the main, avoidant strategies are not good for mental relaxation or living a low stress life.

Old age

Adults classified as avoidant view their aging parents' increasing dependence with some anxiety. Their well-rehearsed defence when confronted by other people's weakness and need is to back off, be critical and disapprove. Insecure adults are less likely than those who are secure to think about providing care for an increasingly dependent parent (Soerensen *et al.* 2002). Compared to secure individuals, the sense of obligation and burden are high. The defensive reaction of avoidant adult children to the perceived 'burden' of caring for their parent can therefore lead to increasing emotional distance. For example, avoidant children of parents with senile dementia are more likely to have them placed in residential care (Markiewicz *et al.* 1997).

On the other hand, if the avoidant child's parent is also avoidant, and assuming that they are not suffering any major mental impairment, they, too, are likely to want to manage on their own for as long as they can. A stubborn independence, admirable in some ways, might well characterize the later years of old people classified as avoidant. Nevertheless, for many, illness and fragility will increase and the old tensions between autonomy and dependence will return. In old age, the balance tips once more towards dependence and vulnerability, difficult for most older people, but particularly problematic for those with insecure and avoidant attachments. For too long they might downplay need and deny distress. Reluctant to seek help, they might delay asking for medical advice or social support.

The attachment style of spousal carers of partners with dementia appears to affect the degree of problem behaviours shown by the deteriorating spouse. As expected, secure partner caregivers are most accepting and compassionate. However, 'the higher the level of the caregivers' avoidance, the higher the level of problem behaviour (specifically agitation/aggression) shown by the care recipient' with dementia (Perren *et al.* 2007: 174). The reluctance to get too involved, emotionally and physically, seems to be sensed by the partner who has dementia. This avoidance can increase feelings of annoyance. Their behaviour grows more stubborn, agitated and even aggressive.

Interestingly, a number of studies report that the proportion of people classified avoidant and dismissing in old age actually increases (see Magai 2008: 534, for a summary). The greater exposure to loss of family and friends might, in part, explain this defensive strategy.

Older people begin to accommodate, by way of detachment, to the loss of those to whom they were close. They adjust to their own increasing frailty. There is also speculation that self-reliance in later life might be a good thing. However, concern is generally expressed that loss of social support networks and disconnecting from family and friends are associated with poorer health, both physical and mental. To this extent, the higher number of avoidantly attached older people should, perhaps, be a cause for concern.

Conclusion

The underlying expectation and worry of avoidant individuals is that making emotional demands on others or appearing vulnerable is likely to lead to rejection or ridicule. To be rejected by other people, particularly those with whom you feel close, is deeply painful and is to be avoided if at all possible. Hence, the avoidant strategy. The best way not to get hurt and yet remain involved is to be self-reliant, keep the lid on showing need, and don't appear weak. This is a tight, tense strategy and comes at some interpersonal, psychological and health cost. There is desire for intimacy but it is just so hard to lower one's defences and let go. The result is either to keep one's emotional distance, or to feel increasingly tetchy whenever intimacy, need and dependence threaten to loom too large in one's life.

10
Ambivalent Attachments in Childhood

Introduction

Parents whose caregiving is uncertain, inconsistent and a little unpredictable pose young babies with a problem. Sometimes when the child has needs and displays attachment behaviour, the parent responds appropriately with both protective and comforting responses. But at other times, the baby's attachment behaviour leads to anxious or flustered responses, irrelevant responses, or even no response at all. This kind of inconsistency and unpredictability is not the same as that occasionally shown by all parents who are sometimes busy or preoccupied with other demands. Secure children receive good enough parenting, which is to say that in principle the caregiver would want to be responsive even though in practice their availability never reaches anything near 100 per cent. But for children whose parents are less predictable, there is no reliable connection between infant displays of attachment and the availability of the caregiver. The caregiver's responses are neither contingent nor congruent. The behavioural challenge for the infant is how to maximize the availability of the caregiver in such a relationship.

Infancy

Parents of babies classified as ambivalent have been described as inept or 'uncertain' in their caregiving style. They lack confidence. Unsure of their own worth and value, these parents are often preoccupied with their own need for love and approval. It is the parents' underlying anxiety, uncertainty and preoccupation with their own feelings and needs which result in this erratic, inconsistent, random, under-involved, and unpredictably responsive caregiving. This anxiety can mean that these parents lose confidence when their babies appear unresponsive and upset. They even feel confused when their babies are self-occupied (for example, playing with a cot mobile). This can lead to intrusive behaviour in which the caregiver impinges on the child's activity and space. Even though the baby might be playing quite contentedly with the cot mobile, the parent nevertheless thrusts a teddy bear in front of the child and jiggles it about. Intrusive caregiving lacks sensitivity and it seriously inhibits children's exploratory, independent play behaviour. Most babies can tolerate some parental intrusion. However, when the intrusion is particularly insensitive, it can distress the infant, triggering attachment behaviour. It is the combination of intrusion and activation of the attachment system that is particularly problematic and predictive of an ambivalent attachment (Beebe *et al.* 2010). In any normal population, between 10 and 15 per cent of children might be classified as ambivalent.

George and Solomon (2008) see the major defence being used by parents of ambivalent children as one of 'cognitive disconnection'. This involves splitting off, or disconnecting attachment and emotionally charged information from their source – the source in this case being the baby. This prevents parents from seeing the 'bigger picture'. They tend to respond to their own arousal rather than step back and analyse its cause. This results in caregiving practices that Solomon and George (1996) describe as 'close protection', a caregiving style that is intrusive, one that anxiously keeps the child in sight and nearby. By keeping children close, babies' attempts to play and flirt with independence are frustrated. Children quickly sense that parents feel anxious whenever they explore and show autonomy. It is only a matter of time, therefore, before children themselves begin to feel anxious whenever they attempt to be independent.

From the caregiver's point of view, too much independent behaviour by children implies that they are not needed as parents, or that they are even no good as parents. These independent behaviours by children feel like abandonment, and it is abandonment that is particularly prone to activate anxiety and uncertainty in the minds of these carers. By frustrating their children's efforts at autonomy, insecure-preoccupied parents are really trying to manage their own anxiety.

Secure babies sense a clear link between their needs and behaviour and the reactions of parents. This helps babies work out how the give-and-take of healthy relationships work. However, in the case of children classified as anxious or ambivalent, these links, these contingent relationships between behaviour and response, are weak and less clear. The caregiving therefore feels arbitrary: sometimes comforting, sometimes intrusive, sometimes angry, sometimes ineffective (Belsky and Cassidy 1994). Synchrony between parent and child is poor.

The problem to solve for children in relationships with unpredictably responsive caregivers is how to engage the attention and protective interest of people whose availability cannot be relied upon, particularly at times of distress. These infants also have the problem of how to avoid and turn away from ('dodge') their parents when the caregiving is experienced as distressing, for example, when caregivers intrude and impinge on their child's activity and space. We know that when needs and levels of anxiety are high, children increase the intensity of their attachment behaviour. One way to get noticed in a relationship where the other person is ignoring you is to protest, express anger, make more noise, refuse to be ignored and generally increase the volume of your presence, that is, raise the intensity of your attachment behaviours to the maximum. And indeed, children whose caregivers' emotional availability and general sensitivity are low do tend to exaggerate their distress and increase the urgency of their demands in order to provoke a response and gain attention. As a result, ambivalent babies and toddlers are often more clingy, whiney, noisy, and attention seeking. They tug clothes. They don't easily let go, physically or emotionally. They refuse to be ignored.

Many ambivalent children also resist being placated because their experience is that once they calm down, they are back to square one with no guarantee that safety, acknowledgement and comfort will be available when they next need it. This is why ambivalent children who use this particular attachment strategy are sometimes said to be showing a *resistant* pattern. It is, of course, an *ambivalent* response because children both want the attention of their caregivers but they are also angry and distressed because of its unreliable availability. Desire for, and anger with caregivers create a feeling of ambivalence.

Young children who don't let up slowly begin to associate their heightened states of arousal and increased attachment behaviour with the increased likelihood of a caregiver response. Behaviourally speaking, some kind of caregiver response is better than no response.

No response equals abandonment, and that is a frightening place to be.

Maternal responses that are erratic and unpredictable are tantamount to putting the baby in a behaviourally random environment. As parents, they are 'noncontingently' responsive, that is their responses are not in tune with the baby's needs and behaviour. Initially, the carer's more responsive behaviours bear no direct relation to the behaviour or condition of the child. The child can therefore establish no connection between what he or she does and the response of the parent other than that increased activation of attachment behaviour seems to provoke a reaction sooner or later. So gradually, the child learns that by maximizing attachment behaviour, the more likely it is that the carer is forced to respond. This reinforces the child's persistence. The strategy of *maximizing* attachment behaviour therefore works well with otherwise inconsistent, erratically available parents. Provocation, petulance, pronounced sulkiness, having temper tantrums, 'going too far', are eventually 'rewarded' with attention of some kind. And having captured the attention of the attachment figure, being cute, coy and clingy might also make it difficult for the caregiver to disengage.

In terms of operant behavioural principles, the caregiver's obligation to respond to some of the child's increasingly intensified attachment behaviours has the effect of reinforcing those behaviours (based on an intermittent or partial reinforcement schedule). This begins to define the child's overall attachment strategy as one of maximization and intensification.

Thus, the infant's anxiety that the carer might not be available at times of distress is reduced by the child *organizing* a defensive strategy that involves quick and easy arousal of attachment behaviours supported by a hyperactivated attachment system (Cassidy and Kobak 1988). The strategy is one of anger and protest, amounting to a 'fight' response designed to force the unresponsive, unreliable, unpredictable parent to take notice. The arousal that accompanies the strategy achieves a secondary *felt security*. By developing attachment systems that are readily activated, the children's behaviour is organized in such a way as to keep inconsistent caregivers maximally available. Their availability is never going to be high, but the strategy is designed to extract the most out of an otherwise wayward caregiving experience.

However, all the emotional effort to force some kind of response from the caregiver comes from the child. The implication therefore is that the infant self is not of sufficient interest or worth to command the automatic love, care and protection of others. The infant remains anxious and uncertain about their own inherent lovability, social value and interpersonal effectiveness. The long-term legacy of being unreliably and inconsistently cared for is to suffer feelings of doubt, despair and inadequacy.

The only state that seems to guarantee some kind of response is one of arousal and being in need of urgent attention. In this sense, behaviour triggered by feelings is more reliable than behaviour planned by thoughts. This is why it feels safer to keep attachment behaviour operating at maximum; at least you won't be ignored or abandoned if you continue to make emotional demands on others. Intimacy (being in close relationship) is preferred to autonomy (experienced as not being in close relationship). Ambivalent children therefore lack independence. Their ability to play, concentrate and persist – with toys, with friends, at school – is low. Children classified as ambivalent are dominated by affect. Cognition fails them. To be alone is to feel abandoned. It is not surprising that ambivalent children respond with great distress to separation or the threat of separation; it prefigures abandonment.

We have already noted that an ambivalent, anxious state of mind is one in which there is both desire for the carer and anger with her inconsistent availability. This can result in confusion between feeling needy and feeling angry so that the experience of one seems to imply the other. These feelings can generalize to all emotionally significant relationships. To be in close relationship with someone whose attachment system is hyperactive, whether that of a baby or adult, is to feel slightly at sea. One minute the ambivalent other is angry with you, the next hurt and needy, and moments later excited and euphoric.

Hyperactivated attachment systems leave less mental energy for play, remembering that in general when attachment behaviour is high, exploratory behaviour is low. Too distressed and too busy fretting about their caregiver's availability, ambivalent children are rather poor when it comes to prolonged, concentrated play. They worry. They lack confidence. When they interact with peers, their play lacks initiative and is correspondingly high on dependency

(McElwain *et al.* 2003). This style of play compromises the development of self-efficacy and planful behaviour. It undermines independence and the acquisition of new social skills.

An ambivalent, resistant or hyperactivated strategy represents attachment behaviour that is *organized* in relation to the set goal of seeking some kind of psychological proximity to an otherwise insensitive, inconsistent carer. It is *insecure* inasmuch as children cannot assume that their own needs will routinely command a response from their caregiver. So long as children's internal working models and behaviour remain organized, they can maintain some kind of functional relationship with others. Young children classified as ambivalent are fretful, emotionally under-regulated and hard to pacify, but they have found a strategy that gets them noticed in relationships that might otherwise neglect them and their needs.

Middle childhood

In the middle years, the parenting of ambivalent children continues to be *permissive* and ineffective. One minute the growing child might be treated like a baby, the next scolded for being ungrateful and annoying. Parental withdrawal of love and affection is used as a weak attempt to discipline the increasingly unruly, provocative child.

Assuming that the parents' caregiving continues to be insensitive, it is likely that children's attachment organization will remain ambivalent. By age 3 and 4, children, of course, are mobile and able to talk. This adds two new behaviours to their hyperactivated attachment repertoire. They can physically follow their carer. And they can shout at their parents in order to gain attention. They can also complain about being ignored and treated unfairly. All of this results in more noise, dependence, provocation, and a reluctance to be quiet and comforted.

One way in which secure caregivers help their children learn to regulate their arousal is to talk about feelings and reflect on them – what's caused them, how do they affect our own and other people's behaviour, how can we manage them. However, this reflective kind of talk is largely absent from the experience of ambivalent children. Their parents tend to 'act out' rather than 'think through' or try to explain their feelings (Crittenden 1995: 386). Therefore children's experience of emotions is immediate. Feelings determine behaviour, not thought. Without an adequate vocabulary, it is hard to think about and manage affective states. Children who miss out on these opportunities to label and reflect on feeling states are said to lack an 'emotional lexicon'. As a result, they find it more difficult to make sense of, and manage their own and other people's emotional states. These deficits are most likely to occur when parents themselves have troubled emotional histories, and find it difficult to deal with, and talk about emotionally charged situations. When interacting with their children, particularly when strong feeling states are involved, these parents appear to employ a vocabulary that is emotionally quite limited. So what ambivalent children do is develop 'episodic models' of how to behave in emotionally anxious relationships. Highly charged emotional 'episodes' of interaction from the past are used to guide behaviour in present situations of arousal and distress: 'I remember feeling like that then, I feel like that now, so I better behave like I did last time I felt that way.' The result is relationships characterized by high drama and intense emotions. There is no reflection, no thought, no flexibility.

Without the conceptual scaffolding that helps us to make sense of our own and other people's feelings and behaviour, self-regulation is difficult. Attempts to manage relationships with an ambivalently classified child by using reason, reflection and rationality are likely to fail, at least initially. The child has learned not to trust words and promises, sensing that only heightened arousal will get other people to react, listen and take note. Ambivalent children therefore tend to have one major mode of response – emotional acting-out.

Coercive strategies

In the preschool years, children begin to use the full range of their attachment behaviours to increase the predictability of otherwise unpredictable parents. Angry, complaining, noisy, provocative, exaggerated needy behaviours are likely to force a response from caregivers. But there is always the danger that parents feel increasingly helpless and crushed by their children's constant demands. Exasperation and exhaustion set in. It is at this point that parents might threaten to abandon the relationship: 'I'm sick and tired of your naughty behaviour. You just never let up. I'm going to shut the door, go out, and leave you, then you'll be sorry!' In response, and with a change of tactic, children classified as ambivalent might prefer to use non-aversive attachment behaviours that emphasize their vulnerability and helplessness. Vulnerability and helplessness are characteristic of babies, and so we see older children sometimes adopting baby-like behaviours to coerce parents back into more protective, engaged responses. By adopting a baby-like voice and vulnerable, submissive, apologetic speech and body language, parental anger is diffused. Infant-like behaviour, particularly smiles, babyish talk, and being cute, are hard to ignore or abandon, and even harder to attack. We all tend to go soft when we are greeted by a wide-eyed, smiling infant.

Similarly, the ambivalent child's frequent claims to be unwell or injured are designed to appeal to people's protective, nurturing instincts. Exaggerating symptoms and claiming to be unwell are used as distress signals to elicit the other's care, nurturance and attention.

So, ambivalent children learn to switch between threatening behaviours to get attention, and coy, disarming behaviours to wrong-foot the exasperated parent. Crittenden (1992b) describes this alternating use of threat and seduction, aggression and helplessness as a *coercive* strategy. On the basis of this awareness, explains Crittenden (ibid.: 583), children organize their behaviour around a strategy of alternately threatening their attachment figures into compliance with angry behaviour, and then bribing them into compliance with disarming, baby-like vulnerable behaviours. Type C coercion therefore maximizes parental responsivity under conditions of unpredictability, complexity, and ambiguity (Spieker and Crittenden 2009: 101; also see Chapter 12).

> By about 2 years of age … children become able to recognize the association between their displays of anger and their mother's responses. So they show more anger. This both attracts their mother's attention and also causes their mothers to be angry with them frequently. The children need a way to terminate parental anger and aggression. Coy behaviour is used to do this. By alternating aggressive-threatening behavior with coy-disarming behavior, children are able to coerce their mothers into doing what they want most of the time.
>
> (Crittenden 1999: 53–4)

The coercive strategy is therefore designed to keep the other involved at all times and reduce the possibility of being abandoned. As a result, most coercive children are preoccupied and emotionally over-involved with their attachment figures. As their needs rise urgently to the surface, they fail to reflect or consider the other person's point of view. This means that they find it difficult to cooperate, negotiate or compromise. They live in a world of the 'emotional now'.

Faced with children's coercive behaviours and feeling constantly wrong-footed and emotionally out-manoeuvred, parents begin to feel increasingly frustrated, manipulated and not in control. Their sense of despair and anger, uncertainty and helplessness increase. Their children feel unmanageable, ungrateful and unloving. The uncertainty that characterized their initial response to caregiving is confirmed.

School and peers

The ambivalent child's anxiety about other people's interest and regard generally means that their focus is more on relationships and less on work. They are easily distracted, moving quickly from one activity to another. Tasks are abandoned in favour of messing about with mates. The child's developing sense of social competence, confidence and exploratory skills are conditional on the presence, support and approval of teachers and caregivers. 'This continuing *dependency* of self on external others retards the development of affective self-regulation capabilities and thus leaves the individual peculiarly vulnerable to stress and emotional lability' (Lopez 1995: 400, emphasis added). Ambivalent children find it difficult to be self-reliant.

Children classified as ambivalent are more comfortable in environments that are high in emotion and low in focus, formality and discipline. With their peers, they tease, giggle, show off, act silly. They like to be the centre of attention. As a result, academic concentration is low. Nevertheless, they can make demands on teachers as they constantly complain that the work is too difficult, or they don't understand. At such times and in a babyish, somewhat pathetic voice, they plead for help: 'Please, miss, this sum's too hard. I don't know to do subtraction. Please, please help me, please.' Not surprisingly, they can easily exasperate and annoy teachers.

However, even though emotionally heightened interactions are preferred, the emotional demands made on others means that relationships, including peer friendships, are forever breaking down. The neediness and vulnerability of ambivalent children put off many would-be friends. Quarrels, being sulky, feigning helplessness, and feeling hurt or possessive or jealous are all part of the emotional highs and lows of a typical day. Ambivalent children experience considerable distress, dissatisfaction and disharmony in their close relationships even though they remain preoccupied with them. More likely to be victims than victimisers, more likely to be bullied than bully, they repeatedly end up feeling hard done by, unfairly picked on, and moan that no-one likes or understands them. All this emotionality leads to regular outbursts of tears, aggression, impulsivity and frustration. And although ambivalent children court a busy, excited social life with peers, they often complain of being neglected, feeling abandoned, and going unloved.

Conclusion

The internal working model of the ambivalent child is one in which an anxious self is viewed as unworthy of love, ineffective and incompetent, while other people are represented as unavailable, withholding and uninterested. An anxious state of mind prevails, and with it, a preoccupation with other people's emotional availability. To the extent that the emotional neediness of ambivalent children risks exasperating and exhausting parents and peers, there is a high chance that the world will continue to be experienced as denying and depriving through into adulthood.

Even as they mature, children classified as ambivalent continue in their failure to make connections between their own and other people's feelings and behaviours. When things go wrong or someone gives up on them, their complaint is that other people are at fault. Ambivalent individuals constantly feel deprived of love and affection. They claim that they never receive enough attention or recognition. Life feels unfair, withholding and denying. The basic, underlying need to feel loved and liked is constantly undermined by the nagging fear that the self commands little value or interest, and rarely registers with other people. Driven by anxiety, the only way to get noticed is to browbeat the world into making a response.

11

Anxious and Preoccupied Attachments in Adulthood

Introduction

The internal working model of those classified as ambivalent is one in which the self is viewed negatively (Park *et al.* 2004). Self-esteem and a sense of self-efficacy are low. Worried that failure of any kind risks abandonment, there is a reluctance to try new tasks or pick up fresh challenges. When self-doubt is high, motivation and concentration tend to be low.

Other people are viewed positively inasmuch there is a strong desire to be close and involved with them. There is also a nagging anxiety that the interest, love and approval of others cannot be taken for granted unless emotional demands are made of them. The result is an emotional overdependence on other people. There is a tendency to ruminate on distress-related thoughts and dwell on the more negative aspects of self (Shaver and Mikulincer 2004: 26). However, running in parallel with the need to feel close, are other feelings that never quite go away – feelings of being unloved, emotionally deprived and somehow neglected.

Adolescence

Insecure-preoccupied or ambivalent adolescents all too readily connect with attachment-related childhood memories (Dykas and Cassidy 2007: 44). These memories and the labile emotions attached to them bubble up and suffuse present thoughts, feelings and behaviour. The emotions associated with childhood attachment experiences – anger, dissatisfaction, jealousy, doubt, uncertainty, neediness, deprivation – constantly rise up, unmonitored, unregulated, uncontained.

Ambivalently classified adolescents are likely to have a negative self-concept. They can appear as rather distressed teenagers, more prone to engage in risky behaviours than most, and more likely to suffer internalizing disorders of anxiety and mood. In adolescence, relationships with parents are still characterized by conflict, argument, need, anxiety, and dissatisfaction (Bernier *et al.* 2005). The enmeshed nature of the parent–adolescent relationship continues to frustrate attempts at independence. In many cases, this emotional need and entanglement can make going off to college or university more fraught and less likely (Bernier *et al.* 2005; Larose *et al.* 2005). And if the adolescent does manage to get away, there is frequent, even excessive contact, by both parent and child.

A variation on these themes is advanced by Crittenden (1992c) who suggests that the aggressive and hostile behaviour shown by some ambivalent adolescents is a maladaptive attempt to get close and be accepted. Their aggression and helplessness are an extreme manifestation of the ambivalent strategy designed to coerce others into responding and paying attention. Their need to self-disclose indiscriminately and get emotionally close, involved and connected can therefore be intense, premature, and for others, just too much (Bauminger *et al.* 2009). The emotional traffic is all one way; anxious adolescents seem intent on getting support but never providing it.

Another way of holding on to and pleasing partners, and avoiding rejection is a ready willingness to have sex, not for its own sake, but as an anxiety-based strategy of keeping the other involved and raising self-esteem (Tracy *et al.* 2003). This is more likely to happen to young women than men. For anxious young men, getting intimately involved with others might be too worrying. This could explain why anxious adolescent males tend to be older than average when they first have sexual intercourse (Gentzler and Kerns 2004; Cooper *et al.* 2006).

Preoccupied adolescents are drawn to peers, even though they are extremely sensitive to perceived slights. As a result, their attachment systems are readily activated, making them emotionally volatile, demanding and not always easy people with whom to be friends. Any hint of a negative reaction feels like abandonment, and abandonment feels like the end of the world. This partly accounts for why rates of depression are relatively high among preoccupied, anxious adolescents (Chango *et al.* 2009).

Certainly by their mid to late teens, ambivalent adolescents are at higher risk of experiencing stress, feeling depressed, and being delinquent. There is fear of failure – at college, at work, in relationships – not helped by the fact that studies and hard work are given low priority (Scharf and Mayseless 2007: 14).

Adulthood

The adult version of ambivalence is often referred to as the *anxious, preoccupied,* or *entangled* (E) pattern. We continue to see a personality type with low self-esteem coupled with a tendency to become emotionally entangled in close relationships (Schmitt and Allik 2005). Individuals with high attachment anxiety remain particularly sensitive to any hint of separation, loss or abandonment. Persistent feelings of anxiety and doubt mean that distress and attachment behaviours tend to be displayed at maximum strength. This results in behaviour that can be interpreted as immature, silly and over-the-top.

'Felt security' is achieved by maintaining a high level of emotionally heightened involvement with other people. But such involvement is also underpinned by an anxiety that unless attention to relationships is maintained at a high, insistent level, other people will lose interest. Anxious individuals believe that intimacy and emotional closeness are more important than autonomy. They often push their desire for intimacy further than their partners feel comfortable with. There is great need for repeated reassurance. As with children, the main characteristics of individuals classified as preoccupied include deep anxiety about the lovability and value of the self. There is a pervasive fear that other people are not sufficiently interested in the self, that their love, availability and attention cannot be taken for granted.

Lurking around every relationship corner is the fear that the other will lose interest. The hyperactivated attachment strategy represents an attempt to keep others involved. The search for love, comfort and approval remains a preoccupation. Any problem or setback in this quest is quickly appraised as a disaster or catastrophe in the making. A husband's failure to return a phone message means he must be having an affair with another woman (fear and jealousy). A pain in the abdomen must be appendicitis (fear and panic). A taxing problem at work suggests uselessness (inadequacy and despair).

In their anxious attempts to provoke others into taking notice and taking care, any emotion connected with neediness and vulnerability is likely to be exaggerated and displayed with intensity. Anxiety, sadness, fear, and shame, but also coyness, cuteness and the like, can all be hitched to this strategy and played at full volume. This results in behaviour that can be chaotic. Efforts to find support remain disorganized and ineffective.

The ability to self-regulate emotional arousal and self-reflect on one's feelings continues to be poor. Individuals find it difficult to calm themselves down. Their attachment system remains hyperactivated until the significant other (parent, partner, lover) responds and becomes emotionally available.

There is a tendency to frown a lot whenever situations feel bothersome or confusing, which they often do (also see Roisman *et al.* 2004). Feelings are *acted out* rather than managed and contained. One negative thought or memory can quickly lead to another, leaving the individual feeling emotionally overwhelmed and confused. As a result, emotions cascade and snowball. Feeling states seem to consume the individual who, nevertheless, remains unable to recognize, name and differentiate the various emotions that swirl around uncontrollably in mind and body.

Thus, when aroused, anxious and preoccupied people find it difficult to collect their thoughts, assess their feelings, and be mentally organized. This anxious pattern can be picked up in speech and conversation when one thought or memory leads uncontrollably to another and another in a free-ranging, incoherent ramble. Caught up, *enmeshed* and *preoccupied* with their anxious feelings and memories, they fail to 'monitor their own discourse' (Main *et al.* 2008). There is little self-reflection. Even after brief acquaintance, anxious individuals are likely to tell their life story. Descriptions of childhood or past relationships can be long, confused and ambiguous. Their willingness to self-disclose indiscriminately is high. Their manner of speech is often cliché prone ('We had a love/hate relationship'). Or it is childish ('Don't be grumpy-wumpy with ickle, little me'). Or it is inclined to 'psychobabble' ('I'm very sensitive and caring. Every time I fill in one of those psychology questionnaires in a magazine, you know, I come out as really, really empathic, which is absolutely me.')

The work environment with its demands and expectations is not an easy one for those classified as anxious and preoccupied. It is the social side of being at work that matters. Although there is a strong desire to be accepted and recognized for doing a job well, the anxiety that this generates hyperactivates the attachment system. This increases the risk of feelings being heightened and, ironically, getting in the way of being able to concentrate, persist, meet deadlines, and complete tasks. As a result, anxious individuals are less likely to get promoted or gain higher salaries. Lack of recognition, perceived slights, alleged deprivations, and imagined injustices in the work context provide further reasons for feeling aggrieved, dissatisfied, under-appreciated and angry.

Intimacy is constantly sought but it rarely brings satisfaction. Uncertainty about other people's love and interest, and doubts about the worth and lovability of the self undermine self-confidence. There is therefore a perceptual bias towards spotting other people's more negative feelings (Fraley *et al.* 2006). This bias and anxious sensitivity lead to an over-reading and mis-reading of other people's emotions and their expression. They are often alleged to be looking bored, uninterested or angry (Meyer *et al.* 2004). Compared to those classified as secure, but similar to other insecure people, anxious individuals have 'less complex mental representations of others' which in turn interferes with their 'accurate understanding of other people's emotions, concerns, and actions' (Mikulincer and Shaver 2007: 176; also see Calabrese *et al.* 2005).

Key relationships, whether past or present, are typically talked about in emotionally extreme terms. Other people are loved and rated as 'the best' when they are experienced as emotionally available and willing to give endless attention. But the moment it feels as if the other person's interest is waning, or they become absorbed in their work, or a new friend appears in their life, then this feels like abandonment. Reactions to feelings of abandonment are characteristically melodramatic, often described in extreme terms: 'I feel torn apart and ripped to pieces.' 'My life isn't worth living without her.' There are no emotional half-measures when the anxious personality gets on to the subject of relationships and feelings. Feeney (2004: 34) offers a typical example of how one preoccupied participant replied to a question about being hurt by a romantic partner:

> I didn't eat for a week. I drank alcohol. I was totally at the bottom of my life. I didn't know what to do – complete depression. I

cannot accurately describe in words how I felt. Words cannot express the depth of my emotions.

Being ignored shakes the ambivalent individual's fragile sense of self and makes them feel anxious and angry. And as other people's apparent loss of interest has caused these unhappy feelings, they are hated, criticized, and berated. Often the same people can, at different times during a conversation, be all good or all bad, loved or hated, giving or denying, generous or withholding, for me or against me, wonderful or horrible. For them, the relationship is all or nothing and there can be no shades of grey. This defence of *splitting* is characteristic. The anxious person finds it difficult to integrate the varied and complex nature of other people's psychological make-up. Hence, who is in or out of favour can change from one day to the next.

The net effect of all of these expectations, assumptions and behaviours is that ambivalent personalities experience themselves in terms of other people's emotional availability. Moods swing up and down depending on the emotional quality of the relationship in which individuals feel themselves currently to be. If a relationship is going well, the mood will be good, the behaviour bubbly. If it isn't running smoothly, feelings will be low, the face downcast.

As we have noted, to be on the receiving end of such emotional need, anxiety and anger can be exhausting. One instinct of the emotionally worn-out partner is to escape. However, this results in the abandonment that the ambivalent person most fears. It is at this point that their coercive strategy is likely to switch, flipping from petulance and anger to one of need and helplessness. The voice becomes weak and babyish. There is much pleading. The body language suggests vulnerability. The implicit message is 'Please don't leave me, please don't hurt me, especially when I'm down. I need you.'

A similar strategy is at work when anxious individuals constantly devalue and put themselves down. 'Oh, I'm useless. I can see why people get fed up with me. Even I don't like me.' Such self put-downs invite other people to be sympathetic and protective, approving and encouraging. Taken together, these behaviours add up to a *hopeless* cognitive style in which passivity, helplessness and uselessness are emphasized (Abramson *et al.* 1989). Believing that they have little personal control over what happens, anxious people feel that their lives are fated. They adopt a passive stance towards all that life sends their way.

Romantic and couple relationships

Anxious, preoccupied individuals believe it is easy to fall in love, something they are prone to do. Because their attachment systems are readily activated, intimate relationships offer the ready promise of being loved and feeling secure. Sex seems a direct way to increase the craved for closeness and intimacy, but it also increases feelings of anxiety about one's own attractiveness and competence. Cuddling and kissing feel most safe (Hazan *et al.* 1994, cited in Mikulincer and Shaver 2007: 357). Sexual intercourse is approached with ambivalence. Sex, therefore, can easily be confused with love, creating a muddled mix of strong but varied feelings.

In spite of an emotional dependence and over-involvement with others, there is anxiety whenever relationships become intimate. The anxious need to be loved, accepted, respected, and not be hurt continues to unsettle even the most ardent of romantic liaisons. For anxious individuals, all emotions tend to be felt and expressed in heightened and exaggerated form in the context of intimate relationships. Declarations of undying love and feelings of possessiveness are as likely as outbursts of mistrust and jealous anger. Both are driven by the anxious need to be loved, reassured and never be abandoned. All of this results in romantic behaviour that is full of self-doubt and in which there is a constant need to be reassured.

For example, once the initial rush of romance and intense attraction is over, anxious and preoccupied individuals might quiz their partner, wanting to know who they have seen and to whom they have spoken, what was said and why. The constant fear is that their partner will leave them. The result is behaviours by the anxious partner that can be jealous, querulous, restricting, and dependent, all suggesting a high reluctance to let go (Pietromonaco *et al.* 2004). At other times, however, when things are going well and there is much togetherness, enmeshed sentimentality gushes over into acts of exaggerated generosity. There is the giving of 'over-the-top' presents; excessive declarations of love and devotion; a willingness to do anything for the loved one; a general flood of feeling; and much coy, disarming, babyish talk. This is particularly pronounced during the courtship and initial dating phase.

Anxious types are the most likely to conduct the romance at the highest levels of intensity. Phone calls and texts full of messages saying 'I love you' and 'I need you and can't live without you' come thick and fast. Gifts shower down. This is all fine so long as it is reciprocated, but as soon as partners relax their response, self-doubts and old anxieties about the reliability of the other and his or her interest and availability return. These anxieties inevitably trigger attachment behaviours, particularly those based on anger and threat quickly followed by vulnerability and abject apology.

These extremes of anxious, irritable jealousy and excitable passion are yet another reminder of the coercive way in which relationships are conducted. The rapid switch between the strong expression of positive and negative feelings, between threat and seduction, regularly lead to rows and *conflict* in which one or the other partner threatens to leave the relationship. Here is a little of Alan's story:

Alan was an only child. His mother was a rather volatile woman who ran her own business and found little time to spend with him. His father suffered ill health. His long periods in hospital meant that on top of her business worries, Alan's mother had to find time to visit her husband. She moaned about the poor hand that fate had dealt her and was forever complaining that no-one really understood the sacrifices she was constantly making to keep everyone else happy.

After a rather poor school career, Alan left to work as a printer's assistant when he was 16. He proved a rather unreliable apprentice – turning up late, taking days off sick, larking about on the job. He was fired after 6 months. He then took a series of short-term jobs that usually ended up with him not turning up for work saying that what he was doing was boring or that he was being exploited or that he'd just heard of a better job.

By the time he was 23, he was in a second marriage, this time to Jackie. Two years later, both his parents died in quick succession. He had inherited enough money to buy a decent size house which is what his wife wanted him to do. However, Alan claimed that the loss of his parents, the depression he felt about losing yet another job through no fault of his own, and the stress he said he was under meant that he needed a fillip, a treat, a bit of cosseting. So he bought himself a large number of expensive electrical goods and a new sports car. The rest of the money he invested in a friend's small business where he expected to make a quick 'killing' and get 'seriously rich'. He first met this 'good mate' at his local pub. The friend had plans to start a business providing IT support for people and their personal computers. The business failed and Alan lost all his money.

All of this put a huge strain on his relationship with his wife. He accused her of having affairs and he became verbally and sometimes physically aggressive. She left him and went to live with her sister. He broke down in tears on hearing the news. Although the sister wouldn't let him in the house, Alan pleaded with Jackie to have him back. On each visit he would cry, bring her flowers, say how sorry he was, that he had learnt his lesson, and that he missed her terribly, couldn't live without her, and had even thought of suicide. After several weeks and many more such visits in which Alan was looking increasingly dishevelled, she returned to live with him.

It is also the case that the uncertainty felt in close relationships by those classified as ambivalent makes them particularly prone to separation anxiety. They worry about being abandoned. Studies that have observed how anxious people react to separations from their lovers, say, at an airport, note higher than average levels of anxiety and distress (e.g. Fraley and Shaver 1998). Similarly, whenever a close relationship is under stress, or there is the threat of abandonment by the other, or there is pressure to become more independent and self-directed (leaving home in late adolescence, a partner deciding to work in another part of the country), or partners hint at their own desire to be more independent and do something on their own, ambivalent personalities experience increased levels of stress and anxiety. The fear of granting partners more autonomy is that they might turn their emotional interest and attention elsewhere. The anxiety this creates leads to heightened emotional need and displays of helplessness, the effect of which is to discourage partners behaving independently or pursuing interests on their own:

Following experiences of repeated separation or threats of separation, it is common for a person to develop intensely anxious and possessive attachment behaviour simultaneously with bitter anger directed against the attachment figure, and often to combine both with much anxious concern about the safety of that figure.

(Bowlby 1998a: 296)

These restless and unsettled feelings encourage constant switches between wanting to control a partner's emotional availability, followed by anxiety that such intrusive behaviours will only serve to annoy them. The anxiety leads to tearful apology and submission, only for the cycle to repeat itself in a further round of emotional need, demand and threat. The result is that relationships feel in a constant state of flux as emotions swing sharply, this way and that (Simpson *et al.* 2006). The strain on the relationship that this creates can bring about what the anxious individual most fears – the breakdown of the romance and abandonment. And when romantic relationships do break up, ambivalent people report a great deal of distress, in contrast to avoidant individuals who often say that they actually feel some relief (Feeney and Noller 1992).

These behaviours and the roller-coaster relationships that they sponsor are most pronounced if both partners are anxious-preoccupied and both compete for support and attention, although turbulence is also experienced when anxious and avoidant people are paired (Bartholomew and Alison 2006). Relationships revolve around the giving and withholding of love and affection, all of which makes for an interesting if somewhat bumpy ride. And as people with an insecure, ambivalent history are often likely to form relationships with other people who are also insecure, the result is partnerships that are full of upset, drama and argument. The presentation of problems and needs to others becomes increasingly exaggerated in attempts to hold other people's attention and force their involvement (Crittenden 1995). Intense signals of distress aim to draw in otherwise inconsistent and unreliable caregivers and attachment figures. A parent, a partner, a truculent teenage daughter, or a hard-to-see doctor all might find themselves in the emotional firing line.

Ambivalent partners feel that in close relationships, they are the victims, that they give everything but receive nothing in return ('It's all give and no take; it's not fair'), that they selflessly meet the other's every need while they remain deprived. 'I have given you so much; how could you do this to me?' (Yunger *et al.* 2005: 106). Simpson and Rholes (2004: 423) report that:

> Regardless of their own attachment scores, men married to more ambivalent women perceived offering less support to their wives, especially during the more stressful postnatal period. They also

viewed their wives as more immature, more dependent, emotionally weaker, and less emotionally stable than did men married to
less ambivalent women.

So, although anxious adults are keen to be seen as energetic carers
and respond to their partner's emotional needs, they tend to get
caught up with their own anxieties. There is the distinct suspicion
that casting themselves in the role of the responsive, extra-sensitive
partner, they are actually being governed by their own unmet attachment needs. Their enmeshment and over-involvement interfere with
their ability to respond in an emotionally useful way (Collins *et al.*
2006). They go over the top, go too far, and so become too much.
Collins *et al.* (2006: 165) state:

> Thus, they are likely to provide care that is intrusive, overinvolved,
> controlling, or otherwise out of synch with their partner's needs
> … For these and many other reasons, the caregiving style of
> anxious individuals is likely to be relatively ineffective, although
> not neglecting.

But in spite of their many dissatisfactions, anxious individuals are
reluctant to give up on romantic relationships. Fears of being abandoned and alone make them more likely to stay in relationships, even
when they are clearly unsatisfactory (Davila and Bradbury 2001).

It is in romantic relationships that we see the behavioural characteristics of the anxious adult being played at their most extreme. We
see personalities that exaggerate feelings, cling anxiously to relationships, and fail to be independent. The self comes across as needy and
helpless. Other people are made to feel responsible for the anxious
individual's emotional well-being. There is no personal growth and
learning about the self never really takes off.

Parenting and caregiving

The ambivalent person's anxious need for intimacy not only means
that they get into sexual relationships at a relatively young age but
also particularly in the case of women, they are likely to have children
before they are too old. Anxious individuals anticipate that they will
be wonderful parents, showering love and affection on their babies,

which of course the young child will appreciate and for which they will be lovingly grateful.

In the mind of the anxious, preoccupied parent, babies, of course, hold out the longed for prospect of a relationship with someone who can be loved and who will return love without the fear of abandonment. Crittenden (1992a) believes that many anxious, insecure adults approach parenthood with the expectation that, finally, they will experience the kind of closeness and intimacy for which they long. The birth of children reawakens old desires. 'In other words, after a history of failed relationships, they will find hope in the birth of children' (Crittenden 1992b: 590).

But in the event, most children of insecure and preoccupied parents fail to provide their parents with the contentment and security for which they yearn.

> Because the arrival of a new child often heightens stress and conflict in many relationships and may elicit memories of deficient caregiving by one's own parents, the transition to parenthood – especially the early post-natal phase – should activate the working models of highly ambivalent people.
>
> (Simpson and Rholes 2004: 421)

The behavioural distress that all babies show begins to be interpreted as infantile ingratitude and further evidence of failure and ineffectiveness on the part of the parent. Children begin to disappoint their parents, unwittingly undermining their confidence. So, even though they have now achieved the longed-for status of parent, nothing seems to have changed. Doubts about competence return. Only if an insecure parent has a secure, responsive and supportive partner are his or her caregiving uncertainties likely to be tempered.

Solomon and George (1996) describe the defensive, helpless style of ambivalent mothers' caregiving as *uncertain*. One minute ambivalent parents are describing their children as wonderful and loving, and the next as difficult and ungrateful. Integrating and dealing with both the positive and negative aspects of looking after children, the parent–child relationship, and the complex feelings that go with caregiving proves difficult.

Anxious, uncertain parents also discourage autonomy in their children. Autonomy implies that as parents, they are no longer needed or loved. Their children's growing bids for independence imply freedom, and with it the loss of the love and intimacy that the idea of children once promised. How ungrateful of them to grow up.

As parental confidence ebbs, uncertainty grows – uncertainty about when to intervene or discipline or let go. Using the only strategy they know in their attempts to control other people's behaviour and regard, parents raise the emotional temperature often by threatening to remove themselves from the relationship. 'None of you ungrateful kids appreciate me and all I do for you. I've had enough of you whining for this and for that. Not one of you ever thinks about me. I've a good mind to walk out and leave you all.' Threats of walking out, withholding love and abandonment only make children more anxious, and anxiety intensifies their already hyperactivated attachment behaviour, making them even less manageable. It is impossible for children to reflect on, and regulate their arousal under such caregiving conditions.

When the primary caregiver is ambivalent and the parenting uncertain, family life is inclined to be busy, fraught and muddled. Some families appear chaotic and disorganized. Other kinship members, particularly maternal grandparents, are often present and active in day-to-day family life, blurring the boundaries between the generations. Pets, particularly energetic and bouncy dogs, are an inevitable presence.

As a result of all this turbulence, family relationships also become *enmeshed* and *entangled*. As well as the anger and competition between members, there is also a good deal of gushing sentimentality. Extravagant presents and cards (particularly ones that are cute, perhaps with a drawing of a doe-eyed, vulnerable bambi or a coy, fluffy rabbit) are bought for birthdays. There are frequent, sentimental expressions of love by parents for their children as well as constant enquiries about whether their children love them. Nevertheless, when both children and parents are using coercive behaviours, the result is relationships that are loud, histrionic, volatile, conflictual, and emotionally exaggerated. Dramatic comings and goings seem to characterize so much of family life, as mum flounces out threatening never to return, or sons provocatively plan to go and live with their girlfriend's family.

It is also often the case in enmeshed families that everyone wants to know what everyone else is feeling and doing – who is being moody, who prefers who, who is being unfair. If I love you in a big demonstrative way, you must show your love for me in an equally exaggerated fashion – otherwise I will doubt your love. Therefore you must tell me of your love, gratitude and need loudly and frequently. There is no psychological privacy. 'Who did you date last night?' asks a mother of her teenage daughter. 'Did you kiss him? Is he sexy? Tell me all about it!'

In enmeshed families, there is rarely a dull moment. Large family gatherings at birthdays, Christmas, and holidays are planned with anticipation and excitement. Surprise parties (anathema to the avoidant mind) are the only kind which to have. Who's in and who's out changes from day to day. Threats and counter-threats about who cares and who does not, who loves and who does not are constantly traded. In the more extreme and chaotic families, to the outside observer it can seem one constant round of noise, need, competition, sentiment, drama, argument, walk-outs, suicide threats, practical jokes, illness, laughter and tears. The result is family life with little structure, few rules, high levels of impulsivity and much disorder.

Physical health

With a tendency to feel helpless in the face of challenge, there is a fatalistic attitude by those who are anxious in their attachments to what happens in life. Decisions are not made. Plans are not followed. Agreements get broken. The helpless stance also means that there is a pessimistic feeling about illness and what can be done about it.

Hyperactivating attachment strategies do not lead to a calm, relaxed approach to life. Preoccupied individuals ruminate over every little worry and anxiety. They see themselves as vulnerable. As a result, relationships are often a cause of stress, and chronic stress is not good for physical health.

Anxious adults are most likely to report symptoms, often with some drama, panic and exaggeration (e.g. Kidd and Sheffield 2005). They are the group most likely to complain – about feeling unwell, being burdened with ill-health, having unsympathetic partners. Physical symptoms cause alarm, being perceived to be more serious and threatening than often they are. It is never a cold, always pneumonia; never a twinge, always a pulled muscle; never a scratch, always a case of bleeding to death. Their ailments baffle and defeat the best medical minds. 'I'm a medical mystery, me. None of them doctors can get to the bottom of what I'm suffering.' These reactions can lead to hypochondria. There are frequent visits to doctors and pharmacists for reassurance, comfort and treatment. Ironically, all of these stressed behaviours increase the risk of leading a careless life style, particularly one that might involve smoking, a lack of exercise, and comfort eating, none of which is conducive to good health.

Mental health

Anxious people suffer chronic low self-esteem. A passive attitude is adopted to life and its problems – things happen and there is nothing that can be done about them. Anxious and preoccupied people are therefore prone to feel helpless, depressed and ineffective. Unable to take other people's support and availability for granted, they feel more alone and vulnerable. They fear disapproval and abandonment, and yet their anxieties and neediness place huge emotional demands on others who otherwise might be there as sources of support.

Whenever negative feelings are triggered, worries grow and become hard to keep under control. Aroused, distressed states can therefore last some time and consume a lot of mental energy. Hyperactivated attachment strategies lead to an intensification of distress and an inability to regulate escalating arousal. Feelings and thoughts can rapidly spin out of control. This can be particularly true when a major loss is suffered, especially when the relationship with the lost other was unhappy and complicated (Dallos and Vetere 2009, Chapter 7). The grief and mourning process become disordered, maladaptive and pathological. Reactions to loss are inclined to be intense and dramatic. Preoccupied individuals can quickly become overwhelmed by memories and strong feelings of irritation, restlessness, recrimination, helplessness, need, love, sadness and pain. 'Conflicted' grief reveals itself in chronic feelings of abandonment and anger, followed by feelings of yearning and loneliness (Parkes and Weiss 1983).

These personality traits are not a recipe for contentment or sound mental health. Unable to regulate their arousal, anxious individuals are liable to act angrily, impulsively or helplessly. They are easily caught up with angry and distressed childhood memories. As a result, their ability to reflect on and process relationship experiences is limited.

There is a particular association between anxious attachments, neuroticism, and the more negative emotions (e.g. Noftle and Shaver 2006). For example, ambivalent attachments in infancy and major separation experiences in childhood have been found to be good predictors of anxiety disorders (fear of danger and mishap when there is no objective evidence to warrant these feelings) in adolescence and adulthood, particularly when combined with an unresolved state of mind with respect to attachment (Bosquet and Egeland 2006; Warren *et al.* 1997).

Simpson and Rholes (2004) suggest that people classified as ambivalent or preoccupied are more at risk of depressive symptoms, particularly if they regularly experience stressful life events. For example, anxious women are more likely to suffer postnatal depression (e.g. Bifulco *et al.* 2004). Driving this risk is the ambivalent personality's anxious preoccupation with relationships, the nagging doubts about one's own worthiness and lovability, and the worry that other people cannot be relied upon to be there at times of need to provide care and support. Anxious people assess their personal well-being in terms of how well or not they believe their relationships are going. There is a belief that happiness is dependent on satisfactory relationships, but as relationships are a regular source of anxiety and uncertainty, feelings of contentment are rare (Simpson and Rholes 2004: 415). The anxious internal working model all too readily supports strong negative thoughts about the self, and negative expectations about the outcome of relationships (cf. Beck *et al.* 1979). It is the constant generation of negative thoughts and feelings of helplessness that increase the risk of depression, eating disorders, and in some cases, talk of suicide.

Even when depressed ambivalent individuals receive support, they are more likely to perceive it as insufficient. For example, over time, partners of depressed ambivalent women are more likely to conclude that 'their ambivalent wives' needs for support are unending and flow from their stable – and perhaps unchangeable – personality traits' (Simpson and Rholes 2004: 425).

Old age

In old age, proportionately fewer people are classified as anxious and preoccupied in their attachments (Zhang and Labouvie-Vief 2004).

This might mean that with age and experience, even some previously preoccupied adults begin to feel more confident in themselves, that it is not always necessary to depend on other people, and that a sense of autonomy grows. However, of those who do remain anxious, we see the familiar hallmark behaviours of the entangled pattern.

Old age is a time when vulnerability is likely to increase. The fears of dependency and abandonment by all old, fragile people activate the attachment system with its goal of trying to maintain the proximity and involvement of potential carers, including adult children, care workers and residential staff. In the case of those with preoccupied attachments, the resurgence of need will be particularly troubling. Their anxieties are liable to get exaggerated. Anxiously attached people, therefore, are often eager to seek care and reassurance from sons and daughters, friends and neighbours (Magai 2008: 543). The old anxieties that other people might not be there for you at times of need, that no-one is interested in you, trigger the usual hyperactivations of the attachment system. Illness creates feelings of alarm and panic. Reduced physical mobility leads to fears of loneliness which, in turn, promotes talk of abandonment and moans that no-one cares what happens to you: 'I'd be better off dead. You'll all be better off without me, I suppose, then none of you will have to bother. I won't be a burden any more.'

These cries of helplessness, growing feelings of anxiety, and the pleas for renewed closeness and attention can frighten off other people. Matters can become particularly entangled if the children of the elderly anxious parent are also insecure, especially if they, too, have an anxious attachment, in which case it will be the adult children's own needs and intensified emotions that will begin to dominate the relationships with their increasingly dependent parent.

As the emotional demands rise, so sons and daughters begin to feel put upon, angry and manipulated. The aging or ill parent begins to feel a burden (Crispi *et al.* 1997). The implied message from the aged parent is that 'you should be grateful for all the things I've ever done for you, so how can you possibly abandon me at my hour of need, unless you really are an ungrateful child?' It is at this time that relationships between the generations can become fraught, particularly when adult children of anxiously attached, later-life parents succumb to the pressures under which they feel. It might be with some reluctance that they agree to have mum live with them. Or, in some cases, the anxious demands might actually cause family and friends to distance themselves, further increasing the insecurity felt by the aging parent. For anxious parents and adult children alike, old age and increasing frailty can be a very difficult time as once again need, fear, ambivalence, sentimentality, deprivation, guilt, and anger confuse relationships between careseekers and caregivers.

Conclusion

In many situations, the personality characteristics shown by mildly preoccupied individuals prove to be both appropriate and even a social asset. People who come alive at social gatherings contribute enormously to the success of parties, celebrations, and socially based websites. Those who like being centre-stage can entertain and excite others. Jobs that involve meeting, helping and becoming involved with the 'public' can be very appealing. Performers, event organizers, and people who run pubs need to be outward-going. Individuals who take the social initiative and give a boost of energy to the flattest of gatherings can be a boon for those who are shy, reserved or even avoidant.

Of course this cod analysis doesn't mean that the majority of people who do such jobs would necessarily be classified as ambivalent, preoccupied and of an emotionally hungry make-up. Rather, jobs perceived to be socially exciting, emotionally expressive and generally people-oriented will have a particular appeal to those who feel more alive, loved, liked, and comfortable when there are people around and they are the centre of attention and in the middle of the action. This reminds us, of course, that in spite of the undoubted bubbliness and emotional transparency of the preoccupied personality, the self exists in a state of doubt and anxiety. Emotional needs are high. Feelings of dissatisfaction and being deprived of love and attention are typical. And there are deep uncertainties about the inherent lovability, worthiness, and effectiveness of the self that bring an intensity, anger, and perhaps even desperation, to most close relationships.

12
Disorganized and Controlling Attachments in Childhood

Introduction

So far we have been exploring attachment patterns and styles that are *organized*, even though some might also be recognized as insecure. We have to remember that attachment behaviours become organized in order to increase proximity to caregivers and the emotional availability of others. For example, as we have seen, one way to increase the responsivity of an unpredictable parent or partner is to increase the frequency and intensity of attachment behavioural displays. The individual still cannot take the partner's availability for granted, hence the insecurity, but the attachment behaviour has been organized in such a way as to increase the chances of the attachment figure responding at times of needs.

However, there are situations in which it proves very difficult to organize an attachment strategy that achieves improved proximity to the caregiver or results in increased parent or partner availability. In these relationships, a need, a stress, or a fear, as expected, activates the attachment system triggering attachment behaviour, but there is no clear or stable pattern, or underlying organization to the behaviour in the presence of the caregiver. When distressed, young children's behaviour might appear odd or seem to lack purpose or goal. The attachment behaviour looks disorganized or disoriented. In the presence of the caregiver, children can look dazed or confused. Recovering proximity to the caregiver normally terminates the attachment system, but in the case of disorganized attachments, because the goal is not achieved, the attachment system remains activated leaving the child in a state of chronic arousal and dysregulation.

The details and dynamics of this category were first described by Mary Main and Judith Solomon (1986, 1990). They were puzzling over some surprising findings from previous studies in which a few cases observed in the strange situation procedure, including a number of abused and neglected babies, were being classified as secure. On the face of it, this seemed both unexpected and unlikely. They reviewed all the videotapes of such cases. Their re-analysis led them to suggest a fourth attachment category in which young children were finding it difficult to find a strategy that increased caregiver availability at times of need and distress. The children's expectations appeared confused, as if they felt some fear of their caregivers and their behaviour, or sensed their parents' psychological unavailability and lack of interest. These children appeared to suffer a loss of attention and a collapse of attachment behaviour. These attachments were therefore described as either *disorganized* or *disoriented*.

In middle-class, non-clinical samples, around 14 per cent of children might be expected to be classified as disorganized (van IJzendoorn *et al.* 1999). This figure rises as children find themselves in more high-risk, stressful environments in which there is poverty, poor parental mental health or environmental stress. When children experience abuse, neglect, maltreatment, have parents who suffer drug addiction, or live in homes where there is domestic violence, rates of disorganization rise to 80 or 90 per cent (Carlson *et al.*. 1989; Cicchetti *et al.* 2006).

Infancy

Some parents appear to 'abdicate' their caregiving at the very moment that their children seek protection, comfort and regulation (Solomon and George 1996). It is as if the parent disconnects from the business in hand and goes into a different mental state. Caregiving and the attachment needs that parenting inevitably throws up, seem to trigger old, unresolved feelings and memories of loss, hurt and trauma that well into consciousness and threaten to overwhelm the parent. These unresolved feelings can be heightened even further when the parent is also in a violent relationship, in the throes of an ugly divorce, trapped in a war zone, feeling depressed, or burdened by relentless poverty.

Under the stress and distress of caregiving, these parents feel unable to cope. They become afraid of their own helplessness. Defensively they resort to the extreme psychological strategy of mental segregation in which individuals opt out of their current mental state with its painful memories and feelings, and occupy another mental state that feels safer, but one which no longer processes the information being generated in the current relationship, that is, the 'outside' interaction with the child that first triggered the distress. *Abdicated caregiving* therefore occurs when the parent goes 'mentally off-line' under the stress of parenting itself.

Solomon and George (1996) recognize two forms of this type of abdicated caregiving: 'dyregulated caregiving' and 'constricted caregiving'. Dysregulated caregiving describes what happens when parents are flooded and overwhelmed by old fears and worries. They begin to feel helpless, vulnerable, in danger, and out of control. They might describe their children as wild, evil, unmanageable.

Constricted caregiving describes parenting that manages to avoid losing control and getting distressed by the demands of parenting, but again it involves abdicating responsibility for key caregiving duties. When their baby cries, parents might go and take a bath and turn on the radio, go to the shops, or put the distressed child in the garden outside in their pram. Or sometimes, parents believe their children don't need care; they are so precociously wonderful that they seem to sense their parents' fragility and so they purportedly care for, soothe, and manage themselves. Children are viewed only in terms of the parents' needs and condition. Children, as separate beings, are thereby rendered 'invisible' (George and Solomon 2008: 847).

It is certainly the case that under less stressful conditions, otherwise disorganized infants are capable of showing more organized attachment behaviours. Indeed, in the manuals that guide researchers in their attempts to classify children and their attachments, there are instructions to assign a secondary 'best-fitting' organized attachment classification. A child, for example, might be classified disorganized-avoidant, disorganized-ambivalent, or even disorganized-secure (see Chapter 4).

Caregiving which fails to offer protection and comfort at times of fear and need, and which fails to offer children a relationship that helps structure, organize and integrate heightened experience, leads to high arousal, sensory overload, and even trauma in young children. Some of the caregiving characteristics seen in disorganized dyads include caregivers whose communications are disturbed and distorted, who look away from their baby for excessively long periods of time, who are facially inexpressive, and who make sudden movements, particularly movements that involve the parent rapidly shifting or 'looming' into the baby's physical and visual space (babies find this alarming). Each of these behaviours is liable to activate the infant's attachment system, although the activation goes unrecognized and unacknowledged by the caregiver. Levels of contingency and degrees of congruence between these caregivers and their babies therefore tend to be low. In extreme cases when the caregiving results in maltreatment, to be cared for by a dangerous or emotionally neglectful parent is to suffer *relational trauma*.

In all such cases, Beebe *et al.* (2010) suggest that the infant's disorganized status 'represents not being sensed and known by the mother, particularly in states of distress. We propose that the emerging internal working model of future D[isorganized] infants includes confusion about their own emotional organization, about their mothers' responses to their distress', all of which sets 'a trajectory in development which may disturb the fundamental integration of the person' (ibid.: 7).

Fear pervades the internal working models of disorganized children. It dysregulates their emotions, overwhelms their cognitive capacities, and damages their ability to develop an integrated state of mind with respect to all attachment matters (Solomon and George 1999). Their defences are fully activated so that as much threatening, painful information as possible (dangerous carer, being abandoned) is excluded from consciousness. Such frightening attachment-related information is kept out of mind. It cannot be integrated into the individual's mental representation of experience. Therefore it is defensively excluded in so complete a way that traumatic memories and painful feelings are segregated and put out of conscious awareness into separate, organized representational systems. Such experiences, feelings and memories therefore cannot be processed, analysed or reflected upon.

Without the safety of a containing relationship, it is too overwhelming to try and process such deeply troubling experiences in which the self is represented as helpless and vulnerable in the face of frightening, unpredictable dangers. The memory of the fear and what caused it doesn't go away. It just lies outside direct conscious awareness. What can and does happen, though, is that any sensory arousal in the context of a current relationship can activate these segregated systems, leading to breaches of the defences with the result that the unresolved fears, and feelings of helplessness and rage can flood into the present, overwhelming both mind, body and behaviour:

> Up to a certain threshold, the more stimulation, through any of its sense organs, that an animal is receiving, the greater its arousal and the more efficient its behaviour: sensory discrimination improves and reaction time is shortened. Above a certain level, however, efficiency may be diminished; and, when in an experimental situation total stimulation is very greatly increased, behaviour becomes completely disorganized. The same occurs when stimulation is much diminished, as in sensory deprivation experiments. These findings suggest that there is an optimum level of sensory input at which responsiveness and efficiency are at their best.
>
> (Bowlby 1997: 96)

Bowlby goes on to discuss why it is important for our emotional arousal to stay within tolerable limits. 'A characteristic of any homeostatic system is that it is capable of effective operation only when the environmental conditions relevant to its operation remain within certain limits. When they do not, the system becomes overstretched and eventually fails' (Bowlby 1998b: 41–2).

For example, our bodies work well within certain temperature ranges. If we get a little bit cold, our metabolic rate increases and our bodies produce heat. If we get too warm, we sweat and we slow down to cool off. However, if the cold or the heat gets too great, our bodies find it increasingly difficult either to generate or lose heat. As a result, we begin to feel distressed and unwell.

> The environmental conditions that produce these physiological states are termed stressors, the states themselves states of stress. The personal experience is one of distress. Since the goal of attachment behaviour is to maintain an affectional bond, any situation that seems to be endangering the bond elicits action designed to preserve it; and the greater the danger of loss appears to be the more intense and varied are the actions elicited to prevent it.
>
> (ibid.: 42).

In essence, disorganization is more likely when parents are experienced as either frightening or frightened, hostile or helpless, abusive or neglectful. The parents themselves possess an unresolved state of mind with respect to attachment, a state of mind that gets triggered by relating to the distressed child and his or her needs. At such moments, the caregiving becomes disorganized, and the caregiver's state of mind is described as *helpless-hostile* (HH) by Lyons-Ruth and her colleagues (2005). It is as if the parent, when under the stress of caregiving, slips between feeling hostile one moment and helpless another. The parent is without a caregiving strategy under the stress of responding to the child's attachment needs. It is also the case that some parents remain in a predominantly hostile state of mind (resulting in emotional, verbal, even physical abuse), while others collapse into one of overall helplessness (resulting in emotional, psychological, supervisory, and physical neglect).

Not surprisingly, listing the various types of frightening and/or frightened caregiving environments that increase the risk of children developing disorganized attachments covers most of the major types of maltreatment: family conflict and domestic violence; physical, emotional and sexual abuse; neglect; parental misuse and abuse of drugs and alcohol; parental depression; parental dissociation; parental self-harming behaviours; and parental threats of abandonment, particularly threats of suicide.

However, children can also experience fear when their caregivers behave in odd, atypical, or distressed ways (Lyons-Ruth *et al.* 1999). These are parents who are not overtly maltreating their children, and the children are not obviously being abused or neglected. Nevertheless, the caregiving is both insensitive and disturbing. Parents might 'loom' menacingly, without explanation. They might encourage a child to approach, and then disengage at the last moment (an affective error). Parents might respond inappropriately to a child's upset, say, by laughing, mocking or criticising them, or behaving in a confused or apprehensive way, or by looking vacant, trance-like, frozen and dissociated. All of these behaviours are described as 'disrupted affective communications' and they put young children at risk of developing disorganized attachments (Madigan *et al.* 2006).

It has to remembered that maltreated children *do* form selective attachments to their caregivers, albeit ones that are insecure (Main and Solomon 1986; Moriceau and Sullivan 2005). Thus, even in cases of abuse where the parent is the actual danger, the caregiver is the 'programmed' haven of safety who *must* be approached (Main *et al.* 2005: 281), even though it is the attachment figure who causes fear in the child in the first place. The child is therefore left in a behavioural dilemma – to escape the source of the fear (the attachment figure) *and* to approach the ostensible source of safety (the very same attachment figure).

It is equally distressing for young children to be met with parental fear and helplessness whenever the infant feels upset and distressed. To all intents and purposes, a helpless parent is emotionally, and sometimes physically abandoning her child at the very moment the child needs the parent to be maximally available. Again, this is frightening for young children. This fear leads to attachment behaviour, the goal of which is proximity with the caregiver who, of course, is not psychologically available as he or she gets lost in his or her own feelings of despair and helplessness.

Bowlby (1997: 97), followed by Main and Hesse (1990), suggests that under all these conditions children experience the simultaneous activation of two incompatible behavioural responses: escape to a place of safety (the response to fear) *and* approach the parent as a source of comfort and safety (as directed by activation of the attachment system). In these cases of frightening and/or frightened parents, children are therefore faced with an irresolvable paradox. They cannot find a behavioural strategy that increases safety. Their heightened arousal therefore goes unregulated. There is a breakdown and collapse of behavioural patterning. And so their attachment behaviour remains disorganized. In the context of the parent–child relationship, the child experiences 'fear without escape' and 'fright without solution' (Main and Hesse 1990).

Organized or disorganized?

So far I have been following the Main and Solomon line describing these escape/approach behaviours as disorganized or disoriented. However, there are other equally interesting ways of thinking about these behaviours. For example, both Radke-Yarrow *et al.* (1985) and Crittenden (1985a, 1985b) prefer to see children's behaviours in these stressful caregiving environments as examples of both avoidant (A) and ambivalent (C) strategies being used as children seek ways of increasing proximity and staying safe. In other words, rather than describe the children's behaviours as disorganized, Crittenden (1992c, 1995) prefers to see them as attempts to 'reorganize' using two or more variants of the organized secure and insecure patterns. For example, upon reunion with his caregiver, a child might show little affect, only then to break down in tears and anger. In relationship with their carers, Crittenden sees maltreated infants strategically organizing their behaviour in order to reduce further maltreatment.

Below, we shall see how Crittenden (2000a, 2000b, 2008; Farnfield *et al.* 2010) in her nimble, clever, and rather elegant Dynamic-Maturational Model (DMM), develops and extends Bowlby's and Ainsworth's original ideas of organized but insecure infant strategies into a lifespan developmental theory of attachment and adaptation. These maturing strategies include various avoidant (Type A), defended, compulsive strategies (compulsive caregiving, compulsive promiscuity, compulsive compliance, compulsive self-reliance), and various ambivalent (Type C), anxious, coercive strategies. It is also possible to see children in complex caregiving environments, in which there is both abuse and neglect, using *both* defended Type A (compulsive avoidant) and coercive Type C (ambivalent) strategies.

The DMM sees danger as a primary organizer of human behaviour along with sex and keeping one's young safe. 'For humans, these result in three related, but sometimes competing, motivations: protecting the self, finding a sexual partner, and protecting one's progeny until their reproductive maturity' (Crittenden 2008: 11). The DMM of attachment and adaptation 'emphasizes developmental change and self-protective organization in response to fear' (Crittenden and Newman 2010: 432). In any current situation, particularly those with other people, an individual's behaviour (often misguided and maladaptive) represents their attempt to adapt and cope as best they can given their assumptions, expectations, previous history, and experiences of surviving. The emphasis, therefore, is on adaptation to current circumstances. Whereas for Main and Hesse (1990) fear is seen as a *disorganizing* mechanism, for Crittenden, fear acts as a powerful *organizing* affect (Shah *et al.* 2010: 331). It is likely, particularly in high-risk cases of maltreatment, that circumstances will be unstable. In the DMM, therefore, it is unlikely that there will be any long-term continuity of a particular attachment pattern:

In DMM terminology, children use one of many A, B, or C strategies and are expected to change strategy when circumstances favour a different solution to the problem of being safe and comfortable and maturation makes more sophisticated solutions possible.

Spieker and Crittenden 2009: 114)

In the case of some individuals in complex environments of unpredictable danger, their vulnerabilities and psychological distortions therefore provoke the use of both compulsive Type A *and* obsessive Type C strategies. Rather than seeing the individual in a disorganized (D) state, with no attachment strategies available to increase safety, in close relationships these combined A and C strategies witness the use of controlling behaviours *and* highly disruptive intrusions of strong negative feelings.

The DMM recognizes two forms of the combined A and C strategies: the A/C and the AC. The A/C form represents a poorly organized set of avoidant and coercive strategies. And lest there be confusion, Crittenden *et al.* are absolutely clear, 'A/C and disorganized are *not* different names for the same construct' (2007: 83, emphasis original). The AC pattern represents a highly integrated form of the compulsive and coercive strategies. This is how Crittenden describes the two forms:

> The two probable forms of this are (a) a poorly organized set of A and C strategies, marked by intrusions of unresolved trauma, and (b) a highly integrated form of the strategy in which behaviour is under very tight control, but marked by violent attempts to achieve closeness and revenge. The former can be thought of as similar to the diagnosis of borderline personality disorder and the latter to the diagnosis of psychopathy.
>
> (Crittenden 2008: 71)]

In the DMM, all attachment strategies are seen as functional in terms of trying to stay safe in the relationship environments in which they are generated. However, in other relationship environments, the use of the more extreme and distorted attachment strategies is likely to be dysfunctional, maladaptive and even dangerous. Thus, argues Crittenden, the DMM methods 'yield more differentiation within clinical samples (as opposed to labelling most clinical cases as "disorganized" or "cannot classify")' (2008: 277).

Hyperarousal

Organized attachment strategies represent ways of maintaining proximity to caregivers and regulating affect. In contrast, and back with the Main and Solomon (1990) model, for children classified as disorganized, whichever attachment strategy they try, their anxiety and distress continue to rise, threatening to overwhelm them. Feelings of fear and helplessness quickly spiral, further amplifying activation of the attachment system. As a consequence, the internal working model developed by these children represents the self, others and relationships as chaotic and incoherent. There appear to be no organized rules based on experience that are available to predict and guide attachment behaviour, no ways in which to regulate distressed affect and increase felt security.

Care which is extremely unresponsive, disruptive or traumatic is likely to see children developing models or representations of themselves as (1) unworthy and frightened, dangerous and bad, powerful but alone, and (2) others as unavailable, frightening, out of control, and exploitative. Nothing else in the environment seems to explain the parent's distress, so children unconsciously conclude that they must be the cause of parental aggression, fear, hostility and helplessness. Children also get the idea that close, dependent relationships are unreliable, unpredictably dangerous and possibly frightening. For these children, therefore, attachment experiences constantly precipitate catastrophic fantasies, often violent in nature with much talk of death, lurking dangers, and an absence of protective adults. Not surprisingly, infants classified as disorganized are at long-term risk of a variety of mental health and behavioural problems.

Further investigation of these cases suggests that the parents of disorganized children react in ways that are experienced as hostile, helpless or out of control because of their own troubled relationship histories (Main and Hesse 1990). It is now clear that many parents of disorganized children suffered loss, abuse, neglect, rejection and trauma during their own childhoods. The unresolved memories of these distressing, painful experiences are triggered by the very act of caring for their own children, particularly during key moments when children are in a state of need, vulnerability and distress. Perversely, it is their child's neediness, fear and vulnerability that activate old unresolved painful memories in the parent's mind triggering their distress, dysregulation, and dangerousness. As the parent's painful memories flood into the present, feelings of fear and distress arise. These might be dealt with defensively by either a fight (hostility), flight (helplessness), or freeze (abandonment) response. Or the parent's response might simply be one of distress and disorganization as his or her ability to reflect, process and mentalize goes 'off-line' (Fonagy 2006).

From the children's point of view, in the case of misattuned and chronically insensitive caregiving, there is no information being given to help them make sense of, and manage their distress. Or what is seen in the parent's mind is hostility. This negative view of the self under attack by the caregiver is incorporated into the self-construct:

> Disturbed and abusive parents obliterate their children's experience with their own rage, hatred, fear, and malevolence …When mirroring is altogether absent, for reasons to do with severe parental psychopathology or other extreme circumstances, the child experiences his inner life as barren and unknowable. Whatever the source, such feelings of alienation and isolation become fundamental to a fragmented and empty sense of self, and to the failure to develop sustaining and nurturing relationships with others.
>
> (Slade 2005: 273)

In the case of chronically insensitive or misattuned caregiving, faults and distortions are created in the construction of the child's self. The infant is forced to internalize the representation of the caregiver's hostile or helpless state of mind as a core part of himself. (Fonagy *et al.* 2002). These early experiences of disturbed caregiving and increased rates of disorganized attachments strongly predict later psychopathology and problems in social adjustment (Green and Goldwyn 2002; Green *et al.* 2007).

Thus, many parents of children classified as disorganized find that the unresolved issues from their own past constantly disturb and disrupt relationships with their children in the present. Maltreating carers might variously communicate to their babies that: 'I do not understand you.' 'I am not able to hear you.' 'Your signals are not meaningful or important to me.' 'You frighten me.' 'I feel helpless.' 'I can't bear your presence.' 'You make me feel so angry and violent.' 'I can't control you; you are unmanageable.'

Children develop a deep lack of confidence in the caregiver's ability to provide protection, safety, love, comfort and attention. In extreme cases, with no caregiver to offer protection or emotional regulation, babies and toddlers develop a variety of self-soothing behaviours. These include rhythmic rocking, head banging, covering the face with hands, and biting the self.

Preschool and middle childhood

The prevailing experience of children with a disorganized attachment status remains one of fear, disorganization and distress in relationship with primary caregivers. The dilemma of having a helpless or out-of-control caregiver is that your attachment strategy is constantly liable to collapse. However, as always, it is rarely the case that one risk factor on its own predicts behavioural and mental health problems. It is the interaction of multiple risk factors that raises the likelihood of increased rates of serious developmental impairment (Deklyen and Greenberg 2008). Nevertheless, an insecure, disorganized attachment is certainly a major worry, particularly if it is combined with other risk factors such as a difficult temperament, neurodevelopment disorder, poverty, family breakdown, and parental violence.

We also need to note that there is something especially frightening to the young mind about the threat of abandonment. Threats to abandon a child can be expressed in a variety of ways (also see Bowlby 1998a: 264). Unless a child is good, he will be taken away to a prison. If a child doesn't behave, a mother might get ill and die and it will be the child's fault. A father might threaten to commit suicide if his children continue misbehaving. It is equally distressing for children to overhear their parents arguing, with one or other threatening to leave. Threats of abandonment might also be used to discipline and frighten young children into compliance: 'Behave, you little bitch, or I'll lock you in the cellar, leave you in the dark with the rats, and then walk out of the house.' Such threats are a recipe for a range of anxiety disorders and other psychopathologies.

As we saw in Chapter 6, secure children do experience their care-givers as protective and comforting. Just as important, their parents are able to mentalize their children's psychological states, their interior worlds. This has the double bonus of both helping secure children regu-late their arousal *and* make sense of the self and other people as complex psychological and emotional beings. The benefits of being in your parent's mind is that you, too, learn to mentalize and cope with stress with increasing skill and competence. So secure children generally expe-rience the least relationship stress and manage it with the most skill.

In contrast, maltreated children experience the highest levels of relationship stress and receive the least help to deal with it or make sense of it. As a consequence, they cope very poorly with the complex business of interacting with others. Close relationships can evoke feelings of fear as well as anger. In defensive attempts to deal with the heightened anxiety that relationships engender, disorgan-ized children begin unconsciously to exclude certain perceptions and experiences from conscious processing. This means that they are not fully, realistically or appropriately engaged with either their own or other people's thinking or feeling states.

It is also the case that early, painful memories can be triggered by current experiences or associated stimuli. These can lead to height-ened arousal, distress and dysregulation akin to Post Traumatic Stress Disorder. Major defensive reactions of fight, flight or freeze are trig-gered which to the casual observer seem way out of proportion to the stimulus that provoked the response. Situations that evoke such memories of early distress and fear are therefore 'felt' rather than 'thought' (LeDoux 1998). Such feelings remain powerful but hard to regulate. So, some children deny danger or their own fear, or they do not acknowledge a parent's failure to love or provide protection. These defensive strategies distort reality, disturb relationships, and bring about no new learning about the self or others.

Controlling strategies

With maturation, disorganized children do gradually develop a range of self-protective, defensive strategies: if my caregiver can't keep me safe, then it is up to me to keep myself safe and comforted. However, these strategies remain fragile and they are liable to break down under the stresses and strains of everyday relationships.

In effect, during the pre-school years, a degree of developmental reorganization begins to take place (Lyons-Ruth 1996: 68). Other people are experienced by children as either irresponsible, helpless and needy, or potentially dangerous and in need of constant monitoring requiring extreme vigilance. In order to survive, children attempt to organize their behaviour in various ways to try and increase parental availability, improve parental predictability, and reduce parental danger in what seems to be a frighteningly unpredictable caregiving environment. The children have to see the self as competent and in control, even though their own attachment needs are neither acknowledged nor met. Not feeling in control is extremely stressful. Children therefore begin to develop strategies that increase their experience of feeling less helpless and more in control. The bottom line of these *controlling* strategies is safety and survival.

It is in the act of caregiving that hostile-helpless parents' own attachment needs get activated. It is the parents' own unresolved feelings of loss, anxiety and fear with which they find themselves having to deal and not the children's attachment needs. This makes parents dangerous (abusive, neglectful, or both). By trying to meet their parents' attachment needs and not their own, children may retain a level of safe proximity and involvement. However, in order to achieve this, children have to strongly deactivate their own attachment needs. Children attempt to 'solve' the behavioural dilemma presented by their frightening, frightened or anxious parents by stepping into or identifying with aspects of the caregiver's role (Main 1995: 433). For example, children may develop caregiving, punitive, bullying, or self-reliant behaviours in their attempts to relate with and *control* their distressed or hostile parent. Mayseless (1996: 211) describes the emergence of such organized adaptations to frightening and helpless caregiving as the 'disorganized-turning-into-controlling' pattern.

By meeting the caregiver's needs (to be comforted or controlled), controlling behaviours represent a way for children to remain engaged with an otherwise unavailable caregiver. Higher order developmental pursuits that might be found in relationships in which there is trust and reciprocity are sacrificed in favour of proximity, safety and self-protection:

Because living with a parent who has unresolved trauma is likely to result in chronic and cumulative experiences of fear, older children may develop strategies for maintaining a relationship with a parent who is unpredictable, frightening or frightened. There is longitudinal evidence that disorganized infants develop controlling-caregiving or controlling-hostile strategies that are thought to provide the child with a way of managing a parent who is a source of fear or alarm (Lyons-Ruth *et al.* 1999).

(Kobak et al. 2004: 410)

For example, being ultra-alert to parental anger and being able to predict parental hostility requires abused children to have a good theory of the malevolent carer's mind, an awareness that 'may prove essential to survival ...The value of quickly detecting (on the caregiver's face) the imminent rise of anger *before* it reaches its full-blown potential (when it has previously led to abusive behaviour from the caregiver) cannot be underestimated' (Steele and Steele 2005b: 158, emphasis original).

So, by the age of 4 or 5, although children may still show disorganized attachment behaviour under stress, under less stressful conditions they also begin to develop more organized attachment strategies around the issue of control (Main and Cassidy 1988). Controlling behaviours consist of either *punitive* behaviours (children behave in a bossy, rejecting, humiliating, sarcastic, aggressive way towards their caregiver), or *caregiving* behaviours (children fuss over, worry about, nervously try to cheer up, assist, nurture and protect the caregiver). These behaviours are often referred to as examples of *role reversal*, that is the child inappropriately behaves towards the parent as a parent might behave towards a child. These role-reversed strategies represent a major distortion in the child–parent relationship. Nevertheless, although controlling behaviours indicate some degree of organization and adaptation, they remain underpinned by mental representations of the self as disorganized and carers as frightening/frightened such that, in many play situations, themes of danger, catastrophe and helplessness continue to be enacted.

Solomon and George (1999) and West and George (1999) also argue that punitive and caregiving behaviours are attempts by otherwise disorganized children to control the parent–child relationship. It is the disorganized child's way of making the caregiver's behaviour more predictable by seeking to control the caregiver. Caregivers experience children's controlling-punitive strategies as ones which leave them not in control, that is, as parents, they have physically or psychologically abdicated care and protection of their child. Children therefore continue to feel abandoned, vulnerable and unprotected. So, instead of children's attachment behaviour activating their parents' caregiving system, it actually triggers the parents' attachment system:

> Overwhelmed by his or her own attachment needs, the parent then fails to provide care and abdicates his or her position as protector precisely at the moment of the child's greatest need … If the parent is feeling vulnerable and unprotected at the moment when the child needs care, it follows that the child would need to develop a mechanism to control the parent's own attachment system in order to reactivate the parent's investment in providing care. Following this thinking, George and Solomon proposed that that punitive or caregiving behaviour directed toward the parent achieves this goal. Punitive acts (sarcasm, insults, hitting, screaming at the parent) and caregiving (stroking, kissing, or making the parent comfortable) are effective means of control because they draw attention back to the child … Although the child develops behaviors to control the parent, mental representations of attachment clearly remain disorganized and disoriented.
>
> (West and George 1999: 143–4)

Compulsive and coercive strategies

These disorganized-controlling attachments are clearly complex. Indeed, discussions still surround their exact nature. We have already noted, for example, that Crittenden (1992b) prefers to see children who are classified disorganized according to the Main and Solomon (1990) and Cassidy *et al.* (1992) models as really showing an underlying logic (i.e. organization) in their behaviour as they attempt to adapt to the adversities of their dangerous or helpless caregiving.

So, although there is much common ground between the main thinkers in this field, there is by no means a consensus about the deeper nature of children's attachment behaviour under conditions of parental disturbance and danger. The developmental pathway that maps a route from 'disorganized' to 'disorganized-turning-into-controlling' to 'controlling' has many supporters. But there is equal interest in the arguments of those who see complex but nevertheless organized attachment strategies being employed even by very young children in situations of abuse and neglect. There have been a few attempts to seek some kind of reconciliation between the various views (for example, Teti 1999), but the debate continues.

Over the intervening years since Teti (1999) first attempted some kind of integration between the two systems, the volume of research and conceptualization concerning disorganized-controlling, and compulsive-coercive notions of attachment behaviour has increased significantly. Although there is overlap between the two systems, it is still the case that significant but interesting differences remain between them. Indeed, Crittenden *et al.* (2007) remain clear that the D-controlling category (in the ABC+D model) is not equivalent or compatible with either the DMM's compulsively compliant/self reliant strategies (A3–4), coercive strategies (C3–4), or the A/C pattern.

The present book is not the place to attempt either an integration or reconciliation between the systems, even if such a thing were possible. Instead, the rendition offered here conflates some of each system's key ideas. Not everyone loves a mongrel, least of all those intent on preserving the purity of the pedigree, but in order to get across some of the complexity as well as importance of this developmental category, the reader is asked to tolerate the shotgun marriage that spawns the hybrid. Of course, there is no real substitute for reading the source materials. Here, the reader will find research rigour and much conceptual elegance (Cassidy *et al.* 1992; Crittenden 1992c, 2000a, 2008; Crittenden and Claussen 2000; Main and Solomon 1990; Solomon and George 1999; West and George 1999).

In the present attempt to conceptualize children's attachment behaviour in caregiving environments that are unpredictable, frightening, hostile and helpless, a rather stripped down, simplified account is given of the basic strategies originally considered by Main and Solomon (1990), Cassidy *et al.* (1992), Solomon and George (1999), and Crittenden (1992, 1995, 2008). These give us four, major sub-optimal caregiving environments, and four *controlling* or organized types of attachment strategy that maturing, 'disorganized' children develop within each sub-optimal caregiving environment:

> *Compulsive caregiving* (on the avoidant, defended spectrum) associated with helpless and hopeless, frightened and neglectful caregiving.

Compulsive compliance (on the avoidant, defended spectrum) associated with hostile and dangerous, frightening and abusive caregiving.
Compulsive self-reliance (on the avoidant, defended spectrum) associated with rejecting and hostile caregiving.
Controlling-punitive and *coercive strategies* (on the ambivalent, enmeshed spectrum) associated with complex environments of maltreatment in which caregiving is both hostile *and* helpless, dangerous *and* unpredictable, frightening *and* frightened, abusive *and* neglectful.]

Children can, and do, develop more than one type of controlling strategy in their attempts to adapt to complex environments of insensitive caregiving and maltreatment. In their attempts to stay safe, children will alternate strategies as the quality and character of the relationship change, sometimes minute by minute.

Compulsive caregiving

Providing some care functions for a parent does not necessarily indicate role reversal. Many children of parents who are ill or disabled provide care for their parents but it is within the bounds of an otherwise healthy parent–child relationship. Children classified as disorganized/controlling-caregiving or compulsive caregiving are more likely to have parents with helpless states of mind, often with issues of unresolved loss (especially loss) and trauma in their history. Parents whose own needs and helplessness dominate their relationship with their children convey the message that they cannot even protect and care for themselves, never mind their children. A mother might be agoraphobic, never leaving the house, or she might be the victim of domestic violence. A parent might have experienced the loss of, or rejection by a mother when she was a child. A father might be alcoholic or depressed.

Many of these parents have unresolved issues of loss, hurt and abuse that become aroused in the act of parenting. Children experience such caregiving as distressed and helpless. In this sense, an unresolved state of mind is similar to that of someone who has suffered Post Traumatic Stress Disorder (PTSD). Old traumatic memories cannot be integrated into a conscious, coherent account of what happened. They remain out of conscious awareness and are unavailable for processing, However, these unresolved, traumatic memories can intrude into present consciousness whenever there are current reminders of need and vulnerability, often experienced at a sensory level (a noise, touch, smell, sight). If the unresolved memory is too painful, the individual becomes lost in the old trauma, absorbed by the memory. In extreme cases, parents might deal defensively with the traumatic arousal by freezing or becoming dissociated. 'Dissociation that occurs when recalling a traumatic event,' suggest Kobak *et al.* (2004: 398), 'impedes the cognitive and emotional processing of the event and is likely to maintain a disorganized trauma memory.' For parents who feel helpless in their role as caregiver, it is their own children's dependence, need and vulnerability that act as an unconscious trigger for the intrusion of the unresolved traumas and the attachment-related anxieties associated with them.

Similar to people suffering from PTSD, unresolved parents are very reactive to stress. Stress therefore might set off a startled, angry, flight or freeze response. 'At moments of high stress, normal coping and monitoring strategies become vulnerable to breakdown that leads to disorganized behaviour or thinking ... The failure or breakdown of coping strategies leaves the individual vulnerable and helpless' (ibid. : 399). The child may therefore cause the parent emotional distress for reasons that are apparent neither to the parent nor the child. It is the parent's own attachment needs that come to the fore when the child displays attachment behaviours. The only adaptive strategy that helps children retain involvement with their dysregulated caregiver is to 'parent the parent', or 'care for the carer'. These are examples of role reversal and compulsive caregiving. In order for this strategy to be successful, children have to suppress their own needs. This is why the strategy is understood as a type of avoidant attachment organization:

> Distressing the parent results in guilt and fear of abandonment by the child. To achieve and maintain closeness to the parent, to avoid passivity and helplessness, the child must offer rather than solicit care; must not expect to receive help in containing and processing anxiety but, on the contrary, must give such assistance. Later on, such children may appear very self-sufficient and choose a partner who is as needy as was the parent. This role-reversal restricts the

child's development, with the inevitable degree of failure increasing guilt and lowering self-esteem. The emotional unavailability of the parent produces an experience of acute and chronic loss. The capacity to ask for care is suppressed, but the need remains strong and unassauged.

(Barnett and Parker 1998: 147–8)]

Disorganized controlling-caregiving and compulsive caregiving children appear overbright, cheerful, solicitous, and prone to clown about to cheer up parents. They worry about other people's needs and well-being more than their own. There is a false, exaggerated, brittle quality to much of the children's determined light heartedness. 'Mummy, are you feeling unwell? Should I get your valium?' However, the anger and hurt felt because their own needs go unmet can occasionally surface, resulting in problem behaviour. A 6-year-old daughter of an alcoholic mother might suddenly break down in tears at school, or slyly pinch other children in the playground. Higher rates of internalizing disorders are also associated with the compulsive caregiving strategy:

Ella's mother suffered anxiety disorders. She was a fretful, nervous woman who showed little pleasure in life. In the mornings she would lie in bed waiting for 7-year-old Ella to make her a cup of tea before the little girl went off to school on her own. She would tell her daughter that she was a 'treasure" 'Mummy wouldn't know what to do without her little angel. You read my mind, don't you?' Ella began to take more and more days off school. And on the days that she did attend, she was anxious and irritable. It was the family doctor who first voiced some concern when Ella was referred to her with stomach pains and headaches for which there seemed no obvious medical cause. During the consultation Ella broke down in tears saying that she didn't want her mummy to die.

There is a long-term risk of some compulsive caregiving children also developing a helpless state of mind in adulthood. With maturation, the strategy of role reversal can generalize so that compulsive caregiving is activated whenever the individual feels anxious about (and responsible for) another person's distress. The concept of *co-dependency* is often associated with a childhood history of compulsive caregiving;

the need to be needed. In the adult version, people become involved with needy, dependent others (alcoholics, addicts, abusers, depressives), but always in the role of giving care (professionally as well as personally), never receiving it.

People who need to be needed have low self-esteem. But they also have suppressed feelings of anger that occasionally erupt in acts of verbal or physical aggression. Nevertheless, it is not being in relationship that raises anxiety. The individual's fear is that she will fall into a 'terrific emptiness because she feels she could not exist alone' (Kasl 1989: 31). There are also long-term mental health risks associated with this type of role reversal including eating disorders, anxiety, and depression, coupled with an increased risk of replication in the next generation, that is, in relationship with them, the parent's own children will develop compulsive caregiving behaviours (Macfie *et al.* 2005).

Compulsive compliance

The main behavioural aim of children who are parented by rejecting, hostile, dangerous, or abusive caregivers is to stay safe. Making demands on hostile, even potentially dangerous caregivers is risky. The child's attachment behaviour might increase the parent's stress to such a level that the caregiver is catapulted into a hyperaroused state of mind. The immediate cause of the parent's distress and dysregulation is the child expressing a need, being dependent, or appearing vulnerable. The parent might deal defensively with their own distress by trying to suppress, attack and subdue its cause, that is the child and his attachment behaviour.

Compliant children are therefore particularly vigilant and wary of their parents' moods and behaviours. Children learn that being open and explicit about their true needs, thoughts and feelings leads to rejection, belittlement, or even assault, whether verbal or physical. Their need to feel protected and loved cannot be expressed. Their strategy is therefore one of avoidance and defence in which they deny feelings of desire, need or anger. They distort their thoughts and perceptions to maintain proximity. Children, by denying their own needs, attempt to behave in ways which they think their parents would accept and approve. They become parent pleasers. Indeed, the intensive efforts to do everything right and not get on the wrong side of their parents may be, according to Crittenden and DiLalla (1988), the basis of compulsive behaviours. Crittenden (2008) also identifies another compulsive strategy that involves inhibition of negative affect that she terms *compulsive performance*. By performing well (behaviourally, academically), children attempt to be as they think their parents want them to be in the hope that this might elicit approval, avoid rejection, and in some cases, decrease the possibility of parental anger and violence. These are high stress strategies. There is a strong risk that these controlled behaviours might unravel in later adolescence. The model schoolgirl becomes the messed-up college student.

Although they have to be good at reading other people's moods, these children are poor at recognizing, understanding and managing their own feelings. However, when not in the presence of the feared parent, they do let go and show anger and aggression. They have learnt that the weak go under and only the strong survive. Such lessons are likely to make bullies of emotionally defended children. Cut off from acknowledging their own emotions, these avoidant children might show little remorse or willingness to change their behaviour:

> Four-year-old Jamie was frightened of his father who would physically chastise him for any sign of need or weakness. His father felt that if Jamie was to be a man, he had to be toughened up. If Jamie cried, his dad would smack him or make him take a cold shower. Jamie quickly learned to stay on the right side of his father, keep a watchful eye on him, and never risk upsetting him. A year later when he started school, Jamie was soon in trouble for hitting other children. It was when he punched a trainee teacher that the school's head finally asked to see his parents who claimed 'he was as good as gold at home.' They concluded that there must be something wrong with the school.

Compulsive self-reliance

If caregivers are experienced as frightening, out-of-control and unavailable, the only person to be trusted is the self. As rejected and hurt children get older, more organized strategies develop with the aim of keeping the self safe. For the child, the only predictable element in the distressed parent–child relationship is the self. Therefore, children begin to feel that the only way to feel remotely safe, physically and psychologically, is *to take control of the self, other people and the situations in which they find themselves.*

For rejected and maltreated children, closeness to others spells potential danger and emotional pain. Intimacy therefore has to be avoided. Love is abjured and self-sufficiency celebrated (Bowlby 1998b: 368). Children attempt to 'care' for and protect themselves by making sure that no-one tries to 'care' for them, for care by others has always led to emotional hurt, trauma, and in severe cases, even threats to one's very survival.

Compulsively self-reliant children therefore begin to organize their attachments along more extreme avoidant lines. They make few demands on their unpredictable, rejecting and possibly dangerous carers for protection or comfort (which paradoxically increases their safety). Ever vigilant and watchful, they operate in constant survival mode. Once again, this is stressful.

A good way to stay safe is always to be in control. This can involve verbal and sometimes physical aggression, often directed at care-givers. It is simply too frightening to let others be in charge, so any hint of letting down one's defences has to be dealt quickly, even violently. Anger begins to feel strong, and safe. It certainly feels powerful. There is contempt for anyone who shows need or vulnera-bility. Compulsively self-reliant children therefore dismiss weakness in others as well as themselves. Some children begin to behave as if they are invulnerable. They engage with the world of people and objects in a reckless manner, with impunity. Fights, playing on busy roads, and a disregard of hazards and danger can lead to a risky life style.

In his autobiography, the novelist J. G. Ballard describes his child-hood in Shanghai not long after China had been invaded by the Japanese. By 1943, many of the European families had been interned at Lunghua camp. One boy made a particular impression on him:

> Bobby was a close friend, though I never really liked him, and found something threatening about his tough and self-reliant mind. I sensed that circumstances had forced him to fight too hard to survive, and that this had made him ruthless not only with others, but with himself … His parents were interned in Peking,

but he never spoke about them, which baffled me at the time, and I suspect that he had forgotten what they were like. Thinking of him now, I realize that part of him had died.

(Ballard 2008: 70)

One of the consequences of going it alone and not having a caregiver who protects you, emotionally regulates you, and who 'has you in mind' is that you find it difficult to make sense of your own and other people's emotional states. And in spite of the compulsive self-reliance, emotions remain a puzzle, self-esteem is low, social cognition is weak, and peer relationships are poor (Jacobvitz and Hazen 1999).

Controlling-punitive and coercive strategies

Some children experience complex environments in which they suffer hostile *and* helpless, abusive *and* neglectful caregiving. Although disorganized attachments might be expected in infancy, maturation sees children beginning to develop more organized, controlling, essentially aggressive and punitive strategies towards their carers in these very troubled parent–child relationships (Howe 2005).

Environments that are felt to be unpredictable and not amenable to our control are experienced as particularly stressful. Stress causes children to have very elevated levels of the hormone cortisol. In such caregiving environments, children can find no logic in their parents' behaviour. All too often, their own attachment needs trigger either helpless or hostile responses. Children sense that whenever they experience need or feel vulnerable, their parent might react with anger or distress. Either way, the vulnerable self feels abandoned at times of need. The stresses evoked overwhelm the self which constantly feels on the edge of disintegration and annihilation. Such experiences are tantamount to relational trauma. Indeed, there is now widespread recognition that there are probably a range of common mechanisms underlying issues of unresolved loss, disorganized attachments and Post Traumatic Stress Disorder (e.g. Kobak *et al.* 2004: 395). Having been caught up in traumatically violent relationships coupled with a deep sense of being abandoned and feeling helpless, the heads of disorganized and controlling-punitive children are full of fear, chaos, aggression and destruction (Allen 2001).

Crittenden (1995), however, prefers to see this *disorganized-controlling* pattern, in which children behave *punitively* towards their carer, as an extreme, but logical extension of the ambivalent-coercive aggressive pattern. We first considered the *coercive* strategy in Chapter 10 where it was described in terms of a childhood ambivalent attachment pattern that takes shape in caregiving environments that are uncertain, under-responsive, and emotionally inconsistent.

However, when the caregiving is not merely uncertain and inconsistent, but is actually dangerous as well as unpredictable, neglectful as well as abusive, more extreme versions of the coercive strategy are called for if children are to cope, survive and adapt. So, for example, when the parent is angry and violent, children need a way to diffuse the danger and promote whatever residual nurturing instincts might be present in the parent's caregiving character. One way to do this is to emphasize the more seductive attachment behaviours – coy smiles, neediness coupled with gratitude, and displays of submission. At the milder end of these 'helpless' strategies are disarming and 'feigned helpless' behaviours. But in more dangerous caregiving relationships, these may evolve into 'seductive' and even 'paranoid' behaviours.

But when the parent flips into feeling helpless, out-of-control, unresponsive and despairing, the more aggressive components of the child's attachment behavioural repertoire come into play. These can range from angry threats to more punitive, menacing behaviours. These aggressive behaviours represent attempts by children to force the parent into making a response (Crittenden 1992, 1995). Some coercive children, adolescents and adults will alternate between aggression (perpetrator) and helplessness (victim) as their feelings and perceptions change. Some individuals might maintain just one dispositional state that produces mainly threatening and aggressive behaviours. Others are governed by dispositions that keep them in a predominantly helpless states of mind in which they feel put upon, deprived, and always the victim.

In the aggressive, punitive mode of the coercive strategy, children appear to be operating on the principle that attack is the best form of defence. It is this element of the coercive strategy that looks similar to the disorganized, controlling-punitive behaviours described by Cassidy *et al.* (1992) in which children seek to control, humiliate and sarcastically belittle their helpless, out-of-control parent.

Coercive and controlling-punitive children might speak to their distraught caregivers in ways that are rude, sarcastic, contemptuous, humiliating, and threatening. For example, in relationship with his angry but helpless mother, 4-year- old Harry was heard ordering her about, shouting: 'Sit down. Be quiet. You do it.' Indeed, if the controlling-punitive, unmanageable, out-of-control 4-year-old can get parents to behave like a 4-year-old by reacting with rage, hostility and helplessness, then 'that's quite an accomplishment' (Keck and Kupecky 1995: 51). Carers feel increasingly harassed and threatened by their children who refuse to be cared for, disciplined or managed as their anxious need to be in control increases.

If the caregiving continues to deteriorate, children begin to add various compulsive strategies to their coercive behaviours including compulsive self-reliance. In these complex, dangerous caregiving environments, children begin to use both compulsive Type A *and* obsessive Type C strategies in their attempts to stay safe. This A/C form, so well described by Crittenden (2008), represents a poorly organized set of avoidant compulsive (Type A) and coercive (Type C) strategies which are often seen in families where children are exposed to unpredictable danger, violence and neglect. This was Harry's eventual fate. His step-father would make periodic appearances and physically abuse him while his mother felt increasingly out of control, and more and more helpless:

> As Harry was approaching his fifth birthday, his mother said his behaviour had become so unmanageable that she wanted him 'taken away'. 'If you don't, I might end up killing him.' This was said in Harry's presence and he laughed saying that he would kill her first. He mocked her anger and frustration. He threw her car keys into the toilet bowl and said she was a 'shitty mum' as he watched her trying to recover them from the far-from clean lavatory pan. He refused to let her tuck him up in bed at night but would wake up frightened by bad nightmares in which a crocodile-like monster would appear in his bedroom and try to eat him. His therapist began to notice that the more aggressive and dismissive Harry was with his mother, the more violent and frightening became his drawings in which he depicted himself as very small and surrounded by men with guns and knives 'who are going to get me – but I'm going to blow them up'.

Matters become even more complicated if relational trauma also involves sexual abuse. Children become confused about the nature and expression of intimacy. This makes the conduct of all close relationships problematic. To form relationships with others implies sex, and yet intimacy inevitably arouses fear, distress and anger. Feelings of love, need, arousal, intimacy, hurt, fear and guilt form a disturbing psychological cocktail that can lead to behaviours that are often sexualized, including the sexual abuse of other children. Some sexually abused children go on to become sexually abusing adults. So, although by no means all sexually abused children become sexual abusers, many sexual abusers have suffered sexual abuse as well as physical abuse when they were children.

In these out-of-control parent–child relationships, children therefore have multiple, sometimes simultaneous experiences of themselves. There is one self that is sometimes frightened, alone and abandoned. There is another self that feels dangerous and bad as that self and its needs seem to cause anger, violence and distress in the parent. There might be brief moments when the self actually feels loved. And yet another self might feel powerful because it can cause such mayhem and panic in the carer. There can even be moments when the child experiences the self as protective and caring as the parent collapses into a helpless state of mind.

As these various senses of self – as frightened, alone, bad, dangerous, powerful, loved, loving – formed under highly stressful conditions, it is not easy for the brain and the overall sense of self to feel all of a piece. In the stress of a relationship, there are moments when one or other self is dominant, one internal working model that is temporarily to the fore. The self therefore feels incoherent. It lacks integration. Each of these senses of self, formed under conditions of traumatic, unpredictable caregiving, are too dysregulating to keep active and together in routine consciousness.

In order to function in these difficult, compound environments of abuse, neglect and rejection, children develop extreme defensive strategies in which each mental representation of the self is kept segregated from the others, and out of immediate awareness. In this way, children don't have to deal all at once with the turmoil that unpredictable and dangerous caregiving and the rapid shifts in attachment strategy that each caregiving style requires. Each self, each internal working model operates independently depending on whether the carer is being hostile, helpless, violent or needy (Liotti 1999).

Bowlby (1980) talked about each representational system being segregated and not routinely accessible to conscious awareness or processing. Segregated systems help keep the full sweep of painful memories and attachment-related information from flooding into consciousness all at once. So what we actually see under the stresses and strains of close relationships is children switching bewilderingly between avoidance and ambivalence, compulsive compliance and compulsive self-reliance, care and coercion, love and hate, sadness and anger, sulkiness and rage, feeling frightened and being frightening as a particular 'self' is forced into consciousness to cope with the immediate demands of a carer who is momentarily being violent, drunk, affectionate, tearful, helpless, or sad.

Therefore, unlike securely attached and organized insecurely attached children (ambivalent and avoidant) who do develop singular and coherent representational models of attachment figures, maltreated and traumatized children

may have conflicting representations of the same caregiver behaving in contradictory ways, i.e. nurturing at times, hurtful at others, or sometimes not seeming to have them in mind at all. As Bowlby (1980) commented, these various representations form multiple models in the child's mind which require more psychic energy than a singular well functioning internal world made up of coherent representations. It could also be that for some of these children, they may suffer from having multiple models from two different sources. Multiple models may, for example, arise as Bowlby postulated from experiences of a caregiver who behaves in markedly contradictory ways, i.e. at times nurturing and at times abusive. Yet another source of multiple models may be seen to arise within the internal world of the child who has the experience of being perpetually in transition. Their representational worlds may contain elements including a range of diverse and possibly conflicting representations from many and often abrupt changes of caregivers, often occurring in a context of confusion and fear.

(Steele *et al.* 2003: 14)

Children who have suffered abuse, neglect, loss, rejection and disrupted attachments are at the highest risk of developing behavioural and mental health problems. These include dissociative symptoms, particularly in cases where children have been traumatized, suffered frightening sexual abuse, and experienced seriously disrupted attachments (Kobak *et al.* 2001). Externalizing disorders, including conduct disorders, are particularly common among children classified as insecure (Fearon *et al.* 2010), disorganized (Fearon *et al.* 2010), and controlling-punitive (Moss *et al.* 2006).

Raised in environments in which emotional climates range from hot to cold, confused to collapsed, abused and neglected children often have great difficulty recognizing and regulating their emotions. Beeghly and Cicchetti (1994) found that children who had experienced severe neglect and abuse used less internal state language and talked less about their own thoughts, feelings and actions than non-maltreated toddlers. These children were also less able to differentiate between feelings of sadness, anger and fear so that to experience one might be to display the other. Disorganized-controlling children therefore tend to misunderstand and misplay many social situations, further adding to their distress, mistrust and sudden displays of intense rage and anger.

Trying to survive in the traumatic moment also means that the ability of these children to see and follow through on the consequences of their own and other people's behaviour is frustrated. Cause-and-effect thinking is therefore difficult. When these children are asked to explain why they did what they did (bite another child, kick the cat), they can't, they really can't 'think' of an answer or make the connections between feelings and behaviour. And although the judgemental component of the following quote from Iris Murdoch's novel *The Black Prince* isn't perhaps morally appropriate, for those who have been traumatized, she does get to the nub of what makes some of us empathic and others not:

> The wicked regard time as discontinuous, the wicked dull their sense of natural causality. The good feel being as a total dense mesh of tiny interconnections.
>
> (Murdoch 1973: 95)

School and peer relationships

The school classroom can be a particularly difficult environment for controlling-punitive children (Cicchetti and Toth 1995). Indeed, the concept of 'school readiness' has been used to examine whether disorganized children will be able to cope with school life. School readiness involves curiosity and the willingness to learn. It requires the ability to communicate, take turns, share with others, show social skills, and follow directions. In their study of children who had just started school, Stacks and Oshio (2009) found that disorganized and controlling children were at risk of not having 'school readiness skills', compared to secure, avoidant and ambivalent children. The lack of these skills significantly raises the risk of poor school performance, dissatisfaction and disengagement.

Although abused children are more likely to be aggressive with their peers (a fight response), children who have suffered neglect are more prone to withdraw and feel helpless (a flight response). In each case children are attempting to reduce engagement with peers (and teachers) to avoid the potential distress and dysregulation that attachment-related encounters cause them. As a result, disorganized-controlling children adjust poorly to school life. Co-operation and collaboration are limited. Poor peer relationship skills correlate with weak academic performance. And problem behaviours are likely to be high. Even so, and although it demands a lot of teachers, there is evidence that if they can tune into and stay with these children, they can act as a safe haven and secure base (Bomber 2007; Geddes 2005). This protective role allows children an increased chance of coping better with school, having improved peer relationships, and maybe surprising themselves as well as others by achieving some success, in spite of the odds being stacked against them (Zionts 2005: 237).

Conclusion

According to Main and Hesse (1990), when attachment figures are the cause of fear, young children find themselves in a difficult, highly distressing situation in which they experience two simultaneous, but incompatible behavioural urges – activation of the fear system demanding an escape response from the caregiver as the source of danger, and activation of the attachment system triggering an approach response to the caregiver as the haven of safety. In this dilemma it is difficult to find an attachment strategy that increases safety and reduces arousal. Attachment behaviour is therefore described as disorganized.

With maturation, disorganized-controlling children gradually develop strategies to help them adapt and survive environments that are mis-attuned and confusing. In more extreme cases, the caregiving actually becomes unpredictable *and* dangerous. The various controlling, adaptive strategies that children develop in these caregiving contexts therefore make sense. More generally, theorists like Crittenden (2000a, 2000b) remind us that all attachment behaviours represent strategies that help children adapt to, and survive their particular worlds. In her Dynamic-Maturational Model (DMM) of attachment and development, Crittenden (2008), rather than see maltreated children's attachments as disorganized, prefers to see them generally developing organized, adaptive and self-protective attachment Type A and Type C strategies, even under conditions of great fear and danger. In the DMM, 'exposure to danger can either be resolved in adaptive ways or remain as "unresolved psychological trauma."' (Crittenden and Newman 2010: 435). Compulsive, coercive and controlling attachments might be the best strategies in places where trust is absent, danger is around every corner, and all the normal rules of civil life have broken down. Compulsively self-reliant and coercive children might be more likely to survive than securely attached children, say, if they find themselves orphaned in a war zone or on the city streets, feral and without family.

So, although the developmental cost of disorganized and controlling, compulsive and coercive strategies might be high in terms of mental health well-being, at least children who develop these strategies are more likely to survive in environments of extreme turbulence and danger. And from an evolutionary perspective, survival is always the behavioural driver. It is only when children whose histories are ones of loss and relational trauma attempt to function in the more benign, everyday environments of the classroom, the peer group, the workplace, and the community that their behaviour, unregulated emotions and desperate needs become a problem. It is this group of children who will make the biggest demands on society's mental health, criminal justice and welfare services.

13

Fearful Avoidant Attachments and Unresolved States of Mind in Adulthood

Introduction

Adults who have suffered childhood losses or traumas which continue to affect them in the present are said to be in an unresolved state of mind with respect to those losses or traumas. This means that any current stress, for example, in the context of a close relationship, can cause the old, distressing memories associated with the original loss or trauma to erupt into, and disturb present consciousness and behaviour. A high degree of continuity seems to characterize this group, certainly when compared with the avoidant and preoccupied groups. This seems to suggest that early loss, abuse, neglect and trauma, if unresolved, retain the power seriously to disturb thought and feeling across the lifecourse. For example, Main *et al.* (2005; also see Weinfield *et al.* 2004) found that the majority of children classified as disorganized as infants, and disorganized controlling aged 6, were coded as 'unresolved' when they reached the age of 19.

It is the stress of relating with close others that is most likely to provoke unresolved issues from childhood, issues of loss, neglect and trauma. In the case of those who remain burdened by painful child-hood memories, uncontrollable feelings of vagueness, confusion, panic, sadness, detachment, anger, violence, or fear might swamp the mind as they deal with their children, relate with their partners, or meet with health professionals. Unbidden and unconscious, these memories disturb behaviour and distort relationships. Fonagy *et al.* (2002) suggest that at such times the ability to reflect and mentalize 'go off-line'. Metacognition (thinking about thinking) is no longer present. The intrusion of these reflective lapses and associated episodes of disorganization and disorientation lead to a collapse of psychological and behavioural coherence (Main 1995). The traumatic events become re-lived in the present.

When individuals are in an unresolved state of mind, they might also entertain irrational beliefs, show an inability to stay with the situation, or break down into a prolonged silence. However, when stress levels are low, the individual's state of mind might recover and become more organized, revealing attachments that are either avoidant, ambivalent, or even secure.

In the Bartholomew and Horowitz (1991) model, there is less talk of unresolved states of mind with respect to attachment and more description of a type of attachment which they refer to as *fearful avoidant*. This group fears both intimacy and being alone. They often appear socially withdrawn and untrusting. But similar to those with unresolved states of mind, they, too, have often suffered difficult and disturbed childhoods. In general, the more disturbed the caregiving environment, the higher the risk of some individuals developing disorganized attachments in childhood and unresolved states of mind and fearful avoidant attachments in adulthood. This is a very vulnerable population of adults. Unless helped or lucky enough to form a close relationship with a reflective, secure other, adults with fearful and avoidant attachments remain at high risk of relationship problems, volatile marriages, poor parenting skills, behavioural difficulties, and mental health problems.

Adolescence

For adolescents, the early teenage years are a time of change, transition, and often conflict. These developmental demands are challenging for most adolescents, even those secure in their attachments and who are buffered by long-established resiliences including high reflective function and self-esteem. Negotiating adolescence is not so easy for young people whose attachment behaviours are disorganized and controlling, compulsive and coercive. They are poorly equipped to deal with challenge and stress, experiences which they generate all too easily lacking, as they do, the skills to manage relationships and regulate emotions (Sroufe *et al.* 2005b). Even in low stress conditions, their attachment styles remain insecure, unstable, and liable to change. Carlivati and Collins state:

In the Minnesota Longitudinal Study, individuals whose attachment classifications changed from secure in infancy to insecure at age nineteen were more likely than nonchangers to have been maltreated in childhood, as well as to have experienced maternal depression and conflictual family functioning in early adolescence (Weinfield 2000 *et al.*) ... In short, attachment representations can be altered by difficult and chaotic life experiences.

(2007: 100)

Major losses and traumas during later childhood in previously non-disorganized individuals can also explain some adolescents being classified as unresolved. Also, suggest Aikins *et al.* (2009), adolescents are exposed to more stressors than other age groups – sexuality, first romantic partners, death of grandparents, school examinations. Or, adolescents may simply be more affected by such events because their emotional and cognitive processing skills are not yet fully developed:

In the face of similar experiences, younger children would garner direct support from parents ... Thus, it may be the unique co-occurrence of limited support and skills for managing these difficulties, along with increased life stressors that puts middle adolescents at particular risk.

(ibid.: 504–5)

The slight increase in unresolved attachments in middle adolescence therefore looks as if it can be explained in a number of ways. For some individuals there is continuity of disorganization in infancy and unresolved status in adolescence. For others, the peculiar stresses of adolescence, the strivings towards autonomy coupled with the (self-imposed) loss of parents as attachment figures, increase feelings of anxiety and vulnerability, all adding to an unresolved state of mind. For many adolescents, this unresolved status is temporary. But for those whose early, middle and later childhoods have been characterized by loss and trauma, attachment issues are likely to remain unresolved, and for some a fearful avoidant attachment beckons.

The abuse and neglect suffered in their early years leaves fearful avoidant and unresolved adults with over-sensitized nervous systems. This makes them highly reactive even to relatively low doses of stress, particularly stress experienced in the context of close relationships. As a result, disorganized-controlling adolescents find that their emotions are typically intense, impulsive, dysregulated, and extreme. Given their emotional volatility, painful memories, and unresolved states of mind, this group is most likely to adopt and pursue more risky life-style choices. Sex at a young age, experimentation with drugs and alcohol, self-harm, antisocial behaviour, and criminality are common.

The addition and interaction of the various risk factors associated with young people who have suffered early maltreatment make them particularly prey to mental health problems. Wallis and Steele (2001), for example, found that all 39 of their sample of young people in a regional psychiatric adolescent unit had an early history of loss or abuse, and of these 59 per cent were classified 'unresolved' with respect to their experiences of loss and trauma.

Adulthood

Individuals with fearful avoidant attachments are likely to have significant relationship problems with peers and friends. Those with unresolved states of mind with respect to attachment, loss and trauma also find themselves easily disturbed and dysregulated by the feelings that inevitably get stirred in close relationships. Past, typically painful memories, and the defences associated with them, constantly invade and disrupt relationships in the present. Thus, although the fearful avoidant and unresolved seek intimacy, often with some intensity, they lack confidence, fear rejection, and experience distress in their relationships. They are nervous about disclosing too much about themselves. Trust is low. Levels of dissatisfaction with peer friendships are therefore high.

Marli was an advice worker in a city centre bureau. This is her description of Dandy, one of her more memorable clients:

> He was never still. Pacing, fidgeting, smoking roll-ups. There were weeks when he'd be in to see me every day. For a chat, for money, for information, for something to do. One day he'd be quite funny, chatty, charming, asking after my health. He would sometimes bring me little presents, then spoil it by saying he'd nicked it from the local supermarket which he said, 'was dead easy to pinch

from'. Then on another day he might suddenly cry and say what a useless life he'd had – a mother who was a druggie, a dad he'd hardly ever seen, in and out of foster homes, kicked out of school. And then out-of-the-blue he'd get in a rage and tell me I was an arsehole, no help whatsoever, I didn't care – never had – just doing it for the money, that I was a slag, 'a fucking waste of time'. I remember after one awful occasion, he came back next day, he said to apologize, but I was away from the office. He shouted at the receptionist, punched his fist through a window, and stormed out. I didn't see him for several months, then one day he popped in. He was holding hands with Kaz. Smiling, as if the cat had got the cream, he said they were going to get married. Kaz, he said, was pregnant. He was going to get a job, no problem. He was going to be the best dad in the world 'cos he knew from his own lousy experience that kids needed good dads. And that was the beginning of another intense episode that ended when Kaz said she was going to leave him because he was 'a nutcase'. Later that afternoon he got arrested for theft and possessing too much cannabis.

Romantic and couple relationships

Close relationships precipitate difficult feelings in those who have suffered pain and confusion in their early years. Individuals typically switch between hyperactivating (ambivalent) and deactivating (avoidant) strategies as first they plunge into the relationship and then agitatedly withdraw, only for the cycle to be repeated over and over again. It is this behaviour that Bartholomew and Horowitz (1991) termed 'fearful avoidance'. The individual enacts 'both strategies in a haphazard, confused, and chaotic manner' (ibid.: 225). At one and the same time, the individual has an anxious, demanding need to be loved, comforted, and protected, and simultaneous feelings of fear about what might happen if love and closeness are achieved that lead to withdrawal, dismissal, and the avoidance of being hurt and rejected. This is a destructive combination and most relationships have a hard time surviving:

> Fearfully avoidant people have especially negative representations of their romantic partners, are more likely than others to be involved in highly distressed and violent couple relationships, are

cognitively closed and rigid, exhibit the least empathy for people who are distressed, and have the most severe personality disorders and poorest mental health.

(Mikulincer and Shaver 2007: 43)

The anxiety that underpins the fearful avoidant pattern is also thought to increase the likelihood of violence in dating couples (e.g. Henderson *et al.* 2005). There is failure to recognize the needs of the partner. Frustration ensues, which leads to aggression before finally tipping over into violence. Bartholomew and Alison (2006: 112) conclude that severe violence meted out in intimate relationships is most likely to occur when both partners are prone to abusive behaviour.

West and George (1999), taking a developmentalist approach, suggest that violence in the context of intimate relationships is rooted in attachment disorganization and the need to control the unavailable, unresponsive, helpless and hostile partner. These controlling strategies include punitive and manipulative responses. 'Similar to disorganized/controlling children, abusive men have been found to evaluate themselves as vulnerable, unprotected, abandoned, helpless, and often wildly out of control of themselves and relationships' (West and Solomon 1999: 145). These hypersensitive individuals become violent when they interpret their partner's behaviour as implying threat, abandonment, humiliation, shame, or embarrassment.

Adding all the above behavioural components together, we see turbulent couple relationships defined by fear, fight and flight responses. There is an anxious need to be loved and protected. There is the fear of being hurt, abandoned and rejected. And there is the defensive use of withdrawal, aggression and contempt.

Parenthood and caregiving

Parenting children is probably one of the most demanding, stressful things that we do. Babies, as we have seen, can only communicate their needs through behaviour, and their behaviour is not always easy to read or manage. Your crying baby might be hungry, tired, unwell, too hot, too cold, uncomfortable, or frightened. If you've tried everything you can think of to soothe and settle the infant, and by now it's 2 o'clock in the morning and your baby is still crying, you're unlikely to be at your best. Coupled with sleep deprivation, your stress level is going to be high.

But babies grow. They learn to walk and talk. They are also full of energy and potential. They set about the world with unrestrained enthusiasm. They begin to sense their independence but have no idea of what's safe, dangerous or annoying. They have learned to say 'no'. These behaviours, too, can easily exasperate even the most patient of parents.

Most mothers and fathers get through these stages in a 'good enough' fashion, not getting it right all of the time, but relating with their children in ways that still manage to convey love and understanding while being firm and fair. This is *authoritative* parenting. It strikes a balance between respecting the child's growing need for freedom and independence on the one hand, and setting reasonable limits and discipline on the other. It is the parents' ability to mentalize their own and their children's psychological states that gives them a buffer, a cushion to help them cope with the more challenging behaviours that children present. Mentalization reduces relationship stress and helps everyone stay connected and real.

But what if your ability to mentalize is weak or easily breaks down under stress? What if your own relationship history is one of rejection or unresolved trauma? How do you deal with the stresses and strains of being a parent? The answer seems to be 'not very well'. We have seen that good enough caregiving describes parents who remain psychologically interested, developmentally fascinated, emotionally available, and fundamentally committed to their children. In their relationships with such parents, children learn to think, feel, reflect, mentalize, plan, concentrate, and persist. Being on the receiving end of social competence and emotional intelligence, children themselves become socially competent, emotionally intelligent, and easier to manage. However, if your parents feel helpless or hostile, desperate and confused as they attempt to deal with both your needs and the stress your needs induces in them, your developmental prospects are poor.

In effect, what we see in cases of 'abdicated' and out-of-control caregiving is parents trying to deal with their own extreme arousal which has been triggered by their children's emotional needs and behavioural demands. The current stress of parenting acts as an unconscious reminder of past traumas. Their out-of-control feelings mean that parents are unable to see, hear or understand their children's emotional needs and attachment signals. The children therefore feel abandoned. When asked about parenting her 3-year-old son, Nadine replied:

> I don't know. He gets to me. Like, I get so angry and I can't see what I'm doing or thinking no more. So wound up, it hurts, I mean hurts so I get headaches and my stomach aches, so I can't control him. He's three! It don't seem fair.

As we saw in Chapter 12, these highly dysregulating feelings are dealt with defensively. Some parents react with a *fight* response, associated with abuse and rejection. Their parenting is *authoritarian*. They fear other people, including their children and their ever-present needs, gaining the upper hand. Although parents exert firm control, they rarely give children any reasons for their harsh discipline and angry reactions. In more extreme cases, discipline might actually involve deliberately frightening the child. For these parents, other people being in control is an unconscious reminder of childhood helplessness, powerlessness, vulnerability and danger. Parents only survived their childhoods by developing compulsively self-reliant, controlling-punitive, or coercive strategies. Contempt and anger for any display of need and weakness, including those shown by children, are therefore a major characteristic of their survival strategy. Their children's attachment needs generate caregiving that is controlling, critical, sarcastic, punitive, aggressive, anxious, rejecting, distant, and lacking in warmth.

Alternatively, the stress of parenting might lead to feelings of helplessness and the defence of *flight*. This results in parental neglect. Or in cases of extreme trauma in childhood, parents might react with a *freeze* response. In these instances, some parents panic, while others dissociate. Whatever the parental reaction, children feel abandoned at the very moment they need their parents to attend and attune.

In summary, those whose minds remain unresolved with respect to attachment and whose attachment styles are ones of fearful avoidance, these parents offer caregiving that is typically distressed. Not only do such parents fail to provide their children with comfort and safety, they are the cause of their children's feelings of fear and upset. Matters are even worse when there is violent conflict between mothers and fathers. Not only does the tension between parents reduce sensitivity, it increases the likelihood that young children's attachments will be disorganized (Finger *et al.* 2009). This is another example of the growing interest that attachment researchers have in the quality of the relationship *between* parents and how it can affect children's attachment and development. As far as children's attachment organization is concerned, it matters how parents get on.

Physical health

People who have suffered early abuse, neglect and trauma not only have easily aroused minds and dysregulated emotions, their bodies and stress systems are also hypersensitive and ultra-reactive. Secure caregivers help babies regulate their bodies as well as their minds. In the early weeks and months of life, patterns of sleeping, waking, feeding, and eating get established. Sensitive parents learn how to recognize their infant's physical needs and read their body language. Secure children gradually develop regulated bodies as well as regulated minds. They begin to deal with stress and manage their arousal. They settle into the rhythms of the day and their bodies stay within tolerable levels of stress and arousal.

In contrast, maltreated and disorganized children do not enjoy the benefits of alert, attuned parenting. Their bodies are not well regulated. They experience high levels of stress and arousal, both physically and psychologically. Indeed, much of this stress is caused by fear of the parent himself of herself. The parent, therefore, both causes the upset and fails to recognize or manage it.

Physiologically, neglected and maltreated children's stress systems get recalibrated to deal with the much higher levels of arousal experienced in relationship with their unpredictable, insensitive, helpless and even hostile caregivers. But these adjustments come at a long-term physiological cost. When stress operates at levels that are both chronic and high, many of the body's systems suffer long-term compromise. Under stress, particularly relationship stress, disorganized children and anxious, avoidant and unresolved adults display irregular patterns and abnormal levels of cortisol. Stress and abnormal cortisol levels can adversely affect physical health. For example, the immune system functions less well when people experience long-term stress. High levels of cortisol make them more susceptible to illness and disease (Sapolsky 1998). Those under stress are also slower to recover from poor health and injury.

More fundamental still, there is growing evidence from the science of epigenetics that early life neglect and trauma increase the long-term risk of adults developing one or more of a range of serious health conditions including heart disease, diabetes and cancer, even when controlling for such things as an unhealthy lifestyle. For any two given populations sharing exactly the same risky lifestyle, such as smoking, those with early child care histories of emotional neglect and trauma are much more likely than their non-neglected counterparts to suffer serious physical ill-health in adulthood.

These are examples in which the psychosocial environment mediates gene expression during key developmental stages, particularly in the first years of life. Early experiences, particularly stressful ones, determine which genes are turned on and off, and even whether some are expressed at all (Meaney 2010; National Scientific Council on the Developing Child 2010). In this model, environmental conditions in early life structurally alter DNA, providing a biological basis for the influence of parental care on gene expression. This approach is known as the 'developmental origin of health and disease' or the DOHaD hypothesis. This postulates that the environment during critical developmental periods is crucial in determining onset of diseases in later life right through into old age. In the case of neglected children, the genes that are expressed, or not expressed, increase the risk of the body, at least in the long run, reacting adversely or unhealthily to a range of subsequent environmental stressors including poor diet, alcohol, smoking, drugs, violent relationships, and emotional pressure.

Perhaps the least surprising finding is that that those who experience anxiety, stress, anger and depression as a result of poor quality caregiving in early life are more likely to develop risky lifestyle habits. These lifestyle choices can represent inappropriate attempts to deal with the hurt, pain and confusion. These are populations that are more likely to drink excessively, take drugs, and self-harm in their attempts to deal with painful memories and unmanageable arousal. Fearful avoidant individuals, for example, are more likely than other attachment groups to take heroin. They often feel helpless and without coping strategies. In these cases, in the absence of safe haven attachment figures, heroin acts as an emotional substitute (Schindler *et al.* 2009).

The diets of those classified unresolved, helpless, hostile, fearful and avoidant are often poor. They are not good at managing their health. Some people suffer a range of somatization problems in which psychological states can be expressed as bodily symptoms. A few develop hypochondria. Others are accident-prone and careless with their safety. Particularly perverse, many people who have suffered relational trauma during childhood are more likely to experience aggression in their adult relationships. For example, many women who have suffered violent sexual abuse by a close relative as a girl are at increased risk of being re-victimized as adults (Follette *et al.* 1996).

For this attachment group, it is the combination of high stress, epigenetic vulnerability, hazardous environments, and poor quality lifestyles that significantly increases the risk of disease, illness and accidents.

Mental health

Unresolved states of mind and fearful avoidance increase the risk of poor mental health and problem behaviour. We've noted that these attachment categories are associated with poor mentalization, particularly at times of stress. Many psychiatric patients report disturbed caregiving and troubled childhoods saturated with loss, abuse and neglect. For example, Carr *et al.* (2009) found that of their sample who had survived institutional abuse as children, 44 per cent were classified as fearful avoidant. This group showed the highest levels of psychopathology in adulthood. In general, researchers have found a strong link between early attachment disorganization in infancy and psychopathology in adulthood, particularly when associated with a difficult temperament (irritability, easily distressed, and poor at coping with novelty and change) (Carlson 1998; Shaw *et al.* 1997; van IJzendoorn *et al.* 1999). More specifically, there are strong suggestions that disorganized attachments in infancy, particularly when associated with abuse, neglect and trauma, increase the risk of dissociative experiences in adulthood (Carlson 1998; Liotti 1995, 2004).

The hypersensitized nervous systems developed by those who have experienced early abuse and neglect make them particularly reactive to stimulation and arousal, even at mild levels. A touch, a sudden noise, an angry look, or a failure to respond can activate old fears of danger, isolation and hurt. These unresolved feelings can suddenly flood into consciousness as defences are breached. Life is therefore experienced as immediate, threatening and stressful. Feelings can quickly overwhelm both body and mind leading to uncontrollable, fearful arousal. Depending on the nature of the memory and the defence originally employed, individuals might react either aggressively or helplessly (Allen 2001). Feelings of anxiety and depression are particularly common. Anxious individuals appear unable to engage those parts of their brain located above the eyes, known as the orbitofrontal cortex. This part of the brain normally helps people become aware of, and self-regulate negative thoughts and feelings (Coan 2008). Unable to self-reflect, self-harm might be one way to self-soothe. Thoughts of suicide can sometimes seem the only way out, while drink or drugs hold the prospect of numbing the pain.

In a study of hospital psychiatric patients and a control group of general hospital outpatients, Fonagy *et al.* (1996) found that 76 per cent of the psychiatric group's interviews were classified as *unresolved/disorganized/disoriented* compared to only 7 per cent of the control group. Some 65 per cent of the psychiatric sample (compared to only 8 per cent of the control sample) reported childhood sexual abuse or severe physical abuse. Patients with anxiety disorders and borderline personality disorders were significantly more likely to have suffered severe physical abuse, sexual abuse, or both in childhood than other psychiatric classifications. In another study by Ward *et al.* (2006), unresolved women accompanied by a classification of 'dismissing' were the group most likely to be diagnosed with a personality disorder. Crittenden and Newman (2010) found that mothers with Borderline Personality Disorder (BPD) recalled more danger, and unresolved psychological trauma tied to danger than other mothers. Using the Dynamic-Maturation Model (DMM) of attachment and adaptation, they explain that the mothers' perceived need to protect themselves using both extreme Type A and Type C strategies not only produces BPD symptoms but also reduces their availability to care for their infants.

People with personality disorders experience great difficulty managing and maintaining good quality relationships. For example, individuals with BPD present with a complex array of symptoms.

There is a pervasive fear of abandonment by an idealized other. 'Because the unstable sense of self is dependent on validation from the idealized other, the threat of abandonment is experienced as potentially devastating. This instability of internal representations is often associated with emotional volatility' (Dozier *et al.* 2008: 733). Individuals with BPD are therefore particularly sensitive to any hints of rejection. People diagnosed with BPD feel needy, unloved and vulnerable. Their self-esteem is low. Some self-harm. They lack trust in others and hold deep anxieties about other people's availability. Relationships are characterized by intensity, chaos and instability. The fearful, anxious, preoccupied, coercive, even hostile-helpless state of mind with respect to past traumas results in the maximization and powerful exaggeration of attachment needs and distresses (Lyons-Ruth *et al.* 2007). The need for and fear of others (as attachment figures) are extreme. One moment, fervent emotional demands are made on a partner, parent or friend. The next, an aggressive, fearful outburst erupts without warning. All of this emotional lability and relationship chaos points to major impairments in the ability to mentalize. And at the core remains a haunting fear of loneliness and abandonment.

Similar findings have been reported for adults with Antisocial Personality Disorder and those who display severe antisocial behavioural problems, including criminal and violent behaviour. The behaviour of people in this group is characterized by impulsivity, deceitfulness, irritability and lack of remorse. The majority of serious and violent offenders in prison report loveless childhoods in which they suffered rejection, abuse (including sexual abuse), and harsh, sometimes violent parenting. The anger and pain associated with early childhood threats, rejection and emotional abandonment remain an unconscious issue. Any current relationship is capable of provoking strong, unprocessed feelings of raw anger, dismissal and contempt.

These hostile behaviours are consistent with a disorganized-avoidant, compulsively self-reliant, dismissing state of mind. The organized attachment pattern most likely to be associated with this group is therefore one in which attachment issues and emotional vulnerability are dismissed as weak. Attachment figures and other key relationships are typically spoken of in contemptuous, derogatory terms. We have seen that whereas ambivalent/preoccupied attachments are more likely to be associated with internalizing disorders, these avoidant/dismissing attachments are more clearly linked to the risk of externalizing disorders (see Dozier *et al.* 2008). And while preoccupied states of mind witness people becoming absorbed by their own needs and feelings, dismissing states of mind are those associated with individuals who try to dampen down or turn away from their pain and distress.

Eating disorders, particularly bulimia and binge eating (more so than anorexia) and substance abuse are two ways in which disorganized, unresolved individuals try to escape from, or physically regulate their emotional pain. In the case of bulimia and binge eating, high levels of anger and idealization have been observed in patients' mental representations of relationships with their mothers, coupled with unresolved issues of loss and trauma (Barone and Guiducci 2009). Along the same lines, a study by Schindler *et al.* (2005) found that the majority of opiate using, drug-dependent adolescents were fearful avoidant in their attachments. In the absence of any attachment strategy to deal with attachment-related distress, emotional instability and feelings of not being in control, drugs are used as a way of coping.

The behavioural and mental problems shown by the majority of those who have suffered early trauma and maltreatment point to the heavy cost, both social and material, that societies pay when children are raised in environments where stress, disadvantage, poverty, violence and neglect are endemic.

Old age

Not a great deal is known about what happens to those with unresolved and fearful avoidant attachments in old age. By dint of experience and a lifetime of relationships, most of us get a little wiser, grow a little calmer. 'The nature, needs, desires and oddities of the self are better understood and, therefore, more easily controlled … the prefrontal cortex becomes better able to control the amygdala. The ego has finally learned to tame the id' (Foley 2010: 207). It might be that even those whose early attachment experiences were troubled gradually develop some insight and reflective function.

We also saw towards the end of Chapter 9 that in old age there is a measure of withdrawal from the pulls and pushes of close relationships. Internal working models evolve to become more avoidant and therefore more organized. Physically, of course, people's health and fitness deteriorate, taking away some of the energy that previously might have been spent on argument and conflict. And, if the arguments of the epigeneticists who suggest that early life experiences contribute significantly to physical health outcomes in the later years age are to be believed, then there is a strong case to be made that those whose attachments are ones of fearful avoidance, who have unresolved states of mind, and whose lifestyles are unhealthy, are less likely to live to a ripe old age.

Conclusion

Individuals who pursue intimacy and closeness, sometimes aggressively and sometimes seductively, are also likely to find relationships difficult and disturbing. The confused, contrasting feelings that all social interaction generates sees fearfully avoidant people crashing in and out of relationships in ways that those on the receiving end experience as unpredictable, disorientating, and exhausting.

Perhaps more than any other attachment group, those profiled as fearful avoidant, many of whom also have unresolved states of mind with respect to attachment, demonstrate the power and potency of early relationships to affect behaviour and personality across the lifecourse, for good or ill. Turn to any prison population of violent offenders, consider any group of maltreating parents, examine any group of non-psychotic psychiatric patients, and you will discover more often than not childhoods in which there was major disturbance, distortion and deprivation. The policy implications of this insight are profound; the political demands challenging. And yet, unless we re-think many of our most established social and educational, economic and family-rearing practices, we condemn ourselves to repeating the problems of the past, failing to reap that which we never managed to sow.

PART III

Issues and Debates

14

Temperament, Disability and Gender

The interaction of nature and nurture

Introduction

As attachment theory has its deep roots in the evolutionary and animal behavioural sciences, an understanding of nature and biology is fundamental to any study of the discipline. But as nature gets played out in the particular environmental contexts in which it finds itself, the nurturing world of social relationships is also critical. Being adaptive, attachment behaviour gets influenced and shaped by the responses of other people, and in the early years no-one is more important in this shaping process than children's primary caregivers. After all, it is the differences in these caregiving environments that give rise to the various patterns of attachment.

The two-way interactions between genes and their environment represent the modern version of the interplay of nature and nurture. The way genes express themselves depends on the environments in which they operate. These environments vary from the biochemical, the nutritional, the behavioural, the emotional, the interpersonal, and the economic. The interactive effects run both ways in the manner so well conceptualized by Bronfrenbrenner (1979) in his ecological models of human behaviour and development.

Thus, although many adults face ostensibly the same life events, they appraise, interpret and react to them differently. These individual differences are partly down to early relationship experiences, attachment styles and their associated internal working models. In these cases, secure people, possessed of greater resilience, might deal with difficult events and situations more resourcefully. More anxious people on the other hand might tackle the same problems less successfully. However, we also have to acknowledge that genetically-based temperamental differences will similarly affect how individuals deal with life's ups and downs. Naturally optimistic, outward-looking people tend to handle new experiences, including negative experiences, reasonably well. Those who are temperamentally more reserved and anxious might feel less confident and more unsettled by radical changes in circumstance.

Nevertheless, there are debates within psychology about the relative effects of nature and nurture. For example, strong versions of the nature and genes argument suggest that the different attachment patterns and their behaviours might reflect biological differences in such things as individual temperament and gender rather than variations in the quality of parenting. Even weaker versions see nature tempering the ways different attachment patterns are expressed.

We shall consider three 'within-child' and 'within-individual' factors as they might influence the caregiving environment and attachment behaviour: temperament, disability, and the sex of the child or adult. The notion of 'within-child' factors is used to convey the idea that children bring their own qualities and attributes to the conduct of relationships. Strong versions of this argument insist that all we are actually seeing when we observe a child's attachment behaviour is some innate, individual difference such as temperament.

Temperament

Temperament refers to the variety of individual differences and personality traits that seem to characterize each of us as we engage with life. We each naturally differ in terms of our sensitivity, reactivity, fearfulness, soothability, sociability, emotionality, and shyness. All parents with more than one child soon realize that each baby is very different in terms of temperament and behaviour. Some are placid and easy going and cope well with change. Others are more reactive, more demanding and cope less well with breaks in routine.

Temperament is often taken to be a 'biological given', heavily influenced by our genes. Fear and many anxiety-related traits appear to be particularly subject to heritability (Stevenson-Hinde 2005). Bowlby (1969) understood the close links between fear behaviour and attachment behaviour insofar as both share the common evolutionary function of protecting us from harm. 'It must be assumed,' wrote Bowlby (1998a: 219), 'that genetic differences play some part in accounting for variance between individuals with regard to suscepti-bility to fear.' Fear compels us to escape from danger. Attachment propels us to seek protection. There will be natural variations in our fearfulness. In turn, this will have implications for how readily, how often and how intensively our attachment systems will be activated.

This natural variation will also have consequences for caregivers, the sensitivity of their caregiving, and the levels of stress experienced by children under taxing conditions. For example, several studies (reported in Stevenson-Hinde 2005) have found higher levels of stress, determined by measuring levels of the hormone cortisol, in children who are naturally more fearful (that is, behaviourally inhib-ited) *and* insecurely attached (that is, in receipt of insensitive caregiv-ing). Both risk factors – behavioural inhibition and insecure attachment – have to be present for stress to be experienced. Supporting this line of analysis, the Minnesota Longitudinal Studies (Sroufe *et al.* 2005b) found that infants classified as ambivalent aged 12 months were at elevated risk of anxiety disorders in their late teens. Thus, it seems that cortisol levels may 'be related to the maintenance or failure of coping strategies. To the extent that security is associated with good coping strategies, protection is offered, even to inhibited children' (Stevenson-Hinde 2005: 207).

Some critics of attachment theory maintain that each attachment pattern is little more than children displaying their natural tempera-mental make-up. Open, optimistic, sociable children are likely to be seen as securely attached when observed by attachment researchers who are mistaking genetic cause for environmental (caregiving) effect. Similarly, naturally sensitive, inhibited and irritable children might easily be seen as insecure and resistant. Children simply vary in their biological susceptibility to distress and their ability to regu-late it. The quality of the caregiving has little to do with it.

Furthermore, attachment critics argue that while temperamen-tally easy children are easy to parent, temperamentally difficult chil-dren are difficult to parent (for example, Kagan 1994; Thomas *et al.* 1968). And as temperament is largely a product of genes and inherited biology, at most the social environment is merely reacting to each child's innate make-up. By the way they react to the responses of their caregiver, children begin to shape and reinforce caregiving responses every bit as much as the caregiving response is shaping the child's attachment behaviour. Even Bowlby was happy to acknowledge the two-way dynamics of parent–child relationships when he wrote: 'The pattern of interaction that gradually develops between an infant and his mother can be understood only as a resultant of the contributions of each, especially of the way each in turn influences the behaviour of the other' (1997: 204).

Attachment theorists accept that parenting to some extent is a reaction to children's innate temperamental character, but they also see the caregiving environment playing a significant and independent role in children's development. In general, however, most researchers now agree that there is likely to be a complex relationship between temperament and attachment, particularly insecure attachments. For example, temperament is likely to affect how children display their distress but not how they regulate it. Or, to take another example, the mother of a child with a difficult, irritable temperament who also finds herself in an unsupportive, conflictual marriage may find that her parenting begins to lack sensitivity. This will increase the likelihood of her children being insecurely attached.

In short, 'parenting and the parent–child relationship are most likely to be adversely affected when *multiple* vulnerabilities exist … that accumulate and undermine the effectiveness of other sources of influence in promoting parental functioning' (Belsky 2005: 81, emphasis original). And conversely, even if a child has a naturally difficult temperament but is parented by a relatively stress-free, autonomous, attuned mother who enjoys extensive spousal and family support, that child is likely to be securely attached.

There is also evidence that the quality of the parents' environment can mediate the quality of the caregiving and the child's temperament. For example, although irritable infants are more likely to be insecure, this is only true in low-resource families. These families experience a number of stressors over and above looking after a difficult baby. Parents who enjoy good material conditions who also have temperamentally irritable babies seem better able to remain sensitive and available, and so their babies are more likely to be secure (e.g. Susman-Stillman *et al.* 1996). Similarly, a supportive, involved father might help an insecure mother and her temperamentally difficult baby stay attuned and available even under moderately high levels of stress. This increases the chances of the baby developing a secure attachment. More generally, the quality of the relationship *between* parents seems to have some effect on a child's security of attachment independent of each parent's caregiving relationship with that child.

A variation on these themes was suggested by Belsky and Rovine (1987). They felt that 'good enough' parenting on the whole would bring about a secure attachment no matter what the innate temperament of the child, but that less optimal caregiving increased the risk of an insecure attachment. However, they argued, which type of insecure attachment developed would depend on the child's temperament. In sub-optimal caregiving environments, children who were less reactive to stress would be more likely to be avoidant while those who were more fearful and reactive to distress with exaggerated responses would end up ambivalent. Further developments suggest a position in which interactive effects are recognized between temperament and attachment. In this model, both temperament and caregiving can directly affect personality, but also temperament can affect caregiving, and caregiving can affect the way temperamental traits are expressed.

Furthermore, the more extreme the environment in terms of abuse and neglect, the more likely it is that the adverse caregiving will swamp children's temperamental dispositions whatever they happen to be. The relational trauma suffered by severely maltreated children overwhelms them physiologically, neurologically and psychologically. This crushes individual differences and the temperaments that support them including the normally protective ones such as cheerfulness, optimism and openness.

It seems, then, that although children's genes and temperament do play a part in the parent–child relationship, the quality of caregiving appears to have the largest effect on children's attachment organization, at least in the early years (Bakermans-Kranenburg *et al.* 2004; Bokhorst *et al.* 2003; Steele and Steele 2005a). By and large, 'attachment and temperament constitute separate domains of development, and that constructs from one domain do not explain individual differences in the other' (Vaughn *et al.* 2008: 210). The character of the attachment relationship is therefore not simply the caregiver's reaction to the child's innate make-up and temperament. 'In general,' write van IJzendoorn and Bakermans-Kranenburg (2004: 208), 'the maternal impact on the infant–mother attachment relationship has been shown to be much larger than the impact of child characteristics such as temperament.'

Another way to explore whether the quality of caregiving is the major force in determining attachment organization is to see what happens to children's attachments when the quality of the caregiving environment changes. During the first few years after birth, parents are more powerful than their children in shaping the child–parent bond. So, for example, when clinicians help parents improve their caregiving sensitivity, we see an increase in the rates of young children's security, suggesting that it is the quality of caregiving and not temperament that determines the attachment type (Bakermans-Kranenberg *et al.* 2003). In similar vein, Dozier and colleagues found that over time there is a correspondence between the caregiving environment generated by foster carers and the attachment organization developed by the children in their care, remembering that in these cases there is no genetic relationship between carer and child (Dozier *et al.* 2001).

Suomi (2008) reports similar findings in his studies of rhesus monkeys. Particularly interesting observations have been made when the experimenters manipulated which babies were cared for by which mothers. For example, up to 50 per cent of baby monkeys born to nonabusive mothers who were then fostered by unrelated abusive mothers grew up to be abusive with their offspring. In contrast, of the baby monkeys born to abusive mothers but who were actually raised by nonabusive mothers, none went on to abuse their offspring (Maestripieri 2005, cited by Suomi 2008). These studies suggest a powerful role for environmental influences over genetic factors.

However, there is still the possibility that the potency of the environment might diminish with age. With maturation, the influence of the family decreases. As children enter adolescence and age into adulthood, they have more control over their choice of relationships and the environment. This growing freedom provides more opportunities for the individual's interests, inclinations and predispositions – many governed by genes – to express themselves, free of parental constraint. Early life experiences and associated attachment styles continue to underpin basic personality organization, but genes and temperament gradually begin to have a greater influence. Nevertheless, although temperamental traits do appear to have a major sway on adult personality and behaviour, attachment organization continues to have an important but independent effect. But yet again, perhaps the more intriguing possibility is that different qualities of caregiving, and the attachments they imply, lead to differences in the way genes express themselves, resulting in different personality types (Meaney 2004, cited in Mikulincer and Shaver 2007: 465). Different personality types both seek out different social environments, and react differently to ostensibly similar social stimuli.

Disability

Although caregiver factors are felt to be more important in determining children's attachment organization, child factors that affect levels of parental stress (which in turn affects the carer's sensitivity and emotional availability) are also thought to play a part. There is evidence that levels of parental stress increase when children with a disability are cared for. Children with speech, language and communication problems along with children who have neuro-developmental disorders might pose particular difficulties for parents and their ability to be sensitive, attuned and appropriately responsive. Children with such impairments might be more difficult to 'read' even for the most sensitive caregivers. Such difficulties are likely to interfere with parents' ability to understand, interpret, and communicate (Johnston *et al.* 2003). It has also been shown that caring for disabled children impacts more generally on the lives of both parents and their families. There are extra economic costs, lack of social support, and increased demands in caring duties (Sloper *et al.* 2003).

It is also the case that children who feel that their needs are unrecognized, ignored or misunderstood by their carers are more likely to become distressed. This intensifies further children's displays of attachment behaviour, adding to the levels of distress and frustration experienced by caregivers. Stress associated with caregiving also activates parents' attachment-based defences. This is likely to be especially the case when parents still have unresolved issues of distress and loss about their child and his or her disability. It is, of course, ironic that children in need of particularly sensitive caregiving might activate unresolved states of mind in their parents, challenging their ability to provide attuned and responsive nurturing. For example, Moran *et al.* (1992) found that for a group of developmentally delayed children, mean levels of maternal sensitivity and security of attachment were relatively low. On the other hand, parents who have resolved their grief reactions and who hold more realistic mental representations of their disabled children are more likely to parent sensitively and more likely to have securely attached children.

Thus, if children with a disability increase the risk of reduced parental sensitivity, protection, attunement and availability, we might expect more disabled children to be classified as insecure compared to general populations. It is only when mothers are able to attribute the stresses of parenting to the inherently demanding but necessary tasks associated with caring for a child with a disability, and separating these out from the child herself, that levels of parental sensitivity and therefore child security rise (Moran *et al.* 1992).

There is a modest body of research that supports the broad thesis that children with a wide variety of congenital medical conditions and disabilities are slightly more likely to be classified insecure in their attachments (Andrew 1989; Huebner and Thomas 1995; Moran *et al.* 1992). Van IJzendoorn *et al.* (1992) conducted a meta-analysis of 13 samples from eight studies of children with a range of disabilities including Down's syndrome, autism, cystic fibrosis, and congenital heart disease. They found that rates of secure attachments were generally lower (less than 50 per cent) compared to children without disabilities (typically around 65 per cent). There was also a slight over-representation of children with disabilities classified as disorganized.

However, when examined in more detail, it was found that disabled children with mothers who had problems (e.g. depression or disturbed caregiving) were the most likely to be classified as insecure, particularly disorganized insecure. When mothers did not have problems, the distribution of attachments, though still tilted a little towards insecure, were much closer to general populations. The authors conclude that 'the mother plays a more important role than the child in shaping the quality of relationships' while allowing for the possibility that more vulnerable parents might find meeting the attachment needs of children with a disability particularly stressful (van IJzendoorn *et al.* 1992: 855).

Barnett *et al.* (1999) reviewed a further seven studies (including children with Down's syndrome, autism, cleft palate, cerebral palsy and congenital heart disease). They found that with the exception of children with cleft lip and palate, those with congenital problems consistently averaged less than 50 per cent secure attachments compared to a rate of 65 per cent found in typically developing children. It was also noted in this analysis that for children with neurological problems – including Down's syndrome, cystic fibrosis, autism – the proportions classified as disorganized ranged between 20 and 33 per cent compared to 15 per cent in normative populations.

However, it has also been observed that the increased severity of a child's disability does not actually predict increased risk of insecurity; indeed, there are some indications that in the case of more severely disabled children, rates of security actually increase. One explanation of this suggests that when a child's disability is unquestionably present and is likely to affect many aspects of their functioning, including the child's ability to communicate their needs, parental recognition, understanding and acceptance increase, and expectations are therefore more realistic.

In Macrae's (2003) study of children totally blind from birth who were cared for by sighted parents, 80 per cent were classified as avoidant compared to only 22 per cent of normative populations. Similarly, deaf children of hearing parents were also more likely to be insecure, particularly in those cases where parents held a negative attitude toward deafness, and when expressions of affection between parent and child were negative (Hadadian 1995). Underpinning the raised rates of insecure attachments, Meadow-Orlans and Steinberg (1993) found that in the case of deaf children of hearing parents, there was some evidence that interactions were less sensitive, warm and flexible. In contrast, deaf children of deaf parents have been found to display normal distributions of attachment patterns (Meadow *et al.* 1984), again suggesting that when communication is clear and reciprocal between parent and child, sensitivity and security increase.

Not surprisingly therefore, when a parent shares the same physical disability or impairment as the child, sensitivity and communication tend to be good, and the rates of secure attachments normal. Similarly, parents who do not share their child's disability but who are good at seeing the world from their child's point of view, also have securely attached children. The lesson here is that the sooner parents of disabled children can be helped and taught to understand and empathize with their child's impairments, the more likely it is that the child will develop a secure attachment. Parents who can see the world from their child's point of view, particularly in terms of how the impairment might affect the child's ability to communicate, show greater sensitivity and attunement.

In general, although higher than normal numbers of disabled children classified as insecure are observed, significant numbers appear securely attached (Howe 2006). Disability on its own, as a within-child factor, is therefore unlikely to be the only risk factor. The characteristics of caregivers, including how they are affected by raised levels of attachment need in others, also play a major role in the quality of parent–child interactions. The dynamics that affect attachment organization are the result of a transaction between both parental and child characteristics. It is only when both parents and children bring vulnerabilities to the transaction that we might expect to see higher rates of insecurity.

Gender

Most studies have found that in the case of securely attached people, there are as many men as women (e.g. Bartholomew and Horowitz 1991; Levy *et al.* 1998). However, when it comes to considering the distribution of insecure attachments, gender might be thought to play a part. On the face of it, it might seem that the stereotypical man is emotionally wooden and less relationally competent, suggesting that men are more likely to be avoidant. Women, on the other hand, might be thought more emotionally open and relationship oriented, making them, for example, more sensitive to men's attachment avoidance and relative lack of emotionality. Thus, it might be felt that women's experience of close relationships is likely to be influenced by their own attachment insecurities and anxieties about their partner's interest and commitment.

However, Mikulincer and Shaver (2007: 311) report that there is no consistent gender difference along these stereotypically expected lines. 'In fact,' they continue, 'the vast majority of studies have yielded significant associations between attachment insecurities and relationship dissatisfaction in both women and men' (ibid.: 311). It is attachment insecurity and anxiety in one or other partner that predict relationship dissatisfaction and not the sex of the partner. Even in matters of physical health, although researchers have found associations between particular attachment styles and well-being, they have observed that men and women who share a particular attachment orientation tend to have similar susceptibilities (or not) to illness and poor health (Sadava *et al.* 2009).

To clinch this gender-neutral picture, Bakermans-Kranenburg and van IJzendoorn (2009) analysed 10,500 Adult Attachment Interviews from over 200 studies. They found no gender differences in the distribution of the major attachment classifications.

Conclusion

The evidence appears to support the argument that the quality and character of close relationships, particularly caregiving relationships in the early years, determine attachment organization. There is even evidence that the mother's attachment organization can predict her child's attachment in the early years. For example, a number of prospective studies have found that in up to 70 per cent of cases, a mother's attachment organization measured before her baby is born predicts a similar attachment in the baby when he or she is 12 months old (for example, Fonagy *et al.* 1991). The more sensitive, responsive and attuned the caregiving, the more likely it will be that the child will show secure attachment behaviour, independent of the attributes of the child. In the case of less sensitive caregiving, children have a higher chance of developing insecure attachments, but the type of insecure attachment might not necessarily be the same one as that of the attachment figure. In their attempts to provoke care and protection from an insensitive parent, some children might adopt strategies that are either more extreme than those being used by their parents, or in some case even the opposite (Crittenden 2000b). A child, for example, in an attempt to stay close and be valued by his mother, might compulsively idealize her (Type A strategy), although she behaves in a coercively helpless fashion (Type C strategy) with both her aggressive partner and the boy himself.

There is also recognition that 'within-child' factors can influence the quality of caregiving such that the caregiving might be more or less sensitive. Children with difficult temperaments or children whose disabilities adversely affect their ability to communicate needs can increase parental stress and mis-attunement. Nevertheless, a responsive, mind-minded caregiver with high reflective function who is able to connect with a child's need for safety, comfort and regulation will over-ride any vulnerability that the child brings to the relationship, allowing the child to develop a secure attachment. Conversely, although temperamentally easy children make caregiving less stressful, even these children experience increasing anxiety and insecurity the more harsh, hostile or helpless the parenting becomes.

Gender, too, has been examined to see whether it is the sex of individuals rather than their relationship history that is acting as the major influence on personality and attachment behaviour. But again, as with temperament and disability, close relationships appear to have a powerful and independent effect on personality development and attachment behaviour. Certainly genes and nature interact with the social environment in ways both interesting and complex, but the impact of close attachment relationships on children's neurological, emotional and interpersonal development appears deep and long-lasting.

15

Attachment Across the Lifecourse

Continuity and discontinuity, stability and change

Introduction

Many studies have found modest but significant levels of attachment continuity across the lifespan, from infancy to adulthood (Shaver and Mikulincer 2004: 41; Grossmann *et al.* 2005). This indicates that attachment organization remains moderately stable for most children and young adults (Ammaniti *et al.* 2000). Whatever your attachment happens to be as a young child, the chances are reasonably strong that you will have that same attachment status twenty or more years later.

However, between the ages of 1 and 4, attachments are prone to be a little more inconsistent between measures, suggesting that young children are particularly sensitive to the subtle relationship changes that ripple through their lives. Baby siblings appear, mum takes a part-time job, dad has a new partner, a parent suffers depression, nursery school begins. If, as a result of major changes in their lives, parents change their caregiving, so will the young child's attachment organization change.

After the age of 4, continuity of attachments becomes more robust such that attachment stability and prediction do not weaken much throughout the rest of childhood and beyond into adulthood (Fraley and Brumbaugh 2004: 115). However, Ammaniti *et al.* (2000) did find a slight increase in dismissiveness for both boys and girls in early adolescence which they thought was related to their increasing need to become independent of their parents. Along with early childhood, adolescence is perhaps the least stable time in terms of attachment continuity (van IJzendoorn and Bakermans-Kranenburg 2010).

The only other refinements to this picture of attachment continuity are the subtle, but interesting long-term changes seen when attachments are examined in old age. In the later life years, the number of people classified as secure or dismissing increases, while the number classified as preoccupied or fearful avoidant marginally decreases (for example, Zhang and Labouvie-Vief 2004).

Overall, the more stable and consistent your relationship environment, the more likely it will be that your attachment style will continue unchanged. This can be seen in middle-class samples where continuity in attachments is generally higher than is found in lower-class and high-risk samples where parents are more likely to experience hardship and stress, and children are more likely to experience relationship instability (Grossmann *et al.* 2005,; Weinfield *et al.* 2004) (also see Chapter 4). Thus, although there is continuity of secure attachments when family life is stable and parents themselves have a secure attachment, this is less likely to be the case in situations of poverty, disadvantage and parental maltreatment where children show less continuity in their attachment organization over time (Crittenden *et al.* 2007).

We have already met and acknowledged the differences between two of attachment's major models: the ABC+D model originating in Main's work (Main and Hesse 1990), and the Dynamic-Maturational Model developed by Crittenden (2008). The two models offer different views on the likelihood of an attachment pattern, particularly an insecure one being stable and continuous from infancy to adulthood.

- The ABC+D model emphasizes the 'transmission' of attachment type from mother to infant, and continuity of attachment across the lifecourse (Main 2000).
- The DMM hypothesizes a much greater likelihood of 'reversal' of attachment type between mother and child in insecure cases along with an expected lack of continuity of attachment across the lifecourse.

Again we find ourselves having to contemplate two diverging theories of attachment (Spieker and Crittenden 2009; see also Chapter 12). Thus, whereas both the ABC+D model and DMM generally expect a *matching* (continuity) between securely attached mothers and securely attached infants, the two models hypothesize different intergenerational patterns in the case of anxious and insecure mothers. As was the case with secure patterns, the ABC+D model also expects matching and continuity in the insecure patterns (the infants of dismissing mothers will be avoidant; the infants of preoccupied mothers will be ambivalent).

In contrast, the DMM predicts more *inversion* or *meshing* in which some infants will develop the *opposite* or *complementary* attachment pattern to that of their mother. For example, there is an expectation in the DMM that many babies of under-responsive, distant, avoidant Type A mothers will organize emotionally intense, demanding and exaggerated ambivalent Type C attachment strategies to increase the probability of a maternal response. Or, in the case of helpless, angry, preoccupied Type C mothers, 'infants may benefit by employing a strategy of caring for (A3) or complying with (A4) their mothers' (Shah *et al.* 2010: 341). Furthermore, the DMM also predicts *change* and *discontinuity* of attachment patterns over time as caregiving and relationship environments change and children mature (Crittenden *et al.* 2007; Shah *et al.* 2010). A small number of studies appear to give some support to the DMM's expectations of inverted, meshed and reversed attachment patterns in which Type C infants have Type A mothers, and Type A infants have Type C mothers (Hautamäki *et al.* 2010; Shah *et al.* 2010).

The two models – ABC+D and the DMM – offer two contrasting explanations and make different predictions, particularly in the case of insecure attachments and their likely stability, continuity and discontinuity across the lifecourse. These differences can be, indeed, are confusing to many people, even those who have a decent grasp of attachment theory, but feel unable to come down on one side or the other. The debate between the two models and their protagonists, and the slow build-up of research evidence will no doubt continue. Meanwhile, we have to conclude that the debate is healthy, albeit bracing, and that it is likely to spur researchers and theorists to ever-sharper thinking and more comprehensive modelling.

Bowlby (1988) believed that attachment patterns and internal working models, although inclined to be self-fulfilling and therefore likely to be relatively stable across the lifecourse, can alter if close relationships and personal circumstances undergo radical change. Continuity and change, therefore, tell us something about our ability to seek out and create social environments that confirm our internal working models, and also our susceptibility to change when we find ourselves in relationships of a radically different quality. A hint of this can be seen in adolescence when young people break away from their parents and explore a variety of new peer relationships. Changes in adolescent representations of attachment can often be put down to shifts in their close relationships (Carlivati and Collins 2007: 94).

It is also understood that although attachment experiences influence the way children and adults approach, relate and interact with subsequent experiences, we also need to acknowledge that early attachment organizations do not directly determine later personality differences. These differences emerge at the end of a long line of developmental *transactions* between individuals and the sum of their experiences to date, and their interaction with current experiences (a new friend, a romantic partner, the death of a parent). Infant–caregiver attachments do not relate inexorably to outcomes, only probabilistically. Sroufe continues this line of thought saying that:

> Within a systemic, organismic view of development, attachment is important precisely because of its place in the initiation of these complex processes. It is an organizing core in development that is always integrated with later experiences and is never lost ... Attachment experiences remain, even in this complex view, vital in the formation of the person.
>
> (2005: 365)

Childhood

As noted above, change in attachment organization is most likely in early childhood, particularly when there are major shifts in the quality of caregiving. For example, Woodward and colleagues (2000) found that parents who separated when their children were young left them at raised risk of attachment insecurity. On the other hand, some older children approaching early adolescence when their parents chose to go their separate ways were at less risk of developing insecure attachments. It appears that the tensions and conflict that exist between separating parents has greater impact on younger than older children.

Bowlby (1997: 348) pointed out that patterns of attachment can, and will change as the quality and character of the parent–child or partner–partner relationship change. Stressful life events increase the likelihood of a caregiver losing sensitivity. As a result, the child feels less recognized and understood, and therefore feels more insecure (Waters *et al.* 2000). A mother falls ill or has an accident. Her partner is unfaithful or becomes violent. Parents divorce. A father suffers a psychiatric illness. A child is abused by a step-father. Under these changed conditions, a previously secure child might become more demanding and a mother more protective. Or a parent struggles with severe depression making him less responsive and the child, initially at least, more clingy.

Egeland and Farber (1984) found that mothers who reported an increase in stressful life events had babies whose attachment organizations shifted from secure to ambivalent over a six-month period. In many of these cases, mothers mentioned that their domestic arrangements had changed from being single to living with a romantic partner. Some mentioned losing interest in their babies as their emotions became more caught up with their new lover.

It is also the case that babies can change from insecure to secure, for example, if their parents become less stressed. There might be an improvement in domestic conditions. Or a previously isolated and fraught young mother decides to move nearer to her own parents and extended family, suddenly enjoying a significant increase in social support and reduction in stress. Interestingly, and perhaps counterintuitively, Ammaniti *et al.* (2005) found that the birth of younger siblings could help children move from insecure to secure. They suggest that a sibling's birth could alter the quality and sensitivity of relationships among family members as parental experience and understanding grow.

So, in general, it seems that changes in the caregiver's environment can either increase or decrease their sensitivity and attunement. Stress can reduce caregiver availability and sensitivity, making it more likely that the baby feels insecure. And when the positives begin to stack up (secure caregiver, good social support, absence of financial worries), parental sensitivity increases and with it the likelihood of a more securely attached child.

Illustrating shifts in relationships, life stressors and attachment organization, Sroufe *et al.* (2005a: 63–4) describe the case of Tony:

As a little boy, Tony enjoyed secure attachments throughout his early years. At school his teachers saw him as socially and academically competent. But then life took a turn for the worse. His parents divorced. There was much tension and conflict. His mother began to lean on him for support. Possibly in reaction to these demands, Tony, aged 13, 'began pushing away from his mother'. Unfortunately, it was at this time his mother died in a car accident, 'which would seem almost certainly to have induced tremendous guilt in Tony' and 'if this were not bad enough, Tony's father then decided to leave the state with the two other children, so that Tony quickly lost his mother, his father and his siblings'. Although an aunt and uncle took him under their wing, they were elderly and he lacked supervision. Throughout his adolescence and late teen-years, Tony went through some very troubled times, at school, with his peers, and with the law. When the researchers saw him age 15, the 'light inside him seemed to have gone out. He was visibly depressed and isolated. Clearly, his history of secure attachment was not enough to protect him from the conse-quences of his middle-childhood and early adolescent trauma.' At 19, Tony was coded by the research team as 'dismissing'. Then jumping ahead to when Tony was 26 years old, the study group found him married with a baby daughter. Although he was rated on the secure/dismissing boundary, the researchers observed that he was an 'extraordinarily supportive father' who had a very posi-tive relationship with his wife.

In telling Tony's story, Sroufe *et al.* (2005a) speculate that his early security, though not sufficiently robust to help him cope with a cata-strophic adolescence, nevertheless possibly did give him enough of a strong foundation and the residual resources to take advantage of the opportunity of a supportive relationship with his wife, enabling him to shift once more towards a more secure attachment.

As well as being attached to their maltreating parent, some abused children might develop additional attachment relationships with trusted, caring, mentalizing adults who understand their plight, people who provide safe havens from which children might 'mentally explore' their painful, abusive experiences. These additional attach-ment figures are adults who can help troubled children think about how rejection has hurt them or abuse has made them frightened, angry and sad. A caring aunt, a sensitive teacher, or a responsive foster carer might allow a child time and space to make sense of, and understand why and how other people can affect us, for good or ill. These opportunities to think and reflect in a safe space give abused and neglected children the chance to grow into adults who recognize that they are vulnerable, but who understand how their vulnerability affects them under stress, even in the present. In other words, they have been helped to develop the capacity to 'mentalize'. Their early life experiences of loss and trauma become resolved. In relationship with a safe other, they can begin to re-appraise and make sense of their early relational pains, hurts and traumas.

Some people, therefore, in spite of the fear and hurt, are able to re-structure their painful experience so that it leaves them stronger and more insightful about the vagaries of human nature. Your hurt, fear or pain might not have gone away, but at least you know you have these fault lines in your psychological make-up, and you recognize what kind of things can activate them. People who have survived early adversity and developed these reflective capacities have been described as 'earned secure' (Main *et al.* 1985; Pearson *et al.* 1994). This helps explain why many parents who have suffered early abuse and neglect do not go on to abuse or neglect their children. They are said to have a resolved state of mind with respect to attachment and their painful childhood memories and experiences. They are able to acknowledge, understand and recognize how these early traumas have affected, and might continue to affect them. They have developed reflective functioning and the capacity to mentalize, and it is these skills and capacities that predict sensitive caregiving and securely attached children (see Koren-Karie *et al.* 2008).

Adoption and foster care

Some of the most revealing, so-called 'natural experiments' in studying stability and change in patterns of attachment are to be found in adoption and foster care research. Children are adopted and fostered for a variety of reasons, although in most modern cases it is because child care authorities have decided that a parent could not, or should not look after their child. The child is removed and, with the authority of the courts and the law, placed either in foster care or for adoption.

Historically, poverty and social stigma often meant that young, unmarried women reluctantly gave up their newborn babies for adoption. In these cases, the adopted child would have a relationship with the adoptive parents more or less from birth and in this respect their attachment prospects would be no different to children born of biological parents. However, with reductions in poverty and social stigma, at least in the developed countries, today there are relatively few baby adoptions. What has markedly increased is the number of older children being fostered and placed for adoption. Older placed children, of course, come with a history of relationships and established patterns of attachment. The majority of these children have pre-placement histories of neglect, abuse and rejection, hence their removal. As might be expected, their attachments at the time of removal tend to be insecure, and often disorganized-controlling. So what happens when they are placed with new carers? Do their attachments change? Do they show developmental recovery and catch-up?

In general, the answer to these questions is 'yes', but with qualifications. It does appear to be the case that when the quality of the caregiving environment changes, so does the child's attachment organization. The plan, of course, is to remove children from substandard caregiving environments to sensitive, responsive ones offered by foster carers and adopters. And indeed, by and large, research tells us that many previously insecure children gradually achieve secure attachments in relationship with nurturing new carers.

However, two factors influence both whether an existing attachment will change in the context of a new caregiving relationship, and in what direction. The first factor concerns what the child brings to the new family in terms of personality, attachment history, psychosocial impairment, defensive behaviour, and sub-optimal neurological development. This factor might affect both the new caregiver's ability to respond sensitively to the child, and the child's ability to engage with, and benefit from sensitive caregiving. The second factor concerns what the new carers bring to the relationship in terms of their personality and attachment organization. The interaction of these factors is likely to be complex and dynamic, and played out over many years.

As a rough rule of thumb: (1) the earlier the age at which young children suffer abuse, neglect or trauma; (2) the more severe the maltreatment; and (3) the more prolonged is this poor quality, pre-placement care, the less likely it is that children will achieve full psychosocial developmental catch-up in the new placement, and the more likely it is that children will have attachment difficulties, including insecure attachments, disorganized attachments, and attachment disorders. For example, children raised in very under-resourced institutional care, who suffered severe deprivation from early babyhood until the age of 4, and who were then adopted have been shown to be at elevated risk of a range of long-term psychosocial problems and attachment difficulties (Dozier and Rutter 2008; O'Connor *et al.* 2003; Rutter *et al.* 2007; Zeanah *et al.* 2005).

In contrast, institutionalized children who enjoyed some security of attachment as babies before being placed in deprived residential care, and children removed from poor quality institutional care while they were still babies tend to fare a lot better in their adoptive placements, often developing secure attachments and showing long-term, good developmental recovery. It appears that these children either developed an early secure core before they entered the institution offering them some short-term protection, or they were not exposed to the toxicity of institutional care sufficiently long for their attachment organization to be undermined. In both of these cases, children seemed to have retained a degree of coherence, security and integration providing them with some resilience to survive the institutional risk. This core of security and the retention of an internal working model in which the self and others continued to be represented positively meant that these particular children were able to respond well when placed with their new carers.

In a rather different set of studies by Stovall and Dozier (2000, see also Dozier *et al.* 2001), we see examples of children bringing to their new placements the insecure attachment strategies that had helped them cope with and, to an extent, survive parental abuse and neglect. There is a natural propensity for new carers to respond in a complementary fashion to children's behavioural signals. This natural tendency risks even secure adopters and foster carers being drawn into their newly placed child's expected relationship schemas. This is how Dozier and her colleagues explain matters.

The emerging consensus is that the developmental outcomes achieved by older placed fostered and adopted children are best understood in terms of a transactional model. A child's 'movement along a particular developmental pathway is determined by the transactions that occur between the child and his or her environment. In a transactional model, the child and the environment co-determine a child's developmental progress' (Stovall and Dozier 1998: 66). Children bring to their adoptions their own unique histories, and the mental states and their associated behavioural and relationship styles formed in their earlier, adverse caregiving environments. Many of these mental states and adaptive strategies will have been forged in situations of abuse, neglect and rejection. Stovall and Dozier believe that although these strategies will have helped children survive in very difficult environments, they can mean that children are ill-equipped to take advantage of good quality, loving and responsive substitute care. In particular, many children seem unable to elicit or respond to sensitive care and protective parenting. Not only are children affected by their caregiving, but also caregiving is affected by children, their needs and behaviour.

This model helps explain the different behavioural and developmental pathways taken by older placed adopted and fostered children. Each child's pathway depends on the type of abuse, neglect and rejection suffered and the particular reactions of the adoptive parents to the behavioural consequences of that abuse, neglect or rejection. For example, an abused and rejected child might have developed an avoidant attachment and a compulsively self-reliant strategy. In the new placement, such a child might behave in an emotionally self-sufficient manner believing that caregivers are not available at times of need and distress. Faced with such a child, an adoptive mother might feel neither needed nor wanted. She might therefore feel disheartened, back off, deactivate her caregiving, or ignore the child. In contrast, a parent who manages not to be drawn into the child's relationship logic, albeit one that has helped him survive past abuse, and instead behaves in a consistent and persistently responsive, caring and protective manner, such caregiving might allow the child to feel safe and less anxious whenever care and protection are needed. This results in a previously insecure child developing a secure attachment.

Steele *et al.* (2003) studied children aged 4–8 who had been maltreated by their birth families and who had been placed with adopters. Prior to placement, the majority of the children were classified as insecurely attached, including many insecure disorganized attachments. Two years after placement, most of the children were showing steady progress. Many had developed more positive representations of their adoptive parents, although alongside these more positive representations, less positive representations continued to exist. Indicators of disorganized attachments were still present and would emerge under conditions of stress. However, in general, children placed with adopters who had resolved, autonomous states of mind with respect to attachment and who were sensitive and attuned, these children were most likely to be developing secure attachments. Warm, responsive, consistent, reliable, predictable and persistent adopters helped children disconfirm their insecure, negative working models of themselves and others. Being loved unconditionally they could learn to love themselves, and by being loved they could feel lovable and loving. In contrast, previously maltreated children placed with adopters who themselves had unresolved attachment issues (of loss, of trauma) were least likely to develop a secure attachment with many still showing high rates of disorganization.

The overall picture suggests that foster carers and adopters who enjoy high levels of reflective function and mentalization, and who provide sensitive, attuned care can help children with insecure attachments, including disorganized attachments gradually become securely organized. However, if children have suffered profound trauma and severe neglect for long periods of time during their early years, recovery, even when children are parented by the most sensitive carers, though present, is likely to be less complete and their attachments more likely to remain insecure, or in the most extreme cases, disordered. Children with insecure attachments who are parented by foster carers or adopters with insecure and unresolved states of mind with respect to attachment will in all likelihood remain insecurely attached.

In summary, adoption and foster care illustrate that children's attachments can and do change, particularly in the direction of insecure to secure. So, although young children are biologically predisposed to attach to any new, full-time carer given time, the type of attachment, as ever, depends on the quality of care. It is testimony to the skills of foster care and adoption agencies that they are able to identify and prepare so many new parents in whose care previously insecure children are able to develop attachments that are judged robust and secure.

Adulthood

Changes in attachment can and do occur in adulthood, but on the whole there is more stability and continuity in attachment organization in this period of our lives We are more likely to be predictable and set in our ways. Generally speaking, if our key relationships and day-to-day environments remain steady and fairly routine, then our dispositional representations and attachment styles are less likely to shift. Indeed, it is the case that with age, our internal working models both expect people to react as they do *and* 'cause' people to behave and react as they do. Avoidant individuals, for example, might be more inclined to be wary of close relationships and be less prepared to engage with peers, even if those peers represent a potentially positive and responsive experience. Avoidant individuals, therefore, are at risk of denying themselves social experiences that might 'disconfirm' their insecure internal working model. So, although change is always possible, it does get harder to the extent that internal working models create their own experience and bring about the social environments they expect. This, in part, explains the increasing likelihood that individuals' attachment organizations remain relatively unchanged the older they become.

Changes, of course, can and do occur from secure to insecure, and insecure to secure in adulthood. In general, major life transitions, including changes in close relationships, can force people to re-evaluate and re-organize their internal working models. A man's wife leaves him. A mother feels under increasing stress after the birth of her fourth child. A partner turns to drink and suffers unemployment. Rejection and criticism can eat away at our confidence and self-belief. Under each and every one of these changed circumstances, an attachment might shift from secure to insecure.

In contrast, love and acceptance boost self-esteem and increase security. A couple's finances improve, allowing them to get out of debt, buy a better house, and enjoy a less stressed relationship. A good experience of psychotherapy can help someone feel more secure and in control. Indeed, the whole purpose of psychotherapy is to help people change their assumptions about themselves, others and relationships. The aim of psychotherapy is to help people alter their attachment organizations from insecure to secure, or at least from very insecure to less insecure. Psychotherapists help clients disconfirm their insecure working models. In effect, therapists who are able to mentalize and who are acting as secure transitional attachment figures are also helping their clients to mentalize, reflect and make sense. Childhood abuse and neglect, therefore, do not necessarily condemn someone to lifelong insecurity, disorganization and unresolved states of mind. Reflective relationships offer the prospect of someone 'earning' a secure state of mind.

In discussing adults who had been classified as 'earned secure', Steele and Steele

> noticed that a defining feature of their [AAI] narratives was the *way* they relied on language as a tool for giving meaning to experience, including the attribution of mental states (beliefs and desires) to attachment figures whose behaviour they did not fully understand, and were threatened by, as children, but have come to understand (if not forgive) as adults.
>
> (2005b: 157, emphasis original)

Those classified as 'earned secure' appeared to have developed 'reflective functioning', that is:

> [The] capacity to monitor thought processes and motivations *in others* as well as the self. Reflective functioning, we showed, was especially important for parents to achieve if there was significant adversity in their past. Without it, there appeared to be little or no chance of having a securely attached infant; by contrast, where reflective functioning was present, the toxic cross-generational effect of emotional conflicts, past trauma, or loss was almost completely eliminated.
>
> (Steele and Steele 2005b: 157, emphasis original;
> see also Fonagy *et al.* 1994)

Conclusion

Attachments form in the context of close relationships. The sensitivity and responsiveness of the significant other will determine whether the attachment is secure or insecure. Young children are particularly sensitive to the quality and character of attachment figures and their caregiving. Changes in nurturing can lead to changes in attachment. However, once children's internal working models have developed and stabilized, attachments tend to acquire a degree of continuity. This is because to some extent internal working models become self-fulfilling. The assumptions and expectations of self, others and relationships built into internal working models mean that they have the power to create the kind of relationship environments that helped create the internal working model in the first place. The stability of attachments, whether secure or insecure, therefore tends to increase with age.

We need to remember that in practice about 60 per cent of any normal population will be secure, and so secure people are more likely to find themselves in close relationship with other secure people. Over time, the chances are that both secure partners' capacity to mentalize and develop reflective functioning will increase as each allows and encourages the other to explore the self and their relationship. The experience will consolidate their secure, autonomous states of mind. Similarly, when both partners are insecurely attached, they are also unlikely to change as they defensively lock themselves into a fixed set of expectations and outlooks in the context of their mutually mis-attuned relationship.

But as we have emphasized, change is always possible. The more significant the relationship with a key other – whether parent, partner, lover, therapist – or the more radical the shift in life circumstances, the more likely it is that an individual's attachment organization will change. Children placed with warm, loving, insightful foster carers gradually develop secure attachments. Insecure people with secure partners might begin to feel loved and valued, and with those feelings their attachment grows more secure, their self more confident. Understanding these processes could have major implications for a whole range of social policies and practices, counselling and psychotherapeutic interventions, teaching and educational experiences, and personal and philosophical approaches to life. If positive change is to happen, it is most likely to take place in the context of a warm, responsive relationship.

Epilogue

Ursula Bowlby, John Bowlby's wife, said that 'John was an explorer, venturing into uncharted territory' with his friend and ally, Mary Ainsworth, providing the signposts (Ursula Bowlby 1999). Robert Hinde, also a long-time friend, collaborator and colleague of Bowlby, observed that 'the essence of John Bowlby's approach was broad-minded eclecticism' (Hinde 2005: 2). This gets to the heart of Bowlby's genius and reminds us that attachment theory's success has been its ability and willingness to remain open to new ideas from across the sciences.

We need to remember that attachment theory was fashioned out of Bowlby's interest in evolutionary theory, ethnology, the animal behav-ioural sciences, developmental and cognitive psychology, and control and systems theory. That is an exotic as well as eclectic mix, but the links he made between each discipline were logical and sound. Together, and when orchestrated by an original mind, they help tell a wonderful story of how young, helpless, unformed infants gradually grow into independent, self-reflective, self-regulating, socially compe-tent, complex psychological beings. I think that if Bowlby were alive today, he would be thrilled by developments in the neurosciences, genetics, epigenetics, and the cognitive sciences. In responding to these developments, attachment theory continues to evolve. And while becoming more refined, it is also playing a key role in the search for an integrated science of human behaviour and development.

Bowlby recognized and continued to marvel at the wonderful complexity of the human mind. Human personality, he said:

> is perhaps the most complex of all complex systems here on earth. To describe the principal components of its construction, to understand and predict the ways in which it works and, above all, to map the multitude of intricate pathways along which any one person may develop, these are all tasks for the future.
>
> (Bowlby 1998a: 419)

He understood that we are still at the beginning of the great quest to understand our psychological make-up and being. This short book has tried to remain true to Bowlby's spirit in its attempts to capture something of the excitement and innovation still being shown by the discipline's leading thinkers. Like them, whether we are just observers of human behaviour or people-minded practitioners, we must resist becoming narrow in our ways. We must fight being blinkered by our theoretical prejudices. We, too, must remain curious, open-minded and retain our sense of wonder.

Further Reading

For those who wish to learn more about attachment theory and the debates that enliven both theory and research, there are a now number of excellent reviews and major texts available. It is impossible to cite them all, but here are some suggestions that capture much of the excitement and creativity that is driving current thinking. The *Handbook of Attachment* edited by Jude Cassidy and Phillip Shaver (New York: Guilford Press, 2008) is the obvious place to begin more advanced study. 'Handbook' might be slightly misleading as it weighs in at over a thousand pages and nearly two kilograms! But what you get for your money is many of the theory's key figures writing with great clarity and authority. The book has become the standard reference on attachment. Mario Mikulincer and Phillip Shaver's jointly authored book, *Attachment in Adulthood* (New York: Guilford Press, 2007) provides an equally impressive digest of the research, theory and clinical practice currently being generated in the field of adult attachments. Pat Crittenden's writing is always stimulating and much of her thinking about the Dynamic-Maturation Model of attachment and adaptation is brought together in her book, *Raising Parents: Attachment, Parenting and Child Safety* (Cullompton: Willan Press, 2008).

Longitudinal studies give us a good picture of attachment across the lifecourse. Here are two examples: *Attachment from Infancy to Adulthood* (New York: Guilford Press, 2005), edited by Klaus Grossmann, Karin Grossmann and Everett Waters, and Alan Sroufe and colleagues, *The Development of the Person: The Minnesota Study of Risk and Adaptation from Birth to Adulthood* (New York: Guilford Press, 2005).

Most attachment researchers have a clinical as well as theoretical focus. There are now many books that consider the clinical and practical applications of attachment theory, so many in fact, it seems invidious to highlight just a small number. The following represent a few recent examples across the range: Lisa Berlin and colleagues' edited volume, *Enhancing Early Attachments: Theory, Research, Intervention, and Policy* (New York: Guilford Press, 2005), Alicia Lieberman and Patricia

Van Horn, *Psychotherapy with Infants and Young Children* (New York: Guildford Press, 2008), Femmie Juffer and colleagues' book, *Promoting Positive Parenting: An Attachment-based Intervention* (London: Psychology Press, 2008), David Oppenheim and Douglas Goldsmith's edited volume, *Attachment Theory in Clinical Work with Children* (New York: Guilford Press, 2007), Joseph Obegi and Ety Berant, editors of *Attachment Theory and Research in Clinical Work with Adults* (New York: Guildford Press, 2008), Susan Johnson and Valerie Whiffen's edited volume, *Attachment Processes in Couples and Family Therapy* (New York: Guildford Press, 2005), Jon Allen, Peter Fonagy and Anthony Bateman's *Mentalizing in Clinical Practice* (Washington, DC: American Psychiatric Publishing, 2008), Howard Steele and Miriam Steele's edited book, *Clinical Applications of the Adult Attachment Interview* (New York: Guildford Press, 2008), Rudi Dallos and Arlene Vetere, *Systemic Therapy and Attachment Narratives* (London: Routledge, 2009), Gillian Schofield and Mary Beek, *Attachment Handbook for Foster Care and Adoption* (London: BAAF, 2006), Kim Golding, *Nurturing Attachments: Supporting Children Who Are Fostered and Adopted* (London: Jessica Kingsley, 2008), Daniel Hughes, *Principles of Attachment-Focused Parenting* (New York: W.W. Norton, 2009), and Susan Bennett and Judith Kay Nelson's edited book, *Adult Attachment in Clinical Social Work Practice* (Berlin: Springer, 2010).

Journals, of course, are the place to visit for the latest research, practice and theorizing. As well as the one dedicated journal, *Attachment and Human Development*, published by Routledge, there are many others in developmental psychology, social psychology, personal relationships, counselling and clinical practice that regularly carry attachment-based papers. A quick glance through the bibliography and reference section of this and other attachment books, or a brief search on any of the major databases will soon tell you which journals are the key ones to check out.

And having got into your attachment stride, there is still no substitute for going back to where much of the intellectual fervour began – John Bowlby's attachment trilogy, *Attachment and Loss:* Vol. 1: *Attachment* (London: Hogarth Press, 1969), *Attachment and Loss:* Vol. 2: *Separation: Anger and Anxiety* (London: Hogarth Press, 1973), and *Attachment and Loss:* Vol. 3: *Loss: Sadness and Depression* (London: Hogarth Press, 1980), and Mary Ainsworth and colleagues' book, *Patterns of Attachment: A Psychological Study of the Strange Situation* (Hillsdale, NJ: Erlbaum, 1978).

Bibliography

Abramson, I. Y., Metalsky, G. L. and Alloy, L. B. (1989) Hopelessness depression: a theory-based subtype of depression. *Psychological Review*, 96: 358–72.

Aguilar, B., Sroufe, L. A., Egeland, B. and Carlson, E. (2000) Distinguishing the early onset/persistent and adolescent-onset antisocial behavior types from birth to 16 years. *Development and Psychopathology*, 12: 109–32.

Aikins, J. W., Howes, C. and Hamilton, C. (2009) Attachment stability and the emergence of unresolved representations during adolescence. *Attachment and Human Development*, 11(5): 491–512.

Ainsworth, M. (1967) *Infancy in Uganda: Infant Care and the Growth of Love*. Baltimore, MD: Johns Hopkins University Press.

Ainsworth, M., Blehar, M., Waters, E. and Wall, S. (1978) *Patterns of Attachment: a Psychological Study of the Strange Situation*. Hillsdale, NJ: Erlbaum.

Ainsworth, M. and Wittig B. A. (1969) Attachment and the exploratory behavior of one-year-olds in a strange situation. In B. M. Foss (ed.) *Determinants of Infant Behavior*, vol. 4. London: Methuen, pp. 113–16.

Allen, J. (2001) *Traumatic Relationships and Serious Mental Disorders*. Chichester; Wiley.

Allen, J., Fonagy, P. and Bateman, A. (2008) *Mentalizing in Clinical Practice* Washington, DC: American Psychiatric Publishing.

Allen, J. G. (2006) Mentalizing in practice. In J. G. Allen and P. Fonagy (eds) *Handbook of Mentalization-Based Treatment*. Chichester: John Wiley & Sons, Ltd, pp. 3–30.

Allen, J. P. and Manning, N. (2007) From Safety to Affect Regulation: attachment from the vantage point of adolescence. In M. Scharf and O. Mayseless (eds) *Attachment in Adolescence: Reflections and New Angles*. San Francisco: Jossey-Bass, pp. 23–39.

Allen, J. P. and Miga, E. M. (2010) Attachment in adolescence: a move to the level of emotion regulation. *Journal of Social and Personal Relationships*, 27: 181–90.

Ammaniti, M., Speranza, A. M. and Fedele, S. (2005) Attachment in infancy and in early and late childhood. In K. A. Kerns and R. A. Richardson (eds) *Attachment in Middle Childhood*. New York: Guilford Press, pp. 113–36.

Ammaniti, M., van IJzendoorn, M., Speranza, A. M. and Tambelli, R. (2000) Internal working models of attachment during late childhood and early adolescence: an exploration of stability and change. *Attachment and Human Development*, 2(3): 328–46.

Andrew, A.K. (1989) Meeting the needs of young deaf-blind children and their parents: I. *Child: Health and Development*, 15(3): 195–206.

Antonucci, T. C., Akiyama, H. and Takahashi, K. (2004) Attachment and close relationships across the lifespan. *Attachment and Human Development*, 6: 353–70.

Aviezer, O., Sagi, A., Resnicj, G. and Gini, M. (2002) School competence in young adolescents: links to early attachment relationships beyond concurrent self-perceived competence and representations of relationships. *International Journal of Behavioral Development*, 26: 397–409.

Bakermans-Kranenburg, M.J. and van IJzendoorn, M. (1993) A psychometric study of the Adult Attachment Interview: reliability and discriminant validity. *Developmental Psychology*, 29: 870–9.

Bakermans-Kranenburg, M. J. and van IJzendoorn, M. H. (2009) The first 10,000 Adult Attachment Interviews: distributions of adult representations in clinical and non-clinical samples. *Attachment and Human Development*, 11(3): 223–63.

Bakermans-Kranenburg, M. J., van IJzendoorn, M., Bokhurst, C. L. and Schuengel, C. (2004) The importance of shared environment in infant–father attachment: a behavioral genetic study of the attachment Q-sort. *Journal of Family Psychology*, 18: 545–9.

Bakermans-Kranenburg, M. J., van IJzendoorn, M. and Juffer, F. (2003) Less is more: meta-analysis of sensitivity and attachment interventions in early childhood. *Psychological Bulletin*, 129: 195–215.

Ballard, J. G. (2008) *Miracles of Life: An Autobiography*. London: Harper Perennial.

Barnett, B. and Parker, G. (1998) The parentified child: early competence or childhood deprivation. *Child Psychology and Psychiatry Review*, 3(4): 146–55.

Barnett, D., Hunt, K. H., Butler, C. M., McCaskill IV, J. W., Kaplan-Estrin, M. and Pipp-Siegel, S. (1999) Indices of attachment disorganization among toddlers with neurological and non-neurological problems. In J. Solomon and C. George (eds) *Attachment Disorganization*. New York: Guilford Press, pp. 189–212.

Barone, L. and Guiducci, V. (2009) Mental representations of attachment in eating disorders: a pilot study using the Adult Attachment Interview. *Attachment and Human Development*, 11(4): 405–17.

Bartholomew, K. (1990) Avoidance of intimacy: an attachment perspective. *Journal of Social and Personal Relationships*, 7: 147–78.

Bartholomew, K. and Alison, C. J. (2006) An attachment perspective on abusive dynamics in intimate relationships. In M. Mikulincer and G. S. Goodman (eds) *Dynamics of Romantic Relationships: Attachment, Caregiving, and Sex*. New York: Guilford Press, pp. 102–27.

Bartholomew, K. and Horowitz, L. M (1991) Attachment styles among young adults: a test of a four-category model. *Journal of Personality and Social Psychology*, 61: 226–44.

Bauminger, N., Finzi-Dottan, R., Chason, S. and Har-Even, D. (2009) Intimacy in adolescent friendship: the roles of attachment, coherence and self-disclosure. *Journal of Social and Personal Relationships*, 25(3): 409–28.

Beck, A. T., Rush, A. J., Shaw, B. F. and Emery, G. (1979) *Cognitive Therapy of Depression*. New York: Guilford Press.

Beebe, B. (2004) Co-constructing mother–infant distress in face to face interactions: contributions of microanalysis. *Zero to Three*, May: 40–8.

Beebe, B., Jaffe, J., Markese, S., Buck, K., *et al.* (2010) The origins of 12-month attachment: a microanalysis of 4-month mother–infant interaction. *Attachment and Human Development*, 12(1–2): 3–141.

Beeghly, M. and Cicchetti, D. (1994) Child maltreatment, attachment and the self system: emergence of an internal state lexicon in toddlers at high social risk. *Developmental Psychopathology*, 6: 5–30.

Belsky, J. (2005) Attachment theory and research in ecological perspective. In K. E. Grossmann, K. Grossmann and E. Waters (eds) *Attachment from Infancy to Adulthood: The Major Longitudinal Studies*. New York: Guilford Press, pp. 71–97.

Belsky, J. and Cassidy, J. (1994) Attachment theory and practice. In M. Rutter and D. Hay (eds) *Development Through Life: A Handbook for Clinicians*. Oxford: Blackwell Science, pp. 373–402.

Belsky, J. and Fearon, R. M. P. (2008) Precursors of attachment security. In J. Cassidy and P. Shaver (eds) *Handbook of Attachment: Theory, Research, and Clinical Applications*. New York: Guilford Press, pp. 295–316.

Belsky, J. and Jaffee, S. (2006) The multiple determinants of parenting. In D. Cicchetti and D. Cohen (eds) *Developmental Psychopathology*, vol. 3, *Risk, Disorder, and Adaptation*. Hoboken, NJ: Wiley, pp. 38–85.

Belsky, J. and Rovine, M. J. (1987) Temperament and attachment security in the strange situation: an empirical rapprochement. *Child Development*, 58: 787–95.

Bennett, S. and Nelson, J. K. (eds) (2010) *Adult Attachment in Clinical Social Work Practice*. Berlin: Springer.

Berlin, L. *et al.* (eds) (2005) *Enhancing Early Attachments: Theory, Research, Intervention, and Policy*. New York: Guilford Press.

Bernier, A., Larose, S. and Whipple, N. (2005) Leaving home for college: a potentially stressful event for adolescents with preoccupied attachment patterns. *Attachment and Human Development*, 7(2): 171–85.

Bifulco, A., Figueredo, B., Guedeney, N., Gorman, I., Hayes, S. and Muzik, M. (2004) Maternal attachment style and depression associated with childbirth: preliminary results from a European and US cross-cultural study. *British Journal of Psychiatry*, 184: 31–7.

Bifulco, A., Jacobs, C., Bunn, A., Thomas, G. and Irving, K. (2008) The Attachment Style Interview (ASI) as an assessment of support capacity: exploring its use for adoption-fostering assessment. *Adoption and Fostering*, 32: 33–45.

Birnbaum, G. E., Orr, I., Mikulincer, M. and Florian, V. (1997) When marriage breaks up: does attachment-style contribute to coping and mental health? *Journal of Social and Personal Relationships*, 14: 643–54.

Bokhurst, C. L., Bakermans-Kranenburg, M. J., Fearon, R., van IJzendoorn, M., Fonagy, P. and Schuengel, C. (2003) The importance of shared environment in mother–infant attachment security: a behavioral genetic study. *Child Development*, 74: 1769–82.

Bomber, L. (2007) *Inside I'm Hurting: Practical Strategies for Supporting Children in Schools*. London: Worth Publishing.

Booth-LaForce, C., Oh, W., Kim, A. H., Rubin, K. H., Rose-Krasnor, L. and Burgess, K. (2006) Attachment, self-worth, and peer group functioning in middle childhood. *Attachment and Human Development*, 8(4): 309–25.

Booth-LaForce, C., Rubin, K. H., Rose-Krasnor, L. and Burgess, K. B. (2005) Attachment and friendship predictors of psychosocial functioning in middle childhood and the mediating roles of social support and self-worth. In K. A. Kerns and R. A. Richardson (eds) *Attachment in Middle Childhood*. New York: Guilford Press, pp. 161–88.

Bosquet, M. and Egeland, B. (2006) The development and maintenance of anxiety symptoms from infancy through adolescence in a longitudinal sample. *Development and Psychopathology*, 18: 517–50.

Bowlby, J. (1958) The nature of the child's tie to his mother. *International Journal of Psycho-Analysis*, 39: 350–73.

Bowlby, J. (1969) *Attachment and Loss: vol. I: Attachment*. London: Hogarth Press.

Bowlby, J. (1973) *Attachment and Loss: vol. 2: Separation: Anger and Anxiety*. London: Hogarth Press.

Bowlby, J. (1979) *The Making and Breaking of Affectional Bonds*. London: Tavistock.

Bowlby, J. (1980) *Attachment and Loss: vol. 3: Loss: Sadness and Depression*. London: Hogarth Press.

Bowlby, J. (1988) *A Secure Base: Clinical Applications of Attachment Theory*. London: Routledge.

Bowlby, J. (1997) *Attachment and Loss: vol. I: Attachment*. London: Hogarth Press; London: Pimlico Edition. (Original edition 1969).

Bowlby, J. (1998a) *Attachment and Loss: vol. 2: Separation: Anger and Anxiety* London: Pimlico Edition. (Original edition 1973).

Bowlby, J. (1998b) *Attachment and Loss: vol. 3: Loss: Sadness and Depression*. London: Pimlico Edition. (Original edition 1980).

Bowlby, U. (1999) Memories of Mary Ainsworth. *Attachment and Human Development*, 1(2): 219.

Bradley, J. M. and Cafferty, T. P. (2001) Attachment among older adults: current issues and directions for future research. *Attachment and Human Development*, 3(2): 200–21.

Bradley, R. H., Caldwell, B. M. and Rock, S. L. (1988) Home environment and school performance: a ten-year follow-up and examination of three models of environmental action. *Child Development*, 59: 852–67.

Brennan, K. A., Clark, C. L. and Shaver, P. R. (1998) Self-report measurement of adult attachment: an integrative overview. In J. A. Simpson and W. S. Rholes (eds) *Attachment Theory and Close Relationships*. New York: Guilford Press, pp. 46–76.

Bretherton, I. (1998) Attachment and psychoanalysis: a reunion in progress. *Social Development*, 7: 132–6.

Bretherton, I., Oppenheim, D., Buchsbaum, H., Emde, R. and the MacArthur Narrative Group (1990) MacArthur Story-Stem Battery (MSSB), unpublished manual, Waisman Center, University of Wisconsin-Madison.

Bronfenbrenner, U. (1979) *The Ecology of Human Development: Experiments in Nature and Design*. Cambridge, MA: Harvard University Press.

Brumbaugh, C. C. and Fraley, R. C. (2006) Transference and attachment: how do attachment patterns get carried forward from one relationship to the next? *Personality and Social Psychology Bulletin*, 32: 552–60.

Calabrese, M. L., Farber, B. A. and Westen, D. (2005) The relationship of adult attachment constructs to object relational patterns of representing self and others. *Journal of the American Academy of Psychoanalysis and Dynamic Psychiatry*, 33: 513–30.

Carlivati, J. and Collins, W. A. (2007) Adolescent attachment representations and development in a risk sample. In M. Scharf and O. Mayseless (eds) *Attachment in Adolescence: Reflections and New Angles*. San Francisco: Jossey-Bass, pp. 91–106.

Carlson, E. A. (1998) A prospective longitudinal study of attachment disorganization/disorientation. *Child Development*, 69, 1107–29.

Carlson, V., Cicchetti, D., Barnett, D. and Braunwald, K. (1989) Disorganized/disoriented attachment relationships in maltreated infants. *Developmental Psychology*, 25: 525–31.

Carnelley, K. B. and Ruscher, J. B. (2000) Adult attachment and exploratory behaviour in leisure. *Journal of Social Behavior and Personality*, 15: 153–65.

Carr, A., Flanagan, E., Dooley, B., Fitzpatrick, M. *et al.* (2009) Profiles of Irish survivors of institutional abuse with different adult attachment styles. *Attachment and Human Development*, 11(2): 183–201.

Cassidy, J. (2008) The nature of the child's ties. In J. Cassidy and P. Shaver (eds) *Handbook of Attachment: Theory, Research, and Clinical Applications*. New York: Guilford Press, pp. 3–22.

Cassidy, J. and Kobak, R. R. (1988) Avoidance and its relationship with other defensive processes. In J. Belsky and T. Nezworski (eds) *Clinical Implications of Attachment*. Hillsdale, NJ: Erlbaum, pp. 300–23.

Cassidy, J., Marvin, R. S. and the Working Group of the John D. and Catherine T. MacArthur Foundation on the Transition from Infancy to Early Childhood. (1992) Attachment organization in three- and four-year olds: coding guidelines, unpublished manuscript. Charlottesville, University of Virginia.

Cassidy, J. and Shaver, P. (2008) *Handbook of Attachment: Theory, Research and Clinical Applications* (2nd edn). New York: Guilford Press.

Chango, J. M., McElhaney, K. B., Allen, J. P. (2009) Attachment organisation and patterns of conflict resolution in friendships predicting adolescents' depressive symptoms over time. *Attachment and Human Development*, 11(4): 331–46.

Cicchetti, D., Rogosch, F. A. and Toth, S. L. (2006) Fostering secure attachment in infants in maltreating families through preventative interventions. *Development and Psychopathology*, 18: 623–49.

Cicchetti, D. and Toth, S. L. (1995) A developmental psychopathology perspective on child abuse and neglect. *Journal of the American Academy of Child Adolescent Psychiatry*, 34(5): 541–65.

Cicirelli, V. C. (1995) Attachment and obligation as daughters' motives for caregiving behaviour and subsequent effect on subjective burden. *Psychology and Aging*, 8: 144–55.

Cicirelli, V. C. (2004) God as the ultimate attachment figure for older adults. *Attachment and Human Development*, 6(4): 371–88.

Coan, J. A. (2008) Towards a neuroscience of attachment. In J. Cassidy and P. Shaver (eds) *Handbook of Attachment: Theory, Research and Clinical Applications*. New York: Guilford Press pp. 241–65.

Cohen, D. L. and Belsky, J. (2008) Avoidant-romantic attachment and female orgasm: testing an emotion-regulation hypothesis. *Attachment and Human Development*, 10(1): 1–10.

Collins, N. C., Guichard, A. C., Ford, M. B. and Feeney, B. C. (2004) Working models of attachment: new developments and emerging themes. In W. S. Rholes and J. A. Simpson (eds) *Adult Attachment: Theory, Research and Clinical Implications*. New York: Guilford Press, pp. 196–239.

Collins, N. C., Guichard, A. C., Ford, M. B. and Feeney, B. C. (2006) Responding to need in intimate relationships: normative processes and individual differences. In M. Mikulincer and G. S. Goodman (eds) *Dynamics of Romantic Love: Attachment, Caregiving, and Sex*. New York: Guilford Press, pp. 149–89.

Cooper, M. L., Albino, A. W., Orcutt, H. K. and Williams, N. (2004) Attachment styles and intrapersonal adjustment: a longitudinal study from adolescence to young adulthood. In W. S. Rholes and J. A. Simpson (eds) *Adult Attachment: Theory, Research and Clinical Implications*. New York: Guilford Press, pp. 438–66.

Cooper, M. L., Pioli, M., Levitt, A., Talley, A. E., Micheas, L. and Collins, N. (2006) Attachment styles, sex motives, and sexual behaviour: evidence for gender specific expressions of attachment dynamics. In M. Mikulincer and G. Goodman (eds) *Dynamics of Romantic Love: Attachment, Caregiving and Sex*. New York: Guilford Press, pp. 243–74.

Craik, K. (1943) *The Nature of Explanation*. Cambridge: Cambridge University Press.

Crispi, E. L., Schiaffino, K. and Berman, W. H. (1997) The contribution of attachment to burden in adult children of institutionalized parents with dementia. *Educational Research*, 37: 52–60.

Crittenden, P. M. (1985a) Maltreated infants: vulnerability and resilience. *Journal of Child Psychology and Psychiatry*, 26: 85–96.

Crittenden, P. M. (1985b) Social networks, quality of parenting, and child development. *Child Development*, 56, 1299–313.

Crittenden, P. M. (1992a) Treatment of anxious attachment in infancy and early childhood. *Development and Psychopathology*, 4: 575–602.

Crittenden, P. M. (1992b) Quality of attachment in the preschool years. *Development and Psychopathology*, 4, 209–41.

Crittenden, P. M. (1992c) Children's strategies for coping with adverse home environments: an interpretation using attachment theory. *Child Abuse and Neglect*, 16: 329–43.

Crittenden, P. M. (1995) Attachment and psychopathology. In S. Goldberg, R. Muir and J. Kerr (eds) *Attachment Theory: Social, Developmental and Clinical Perspectives*. Hillsdale, NJ: Analytic Press, pp. 367–406.

Crittenden, P. M. (1997) Patterns of attachment and sexual behaviour: risk of dysfunction versus opportunity for creative integration. In L. Atkinson and K. Zucker (eds) *Attachment and Psychopathology*. New York: Guilford Press, pp. 47–93.

Crittenden, P. M. (1999) Child neglect: causes and contributors. In H. Dubowitz (ed.) *Neglected Children: Research, Practice and Policy*. Thousand Oaks, CA: Sage, pp. 47–68.

Crittenden, P. M. (2000a) A dynamic-maturational model of the function, development, and organization of human relationships. In R. S. L. Mills and S. Duck (eds) *Developmental Psychology of Personal Relationships*. Chichester: Wiley, pp. 199–218.

Crittenden, P. M. (2000b) A dynamic-maturational exploration of the meaning of security and adaptation: empirical, cultural and theoretical considerations. In P. M. Crittenden and A. A. Claussen (eds) *The Organization of Attachment Relationships: Maturation, Culture, and Context*. New York: Cambridge University Press.

Crittenden, P. M. (2008) *Raising Parents: Attachment, Parenting and Child Safety*. Cullompton: Willan Press.

Crittenden, P. M. and Claussen, A. H. (eds) (2000) *The Organization of Attachment Relationships: Maturation, Culture, and Context*. New York: Cambridge University Press.

Crittenden, P. M., Claussen, A. H. and Kozlowska, K. (2007) Choosing a valid assessment of attachment for clinical use: a comparative study. *Australia and New Zealand Journal of Family Therapy*, 28: 78–87.

Crittenden, P. M. and DiLalla, D. L. (1988) Compulsive compliance: the development of an inhibitory coping strategy in infancy. *Journal of Abnormal Child Psychology*, 16: 585–99.

Crittenden, P. M. and Newman, L. (2010) Comparing models of borderline personality disorder: mothers' experience, self-protective strategies, and dispositional representations. *Clinical Child Psychology and Psychiatry*, 15(3): 433–51.

Dallos, R. and Vetere, A. (2009) *Systemic Therapy and Attachment Narratives*. London: Routledge.

Davila, J. and Bradbury, T. N. (2001) Attachment insecurity and the distinction between unhappy spouses who do and do not divorce. *Journal of Family Psychology*, 15: 371–93.

DeKlyen, M. and Greenberg, M. T. (2008) Attachment and pathology in childhood. In J. Cassidy and P. Shaver (eds) *Handbook of Attachment: Theory, Research, and Clinical Applications* (2nd edn). New York: Guilford Press, pp. 637–65.

DeOliveira, C. A., Moran, G. and Pederson, D. R. (2005) Understanding the link between maternal adult attachment classifications and thoughts and feelings about emotions. *Attachment and Human Development*, 7(2): 153–70.

de Rosnay, M. and Harris, P. L. (2002) Individual differences in children's understanding of emotion: the role of attachment and language. *Attachment and Human Development*, 4(1): 39–54.

Diamond, L. M. and Fagundes, C. P. (2010) Psychobiological research on attachment. *Journal of Social and Personal Relationships*, 27(2): 218–25.

Diamond, L. M. and Hicks, A. M. (2004) Psychobiological perspectives on attachment. In W. S. Rholes and J. A. Simpson (eds) *Adult Attachment: Theory, Research and Clinical Implications*. New York: Guilford Press, pp. 240–63.

Dozier, M. (1990) Attachment organization and treatment use for adults with serious psychopathological disorders. *Development and Psychopathology*, 3: 47–60.

Dozier, M. and Rutter, M. (2008) Challenges of the development of attachment relationships faced by young children in foster and adoptive care. In J. Cassidy and P. Shaver (eds) *Handbook of Attachment: Theory, Research, and Clinical Applications*. New York: Guilford Press, pp. 698–717.

Dozier, M., Stovall, K. C., Albus, K. and Bates, B. (2001) Attachment for infants in foster care: the role of caregiver state of mind. *Child Development*, 72: 1467–77.

Dozier, M., Stovall-McClough, K.C., and Albus, K. (2008) Attachment and psychopathology in adulthood. In J. Cassidy and P. Shaver (eds) *Handbook of Attachment: Theory and Research*. New York: Guilford Press, pp. 718–44.

Dykas, M. J. and Cassidy, J. (2007) Attachment and the processing of social information in adolescence. In M. Scharf and O. Mayseless (eds) *Attachment in Adolescence: Reflections and New Angles*. San Francisco: Jossey-Bass, pp. 41–56.

Egeland, B. and Farber, E. A. (1984) Infant–mother attachment: factors related to its development and change over time. *Child Development*, 55: 753–71.

Elicker, J., Englund, M. and Sroufe, L. A. (1992) Predicting peer competence and peer relationships. In R. D. Parke and G. W. Ladd (eds) *Family-Peer Relationships*. Hillsdale, NJ: Erlbaum, pp. 77–106.

Elliot, A. J. and Reis, H. T. (2003) Attachment and exploration in adulthood. *Journal of Personality and Social Psychology*, 85: 317–31.

Farnfield, S., Hautamäki, A., Norbech, P. and Sahhar, N. (2010) Dynamic-Maturation Model methods for assessing attachment. *Clinical Child Psychology and Psychiatry*, 15(3): 313–28.

Fearon, R. P., Bakermans-Kranenburg, van IJzendoorn, M. J., M., Lapsley, A-M. and Roisman, G. I. (2010) The significance of insecure attachment and disorganization in the development of children's externalizing behaviour: a meta-analytic study. *Child Development*, 81(2): 435–56.

Feeney, B. C. and Collins, N. L. (2001) Predictors of caregiving in adult intimate relationships: an attachment theoretical perspective. *Journal of Personality and Social Psychology*. 80: 972–94.

Feeney, B. C. and Collins, N. L. (2003) Motivations for caregiving in adult intimate relationships: influences on caregiving behaviour and relationship functioning. *Personality and Social Psychology Bulletin*, 29: 950–68.

Feeney, B. C. and Kirkpatrick, L. A. (1996) Effects of adult attachment and presence of romantic partners on physiological responses to stress. *Journal of Personality and Social Psychology*, 70: 255–79.

Feeney, B. C. and Van Vleet, M. (2010) Growing through attachment: the interplay of attachment and exploration in adulthood. *Journal of Social and Personal Relationships*, 27(2): 226–34.

Feeney, J. A. (2004) Adult attachment and relationship functioning under stressful conditions. In W. S. Rholes and J. A. Simpson (eds) *Adult Attachment: Theory, Research and Clinical Implications*. New York: Guilford Press, pp. 339–64.

Feeney, J. A. and Noller, P. (1992) Attachment style and romantic love: relationship dissolution. *Australian Journal of Psychology*, 44: 69–74.

Feeney, J. A., Noller, P. and Hanrahan, M. (1995) Assessing adult attachment. In M. Sperling and M. Berman (eds) *Attachment in Adults: Theory, Assessment and Treatment*. New York: Guilford Press, pp. 128–52.

Finger, B., Hans, S. L., Bernstein, V. J. and Cox, S. M. (2009) Parent relationship quality and infant–mother attachment. *Attachment and Human Development*, 11(3): 285–306.

Foley, M. (2010) *The Age of Absurdity: Why Modern Life Makes It Hard to Be Happy*. London: Simon & Schuster.

Follete, V. M., Polusny, M. A., Bechtle, A. E. and Naughle, E. (1996) Cumulative trauma: the impact of child sexual abuse, adult sexual assault, and spouse abuse. *Journal of Traumatic Stress*. 9: 25–35.

Fonagy, P. (2006) The mentalization-focused approach to social development. In J. G. Allen and P. Fonagy (eds) *Handbook of Mentalization-Based Treatment*. Chichester: John Wiley & Sons, Ltd, pp. 53–100.

Fonagy, P., Gergely, G., Jurist, E. and Target, M. (2002) *Affect Regulation, Mentalization, and the Development of the Self*. New York: Other Press.

Fonagy, P., Leigh, T., Steele, M. *et al.* (1996) The relation of attachment status, psychiatric classification, and responses to psychotherapy. *Journal of Consulting and Clinical Psychology*, 64(1): 22–31.

Fonagy, P., Steele, H. and Steele, M. (1991) Maternal representations of attachment during pregnancy predict the organization of infant–mother attachment at age one year of age. *Child Development*, 62: 891–905.

Fonagy, P., Steele, H., Steele, M., Higgit, A. and Target, M. (1994) The theory and practice of resilience [The Emmanuel Miller Memorial Lecture 1992]. *Journal of Child Psychology and Psychiatry*, 35(2): 231–57.

Fonagy, P., Steele, M., Steele, H., Leigh, T., Kennedy, R., Matoon, G. and Target, M. (1995) Attachment, the reflective self, and borderline states. In S. Goldberg, R. Muir and J. Kerr (eds) *Attachment Theory: Social, Developmental, and Clinical Perspectives*. Hillsdale, NJ: Analytic Press, pp. 233–78.

Fonagy, P. and Target, M. (1997) Attachment and reflective function: their role in self-organization. *Development and Psychopathology*, 9: 679–700.

Fonagy, P. and Target, M. (2005) Bridging the transmission gap: an end to an important mystery of attachment research. *Attachment and Human Development*, 7(3): 333–43.

Fox, N. A. and Hane, A. A. (2008) Studying the biology of human development. In J. Cassidy and P. Shaver (eds) *Handbook of Attachment: Theory, Research and Clinical Applications*. New York: Guilford Press, pp. 217–40.

Fraley, C. and Brumbaugh, C. C. (2004) A dynamical systems approach to conceptualizing and studying stability and change in attachment security. In W. S. Rholes and J. A. Simpson (eds) *Adult Attachment: Theory, Research and Clinical Implications*. New York: Guilford Press, pp. 86–132.

Fraley, R. C., Niedenthal, P. M., Marks, M., Brumbaugh, C. and Vicary, A.

(2006) Adult attachment and the perception of emotional expressions: probing the hyperactivating strategies underlying anxious attachment. *Journal of Personality*, 74: 1163–90.

Fraley, R. C. and Shaver, P. (1998) Airport separations: a naturalistic study of adult attachment dynamics in separating couples. *Journal of Personality and Social Psychology*, 75: 1198–212.

Geddes, H. (2005) *Attachment in the Classroom*. London: Worth Publishing.

Gentzler, A. L. and Kerns, K. A. (2004) Associations between insecure attachment and sexual experiences. *Personal Relationships*, 11: 249–65.

George, C. (1996) A representational perspective of child abuse and prevention: internal working models of attachment and caregiving. *Child Abuse and Neglect*, 20(5): 411–24.

George, C. (2009) Couple relationships and the family system: commentary from a behavioral systems perspective. *Attachment and Human Development*, 11(1): 103–10.

George, C., Kaplan, N. and Main, M. (1984) Adult Attachment Interview Protocol, unpublished manuscript, University of California at Berkeley.

George, C. and Solomon, J. (2008) The caregiving system: a behavioral systems approach to parenting. In J. Cassidy and P. Shaver (eds) *Handbook of Attachment*. New York: Guilford Press, pp. 833–56.

Gerhardt, S. (2004) *Why Love Matters: How Affection Shapes a Baby's Brain*. New York: Brunner-Routledge.

Golding, K. (2008) *Nurturing Attachments: Supporting Children Who Are Fostered and Adopted*. London: Jessica Kingsley.

Goldberg, S. (2000) *Attachment and Development*. London: Arnold.

Gottman, J. M. (1994) *What Predicts Divorce? The Relationship between Marital Processes and Marital Outcome*. Hillsdale, NJ: Erlbaum.

Green, J. and Goldwyn, R. (2002) Attachment disorganization and psychopathology: new findings in attachment research and their potential implications for developmental psychopathology in childhood. *Journal of Child Psychology and Psychiatry*, 43: 835–46.

Green, J., Stanley, C. and Peters, S. (2007) Disorganized attachment representation and atypical parenting in young school aged children with externalizing disorder. *Attachment and Human Development*, 9(3): 207–22.

Grienenberger, J., Kelly, K. and Slade, A. (2005) Maternal reflective functioning, mother–infant affective communication, and infant attachment: exploring the link between mental states and observed caregiving behaviour in the intergenerational transmission of attachment. *Attachment and Human Development*, 7: 299–311.

Grossmann, K., Grossmann, K. E., and Kindler, H. (2005) Early care and the roots of attachment partnership representations: the Bielefeld and Regensberg longitudinal studies. In K. E. Grossmann, K. Grossmann and

E. Waters (eds) *Attachment from Infancy to Adulthood: The Major Longitudinal Studies*. New York: Guilford Press, pp. 98–136.

Grossmann, K. E., Grossmann, K. and Waters, E. (eds) (2005) *Attachment from Infancy to Adulthood: The Major Longitudinal Studies*. New York: Guilford Press.

Guerrero, L. K. (1996) Attachment-style differences in intimacy and involvement: a test of the four-category model. *Communication Monographs*, 63: 269–92.

Gump, B. B., Polk, D. E., Kamarck, T. W. and Shiffman, S. M. (2001) Partner interactions are associated with reduced blood pressure in the natural environment: ambulatory monitoring evidence from a healthy, multiethnic adult sample. *Psychosomatic Medicine*, 63: 423–33.

Hadadian, A. (1995) Attitudes toward deafness and security of attachment relationships among young deaf children and their parents. *Early Education and Development*, 6(2): 181–91.

Hautamäki, A., Hautamäki, L., Neuvonen, L. and Maliniemi-Piispanen, S. (2010) Transmission of attachment across three generations: continuity and reversal. *Clinical Child Psychology and Psychiatry*, 15(3): 347–54.

Hazan, C., Campa, M. and Gur-Yaish, N. (2006) What is adult attachment? In M. Mikulincer and G. S. Goodman (eds) *Dynamics of Romantic Love: Attachment, Caregiving and Sex*. New York: Guilford Press, pp. 47–70.

Hazan, C. and Shaver, P. (1987) Romantic love conceptualized as an attachment process. *Journal of Personality and Social Psychology*, 52: 511–24.

Hazan, C. and Zeifman, D. (1994) Sex and the psychological tether. In K. Bartholomew and D. Perlman (eds) *Advances in Personal Relationships:* vol. 5: *Attachment Processes in Adulthood*. London: Jessica Kingsley, pp. 151–77.

Hazan, C., Zeifman, D. and Middleton, K. (1994) Adult romantic attachment, affection, and sex. Paper presented at the 7th International Conference on Personal Relationships, Gröningen, The Netherlands, July.

Henderson, A. J. Z., Bartholomew, K., Trinke, S. and Kwong, M. J. (2005) When loving means hurting: an exploration of attachment and intimate abuse in a community sample. *Journal of Family Violence*, 20: 219–30.

Hesse, E. (2008) The Adult Attachment Interview: protocol, method of analysis, and empirical studies. In J. Cassidy and P. Shaver (eds) *Handbook of Attachment: Theory, Research and Clinical Applications*. New York: Guilford Press, pp. 552–98.

Hinde, R. A. (2005) Ethology and attachment theory. In K. E. Grossmann, K. Grossmann and E. Waters (eds) *Attachment from Infancy to Adulthood: The Major Longitudinal Studies*. New York: Guilford Press, pp. 1–12.

Hock, E., Eberly, M., Bartle-Haring, S., Ellwanger, P. and Widaman, K. F. (2001) Separation anxiety in parents of adolescents: theoretical significance and scale development. *Child Development*, 72: 284–98.

Hodges, E. V. E., Finnegan, R. A., and Perry, D. G. (1999) Skewed autonomy-relatedness in preadolescents' conceptions of their relationships with mother, father and best friend. *Developmental Psychology*, 35: 737–48.

Howe, D. (2005) *Child Abuse and Neglect: Attachment, Development and Intervention*. Basingstoke: Palgrave Macmillan.

Howe, D. (2006) Disabled children, parent–child interaction and attachment. *Child and Family Social Work*, 11(2): 95–106.

Howe, D., Brandon, M., Hinings, D. and Schofield, G. (1999) *Attachment Theory, Child Maltreatment and Family Support*. Basingstoke: Palgrave Macmillan.

Hrdy, S. (2005) Evolutionary context of human development: the cooperative breeding model. In C. S. Carter, L. Ahnert, K. Grossmann, S. Hrdy, and M. Lamb (eds) *Attachment and Bonding: A Synthesis*. Cambridge, MA: MIT Press, pp. 9–32.

Huebner, R.A. and Thomas, K.R. (1995) The relationship between attachment, psychopathology, and childhood disability. *Rehabilitation Psychology*, 40(2): 111–24.

Hughes, D. (2009) *Principles of Attachment-Focused Parenting*. New York: W.W. Norton.

Jacobvitz, D., Curran, M. and Moller, N. (2002) Measurement of adult attachment: the place of self-report and interview methodologies. *Attachment and Human Development*, 4: 207–15.

Jacobvitz, D. and Hazen, N. (1999) Developmental pathways from infant disorganization to childhood peer relationships. In J. Solomon and C. George (eds) *Attachment Disorganization*. New York: Guilford Press, pp. 127–59.

Johnson, S. and Whiffen, V. (eds) (2005) *Attachment Processes in Couples and Family Therapy*. New York: Guildford Press.

Johnson, S. M. (2004) Attachment theory: a guide to healing couple relationships. In W. S. Rholes and J. A. Simpson (eds) *Adult Attachment: Theory, Research and Clinical Implications*. New York: Guilford Press, pp. 367–87.

Johnston, C., Hessl, D., Blasey, C., Eliez, S., Erba, H. *et al.* (2003) Factors associated with parenting stress in mothers of children with Fragile X Syndrome. *Journal of Developmental and Behavioral Pediatrics*, 24(4): 267–75.

Juffer, F. *et al.* (2008) *Promoting Positive Parenting: An Attachment-based Intervention*. London: Psychology Press.

Kagan, J. (1994) *Galen's Prophecy*. New York: Basic Books.

Kaitz, M., Bar-Haim, Y., Lehrer, M. and Grossman, E. (2004) Adult attachment style and interpersonal distance. *Attachment and Human Development*, 6(3): 285–304.

Kasl, C. (1989) *Women, Sex and Addiction*. New York: Mandarin.

Keck, G. and Kupecky, R. (1995) *Adopting the Hurt Child*. Colorado Springs, CO: Pinon Press.

Kidd, T. and Sheffield, D. (2005) Attachment style and symptom reporting: examining the mediating effects of anger and social support. *British Journal of Health Psychology*, 10: 531–41.

Kim, Y. (2006) Gender, attachment, and relationship duration on cardiovascular reactivity to stress in a laboratory study of dating couples. *Personal Relationships*, 13: 103–14.

Klohen, E. C. and Luo, S. (2003) Interpersonal attraction and personality: what is attractive – self similarity, ideal similarity, complementarity or attachment security? *Journal of Personality and Social Psychology*, 31(12): 709–22.

Kobak, R., Cassidy, J., Lyons-Ruth, K. and Ziv, Y. (2006) Attachment, stress and psychopathology: a developmental-pathways model. In D. Cicchetti and D. Cohen (eds) *Developmental Psychopathology* (2nd edn). Hoboken, NJ: Wiley, pp. 333–69.

Kobak, R., Cassidy, J. and Ziv, Y. (2004) Attachment-related trauma and Posttraumatic Stress Disorder. In W. S. Rholes and J. A. Simpson (eds) *Adult Attachment: Theory, Research and Clinical Implications*. New York: Guilford Press, pp. 388–407.

Kobak, R., Little, M., Race, E., and Acosta, M. C. (2001) Attachment disruptions in seriously emotionally disturbed children: implications for treatment. *Attachment and Human Development*, 3(3): 243–58.

Kobak, R., Rosenthal, N. and Serwik, A. (2005) The attachment hierarchy in middle childhood. In K. A. Kerns and R. A. Richardson (eds) *Attachment in Middle Childhood*. New York: Guilford Press, pp. 71–88.

Kobak, R., Rosenthal, N. L., Zajac, K. and Madsen, S. D. (2007) Adolescent attachment hierarchies and the search for an adult-pair bond. In M. Scharf and O. Mayseless (eds) *Attachment in Adolescence: Reflections and New Angles*. San Francisco: Jossey-Bass, pp. 57–72.

Koren-Karie, N., Oppenheim, D. and Getzler-Yosef, R. (2008) Shaping children's internal working models through mother–child dialogues: the importance of resolving past maternal trauma. *Attachment and Human Development*, 10(4): 465–83.

Kuczynski, L., Kochanska, G., Radke-Yarrow, M. and Girnius-Brown, O. (1987) A developmental interpretation of young children's non-compliance. *Developmental Psychology*, 23: 799–806.

Larose, S., Bernier, A. and Tarabulsy, G. M. (2005) Attachment state of mind, learning dispositions, and academic performance during college transition. *Developmental Psychology*, 41: 281–9.

LeDoux, J. (1998) *The Emotional Brain*. London: Weidenfeld and Nicolson.

Levy, K. N., Blatt, S. J. and Shaver, P. R. (1998) Attachment style and parental representations. *Journal of Personality and Social Psychology*, 74: 407–19.

Lewis, C. S. (1961) *A Grief Observed*. London: Faber and Faber.

Lieberman, A. (1992) Infant–parent psychotherapy with toddlers. *Development and Psychopathology*, 4: 559–74.

Lieberman, A. and Van Horn, P. (2008) *Psychotherapy with Infants and Young Children*. New York: Guildford Press.

Liebowitz, J., Ramos-Marcuse, F. and Arsenio, W. F. (2002) Parent–child emotion communication, attachment, and affective narratives. *Attachment and Human Development*, 4(1): 55–67.

Liotti, G. (1995) Disorganized/disoriented attachment in the psychotherapy of dissociative disorders. In S. Goldberg, R. Muir and J. Kerr (eds) *Attachment Theory: Social, Developmental and Clinical Perspectives*. Hillsdale, NJ: The Analytic Press, pp. 343–66.

Liotti, G. (1999) Disorganization of attachment as a model for understanding dissociative psychopathology. In J. Solomon and C. George (eds) *Attachment Disorganization*. New York: Guilford Press, pp. 291–317.

Liotti, G. (2004) Trauma, dissociation, and disorganized attachment: three strands of a single braid. *Psychotherapy: Theory, Research, Practice and Training*, 41: 472–86.

Lopez, F. G. (1995) Contemporary attachment theory: an introduction with implications for counselling psychology. *Counseling and Psychologist*, 23(3): 395–415.

Lyons-Ruth, K. (1996) Attachment relationships among children with aggressive behaviour problems: the role of disorganized early attachment patterns. *Journal of Consulting and Clinical Psychology*, 64: 64–73.

Lyons-Ruth, K., Bronfman, E. and Parsons, E. (1999) Maternal disrupted affective communication, maternal frightened or frightening behaviour, and infant disorganized strategies. In J. Vondra and D. Barnett (eds) *Atypical Patterns of Infant Attachment, Monographs of the Society for Research and Implications for Clinical Work*, 64(3): 67–96.

Lyons-Ruth, K. and Jacobvitz, D. (2008) Attachment disorganization. In J. Cassidy and P. Shaver (eds) *Handbook of Attachment: Theory, Research, and Clinical Applications*. New York: Guilford Press, pp. 666–97.

Lyons-Ruth, K., Melnick, S., Bronfman, S., Sherry, S. and Lianas, L. (2004) Hostile-helpless relational models and disorganized attachment patterns between parents and their young children: review of research and implications for clinical work. In L. Atkinson and S. Goldberg (eds) *Attachment Issues in Psychopathology and Intervention*. Hillsdale, NJ: Lawrence Erlbaum, pp. 65–94.

Lyons-Ruth, K., Melnick, S., Patrick, M. and Hobson, R. P. (2007) A controlled study of hostile-helpless states of mind among borderline and dysthymic women. *Attachment and Human Development*, 5: 1–19.

Lyons-Ruth, K., Yellin, C., Melnick, S., and Atwood, G. (2005) Expanding the concept of unresolved mental states: hostile/helpless states of mind on the Adult Attachment Interview are associated with atypical maternal behaviour and infant disorganization. *Development and Psychopathology*, 17: 1–23.

Macfie, J., McElwain, N. L., Houts, R. M. and Cox, M. J. (2005) Intergenerational transmission of role reversal between parent and child. *Attachment and Human Development*, 7(1): 51–65.

Macrae, K. A. M. (2003) Attachment in blind infants: a systematic investigation using Ainsworth's strange situation. *Dissertation Abstracts International: Section B: The Sciences and Engineering* 63(12-B): 6121.

Madigan, S., Bakermans-Kranenburg, M. J., van IJzendoorn, M., Moran, G., Pederson, D. and Benoit, D. (2006) Unresolved states of mind, anomalous parental behaviour, and disorganized attachment: a review and meta-analysis. *Attachment and Human Development*, 8: 89–111.

Maestripieri, D. (2005) Early experience affects the intergenerational transmission of infant abuse in rhesus monkeys. *Proceedings of the National Academy of Sciences USA*, 102: 9726–9.

Magai, C. (2008) Attachment in middle and later life. In J. Cassidy and P. Shaver (eds) *Handbook of Attachment: Theory, Research, and Clinical Applications*. New York: Guilford Press, pp. 532–51.

Maier, M. A., Bernier, A., Pekrun, R., Zimmermann, P., Strasser, K. and Grossmann, K. (2005) Attachment state of mind and perceptual processing of emotional stimuli. *Attachment and Human Development*, 7(1): 67–82.

Main, M. (1991) Metacognitive knowledge, metacognitive monitoring, and singular (coherent) vs multiple (incoherent) models of attachment. In C. Parker, J. Stevenson-Hinde and P. Marris (eds) *Attachment Across the Life Cycle*. London: Tavistock, pp. 407–74.

Main, M. (1995) Recent studies in attachment: overview, with selected implications for clinical work. In S. Goldberg, S. Muir and J. Kerr (eds) *Attachment Theory Across the Life Cycle: Social, Developmental and Clinical Perspectives*. Hillsdale, NJ: Analytic Press, pp. 407–74.

Main, M. (2000) The organized categories of infant, child, and adult attachment: flexible vs. inflexible attention under attachment stress. *Journal of the American Psychoanalytic Association*, 48: 1055–96.

Main, M. and Cassidy, J. (1988) Categories of response to reunion with the parent at age six: predictable from infant attachment classifications and stable over a 1-month period. *Developmental Psychology*, 24: 415–26.

Main, M., Goldwyn, R. and Hesse, E. (2008) The Adult Attachment Interview: Scoring and Classification System, Version 8. Unpublished manuscript: University of California at Berkeley.

Main, M. and Hesse, E. (1990) Parents' unresolved traumatic experiences are related to infants' disorganized attachment status: Is frightened and/or frightening parental behaviour the linking mechanism? In M. Greenberg,

D. Cicchetti and E. Cummings (eds) *Attachment in the Pre-School Years*. Chicago: University of Chicago Press, pp. 161–82.

Main, M., Hesse, E. and Kaplan, N. (2005) Predictability of attachment behaviour and representational processes at age 1, 6 and 18 years of age: the Berkeley Longitudinal Study. In K. E. Grossmann, K. Grossmann and E. Waters (eds) *Attachment from Infancy to Adulthood*. New York: Guilford Press, pp. 245–304.

Main, M., Kaplan, N. and Cassidy, J. (1985) Security in infancy, childhood and adulthood: a move to the level of representation. In I. Bretherton and E. Waters (eds) Growing points of attachment theory and research. *Monographs of the Society for Research in Child Development*, 50: 66–104.

Main, M. and Solomon, J. (1986) Discovery of an insecure-disorganized/ disorientated pattern. In T. Brazelton and M. Yogman (eds) *Affective Development in Infancy*. Norwood, NJ: Ablex, pp. 95–124.

Main, M. and Solomon, J. (1990) Procedures for identifying infants as disorganized/disoriented during the Ainsworth Strange Situation. In M. T. Greenberg, D. Cicchetti and E. M. Cummings (eds) *Attachment in the Preschool Years*. Chicago: University of Chicago Press, pp. 121–60.

Markiewicz, D., Reis, M. and Gold, D. P. (1997) An exploration of attachment styles and the personality traits in caregiving for dementia patients. *International Journal of Aging*, 24: 429–45.

Mayseless, O. (1996) Attachment patterns and their outcomes. *Human Development*, 36: 206–23.

Mayseless, O. (2005) Ontogeny of attachment in middle childhood. In K. A. Kerns and R. A. Richardson (eds) *Attachment in Middle Childhood*. New York: Guilford Press, pp. 1–23.

McElwain, N. L., Cox, M. J., Burchinal, M. R. and Macfie, J. (2003) Differentiating among insecure mother–infant attachment classifications: a focus on child–friend interaction and exploration during solitary play at 36 months. *Attachment and Human Development*, 5(2): 136–64.

Meadow, K. P., Greenberg, M. T. and Erting, C. (1984) Attachment behaviour of deaf children with deaf parents. *Annual Progress in Child Psychiatry and Child Development*, 22: 176–87.

Meadow-Orlans, K. P. and Steinberg, A. G. (1993) Effects of infant hearing loss and maternal support on mother–infant interactions at 18 months. *Journal of Applied Developmental Psychology*, 14: 407–26.

Meaney, M. J. (2004) The nature of nurture: maternal effects and chromatin remodelling. In J. T. Caccioppo (ed.) *Essays in Social Neuroscience*. Cambridge, MA: MIT Press, pp. 1–14.

Meaney, M. J. (2010) Epigenetics and the biological definition of gene x environment interactions. *Child Development*, 81(1): 41–79.

Meins, E. (1997) *Security of Attachment and the Social Development of Cognition*. Hove: Psychology Press.

Meins, E. (1999) Sensitivity, security and internal working models: bridging the transmission gap. *Attachment and Human Development*, 1(3): 325–42.

Meyer, B., Pikonis, P. A. and Beevers, C. G. (2004) What's in a (neutral) face?: Personality disorders, attachment styles, and the appraisal of ambiguous social cues. *Journal of Personality Disorders*, 18: 320–36.

Miesen, B. M. L. (1992) Attachment theory and dementia. In G. M. M. Jones and B. M. L. Miesen (eds) *Care-giving in Dementia: Research and Applications*. London: Tavistock, pp. 38–58.

Mikulincer, M. (1998) Adult attachment style and individual differences in functional versus dysfunctional experiences of anger. *Journal of Personality and Social Psychology*, 74: 1209–24.

Mikulincer, M. and Shaver, P. (2007) *Attachment in Adulthood: Structure, Dynamics, and Change*. New York: Guilford Press.

Mikulincer, M. and Shaver, P. (2008) Adult attachment and affect regulation. In J. Cassidy and P. Shaver (eds) *Handbook of Attachment*. New York: Guilford Press, pp. 503–31.

Miller, J. B. (2001) Attachment models and memory for conversation. *Journal of Social and Personal Relationships*, 18: 404–22.

Millings, A. and Walsh, J. (2009) A dyadic exploration of attachment and caregiving in long-term couples. *Personal Relationships*, 16(3): 437–53.

Mohr, J. J. (2008) Same-sex romantic attachment. In J. Cassidy and P. Shaver (eds) *Handbook of Attachment: Theory, Research, and Clinical Applications*. New York: Guilford Press, pp. 482–502.

Mohr, J. J. and Fassinger, R. E. (2003) Self-acceptance and self-disclosure of sexual orientation in lesbian, gay and bisexual adults: an attachment perspective. *Journal of Counseling Psychology*, 50: 482–95.

Moran, G., Pederson, D. R., Pettit, P. and Krupka, A. (1992) Maternal sensitivity and infant–mother attachment in a developmentally delayed sample. *Infant Behavior and Development*, 15: 427–42.

Moriceau, S. and Sullivan, R. M. (2005) Neurobiology of infant attachment. *Developmental Psychobiology*, 47: 230–42.

Moss, E., Smolia, N., Cyr, C., Dubois-Comtois, K., Mazzarello, T. and Berthiaume, C. (2006) Attachment and behaviour problems in middle childhood as reported by adult and child informants. *Development and Psychopathology*, 18: 425–44.

Murdoch, I. (1973) *The Black Prince*. London: Chatto and Windus.

National Scientific Council on the Developing Child (2010) *Early Experiences Can Alter Gene Expression and Affect Long-Term Development: Working Paper No. 10*. Available at: http://www.developingchild.net.

Noftle, E. E. and Shaver, P. R. (2006) Attachment dimensions and the Big Five personality traits: associations and comparative ability to predict relationship quality. *Journal of Research in Personality*, 40: 179–208.

Obegi. J. and Berant, E. (eds) (2008) *Attachment Theory and Research in Clinical Work with Adults.* New York: Guildford Press.

O'Connor, T. G., Marvin, R. S., Rutter, M., Olrick, J. T. and Britner, P. A. (2003) Child–parent attachment following institutional deprivation. *Development and Psychopathology*, 15: 19–38.

Oppenheim, D. and Goldsmith, D. (eds) (2007) *Attachment Theory in Clinical Work with Children.* New York: Guilford Press.

Park, L. E., Crocker, J. and Mickelson, K. D. (2004) Attachment styles and contingencies of self-worth. *Personality and Social Psychology Bulletin*, 30: 1243–54.

Parkes, C. M. (2006) *Love and Loss: The Roots of Grief and its Complications.* New York: Taylor and Francis.

Parkes, C. M. and Weiss, R. S. (1983) *Recovery and Bereavement.* New York: Basic Books.

Pearson, J. L., Cohn, D. A., Cowan, P. A. and Cowan, C. P. (1994) Earned and continuous-security in adult attachment: relation to depressive symptomatology and parenting style. *Development and Psychopathology*, 6: 359–73.

Perren, S., Schmid, R., Herrmann, S. and Wettstein, A. (2007) The impact of attachment on dementia-related problem behaviour and spousal caregiver's well-being. *Attachment and Human Development*, 9(2): 163–78.

Perry, B. and Szalavitz, M. (2006) *The Boy Who Was Raised as a Dog.* New York: Basic Books.

Pietromonaco, P. R., Greenwood, D. and Barrett, L. S. (2004) Conflict in adult close relationships: an attachment perspective. In W. S. Rholes and J. A. Simpson (eds) *Adult Attachment: Theory, Research and Clinical Implications.* New York: Guilford Press, pp. 267–99.

Prior, V. and Glaser, D. (2006) *Understanding Attachment and Attachment Disorders.* London: Jessica Kingsley.

Radke-Yarrow, M., Cummings, E. M., Kuczynski, L. and Chapment, M. (1985) Patterns of attachment in two- and three-year-olds in normal families and families with parental depression. *Child Development*, 56: 591–615.

Raikes, H. A. and Thompson, R. A. (2008a) Attachment security and parenting quality predicts children's problem-solving, attributions, and loneliness with peers. *Attachment and Human Development*, 10(3): 319–44.

Raikes, H. A. and Thompson, R. A. (2008b) Conversations about emotion in high-risk dyads. *Attachment and Human Development*, 10(4): 359–77.

Robertson, J. (producer) (1953) *A Two-Year Old Goes to Hospital: A Scientific Film Record.* [Film]. Nacton, UK, Concord Film Council.

Roisman, G. I., Tsai, J. L. and Chiang, K. H. S. (2004) The emotional integration of childhood experience: physiological, facial expressions, and self-reported emotional response during the Adult Attachment Interview. *Developmental Psychology*, 40: 776–89.

Rutter, M., Colvert, E., Kreppner, J., Beckett, C., Castle, J. and Groothues, C. (2007) Early adolescent outcomes for institutionally-deprived and non-deprived adoptees: I. Disinhibited attachment. *Journal of Child Psychology and Psychiatry*, 48: 17–30.

Sable, P. (2007) Accentuating the positive in adult attachments. *Attachment and Human Development*, 9(4): 361–74.

Sadava, S. W., Busseri, M. A., Molnar, D. S., Perrier, C. P. K., and DeCourville, N. (2009) Investigating a four-pathway model of adult attachment orientation and health. *Journal of Social and Personal Relationships*, 26(5): 604–33.

Sagi-Schwartz, A. and Aviezer, O. (2005) Correlates of attachment to multiple caregivers in kibbutz children from birth to emerging adulthood: the Haifa Longitudinal Study. In K. E. Grossmann, K. Grossmann and E. Waters (eds) *Attachment from Infancy to Adulthood: The Major Longitudinal Studies*. New York: Guilford Press, pp. 165–97.

Sapolsky, R. M. (1998) *Why Zebras Don't Get Ulcers*. New York: W. H. Freeman.

Scharf, M. and Mayseless, O. (2007) Putting eggs in more than one basket: a new look at development processes of attachment in adolescence. In M. Scharf and O. Mayseless (eds) *Attachment in Adolescence: Reflections and New Angles*. San Francisco: Jossey-Bass, pp. 1–22.

Scharf, M., Mayseless, O. and Kivenson-Baron, I. (2004) Adolescent attachment representations and development tasks in emerging adulthood. *Developmental Psychology*, 40: 430–44.

Schindler, A., Thomasius, R., Petersen, K., and Sack, P-M. (2009) Heroin as an attachment substitute? Differences in attachment representations between opioid, ecstasy, and cannabis abusers. *Attachment and Human Development*, 11(3): 307–30.

Schindler, A., Thomasius, R., Sack, P-M., Gemeinhardt, B., Küstner, U. and Eckert, J. (2005) Attachment and substance use disorders. *Attachment and Human Development*, 7(3): 207–28.

Schmitt, D. P. and Allik, J. (2005) Simultaneous administration of the Rosenberg Self-Esteem Scale in 53 nations: exploring the universal and culture-specific features of global-self-esteem. *Journal of Personality and Social Psychology*, 89: 623–42.

Schofield, G. and Beek, M. (2006) *Attachment Handbook for Foster Care and Adoption*. London: BAAF.

Schoon. I. (2006) *Risk and Resilience: Adaptations in Changing Times*. Cambridge: Cambridge University Press.

Schore, A. (1999) Attachment and the regulation of the right brain. *Attachment and Human Development*, 2(1): 23–47.

Schore, A. (2001) Effects of a secure attachment relationship on right brain development, affect regulation, and infant mental health. *Infant Mental Health Journal*, 22(1–2): 7–66.

Schore, A. (2003) *Affection Regulation and the Repair of the Self.* New York: Norton.

Shah, P. E., Fonagy, P. and Strathearn, L. (2010) Is attachment transmitted across the generations? The plot thickens. *Clinical Child Psychology and Psychiatry,* 15(3): 329–45.

Shaver, P. R. and Fraley, R. C. (2008) Attachment, loss and grief. In J. Cassidy and P. Shaver (eds) *Handbook of Attachment: Theory, Research and Clinical Applications.* New York: Guilford Press, pp. 48–77.

Shaver, P. and Mikulincer, M. (2003) Dialogue on adult attachment: diversity and integration. *Attachment and Human Development,* 4(2): 243–57.

Shaver, P. and Mikulincer, M. (2004) What do self-report attachment measures assess? In W. S. Rholes and J. A. Simpson (eds) *Adult Attachment: Theory, Research and Clinical Implications.* New York: Guilford Press, pp. 17–54.

Shaw, D. S., Keenan, K., Vondra, J. I., Delliquadri, E., and Giovanelli, J. (1997) Antecedents of preschool children's internalizing problems. *Journal of the American Academy of Child and Adolescent Psychiatry,* 36: 1760–67.

Simpson, J. A., Campbell, L and Weisberg, Y. J. (2006) Daily perceptions of conflict and support in romantic relationships: the ups and downs of anxiously attached individuals. In M. Mikulnicer and G. Goodman (eds) *Dynamics of Romantic Love: Attachment, Caregiving, and Sex.* New York Guilford Press, pp. 216–39.

Simpson, J. A. and Rholes, W. S. (2004) Anxious attachment and depressive symptoms: an interpersonal perspective. In W. S. Rholes and J. A. Simpson (eds) *Adult Attachment: Theory, Research and Clinical Implications.* New York: Guilford Press, pp. 408–37.

Simpson, J. A., Rholes, W. S. and Phillips, D. (1996) Conflict in close relationships: an attachment perspective. *Journal of Personality and Social Psychology,* 71(5): 899–914.

Slade, A. (2005) Parental reflective functioning: an introduction. *Attachment and Human Development,* 7(3): 269–81.

Sloper, P., Jones, L., Triggs, S., Howarth, J. and Barton, K. (2003) Multi-agency care coordination and key worker services for disabled children. *Journal of Integrated Care,* 11: 9–15.

Soerensen, S., Webster, J. D. and Roggman, L. A. (2002) Adult attachment and preparing to provide care for older relatives. *Attachment and Human Development,* 4: 84–106.

Solomon, J. and George, C. (1996) Defining the caregiving system: toward a theory of caregiving. *Infant Mental Health Journal,* 17: 183–97.

Solomon, J. and George, C. (1999) The place of disorganization in attachment theory: linking classic observations with contemporary findings. In J. Solomon and C. George (eds) *Attachment Disorganization.* New York: Guilford Press, pp. 3–32.

Solomon, J. and George, C. (2008) The measurement of attachment security and related constructs in infancy and early childhood. In J. Cassidy and P. Shaver (eds) *Handbook of Attachment*. New York: Guilford Press, pp. 383–416.

Solomon, J., George, C. and DeJong, A. (1995) Symbolic representation of attachment in children classified as controlling at age 6: evidence of disorganization of representation strategies. *Development and Psychopathology*, 7, 447–64.

Spieker, S. and Crittenden, P. M. (2009) Comparing two attachment classification methods applied to preschool strange situations. *Clinical Child Psychology and Psychiatry*, 15(1): 97–120.

Sroufe, L. A. (2005) Attachment and development: a prospective, longitudinal study from birth to adulthood. *Attachment and Human Development*, 7(4): 349–67.

Sroufe, L. A., Carlson, E., Levy, A. and Egeland, B. (1999) Implications of attachment theory for developmental psychopathology. *Development and Psychopathology*, 11(1): 1–14.

Sroufe, L. A., Egeland, B., Carlson, E. and Collins, W. A. (2005a) Placing early developmental experiences in developmental context. In K. E. Grossmann, K. Grossmann and E. Waters (eds) *Attachment from Infancy to Adulthood: The Major Longitudinal Studies*. New York: Guilford Press, pp. 48–70.

Sroufe, L. A., Egeland, B., Carlson, E. and Collins, W. A. (2005b) *The Development of the Person: The Minnesota Study of Risk and Adaptation from Birth to Adulthood*. New York: Guilford Press.

Stacks, S. and Oshio, T. (2009) Disorganized attachment and social skills as indicators of Head Start children's school readiness skills. *Attachment and Human Development*, 11(2): 143–64.

Steele, H., Phibbs, E. and Woods, R. T. (2004) Coherence of mind in daughter caregivers of mothers with dementia: links with their mother's joy and relatedness on reunion in a strange situation. *Attachment and Human Development*, 6(4): 439–50.

Steele, H. and Steele, M. (2005a) The construct of coherence as an indicator of attachment security in middle childhood. In K. A. Kerns and R. A. Richardson (eds) *Attachment in Middle Childhood*. New York: Guilford Press, pp. 137–60.

Steele, H. and Steele, M. (2005b) Understanding and resolving emotional conflict: The London parent–child project. In K. E. Grossmann, K. Grossmann and E. Waters (eds) *Attachment from Infancy to Adulthood: The Major Longitudinal studies*. New York: Guilford Press, pp. 137–64.

Steele, H. and Steele, M. (eds) (2008) *Clinical Applications of the Adult Attachment Interview*. New York: Guildford Press.

Steele, H., Steele, M., Croft, C. and Fonagy, P. (1999) Infant–mother attachment at one year predicts children's understand of mixed emotions at six years. *Social Development*, 8: 161–77.

Steele, M., Hodges, J., Kaniuk, J., Hillman, S. and Henderson, K. (2003) Attachment representations and adoption: associations between maternal states of mind and emotion narratives in previously maltreated children. *Journal of Child Psychotherapy*, 29(2): 187–205.

Stevenson-Hinde, J. (2005) The interplay between attachment, temperament, and maternal style. In K. E. Grossmann, K. Grossmann and E. Waters (eds) *Attachment from Infancy to Adulthood: The Major Longitudinal Studies*. New York: Guilford Press, pp. 198–222.

Stovall, K. C. and Dozier, M. (1998) Infants in foster care: an attachment theory perspective, *Adoption Quarterly*, 2(1): 55–88.

Stovall, K. C. and Dozier, M. (2000) The evolution of attachment in new relationships: single subject analyses for ten foster infants. *Development and Psychopathology*, 12: 133–56.

Stroebe, M., Folkman, S., Hansson, R. O. and Schut, H. (2006) The prediction of bereavement outcome: development of an integrative risk factor framework. *Social Science and Medicine*, 63: 2440–51.

Suomi, S. J. (2008) Attachment in rhesus monkeys. In J. Cassidy and P. Shaver (eds) *Handbook of Attachment: Theory, Research and Clinical Applications*. New York: Guilford Press, pp. 173–91.

Susman-Stillman, A., Kalkose, M., Egeland, B. and Waldman, I. (1996) Infant temperament and maternal sensitivity as predictors of attachment. *Infant Behavior and Development*, 19: 33–47.

Teti, D. M. (1999) Conceptualizations of disorganization in the preschool years: an integration. In J. Solomon and C. George (eds) *Attachment Disorganization*. New York: Guilford Press, pp. 213–42.

Thomas, A., Chess, S. and Birch, H. G. (1968) *Temperament and Behaviour Disorders in Children*. New York: New York University Press.

Thompson, R. A. and Raikes, H. A. (2003) Toward the next quarter-century: conceptual and methodological challenges for attachment theory. *Development and Psychopathology*, 15: 691–718.

Tracy, J. L., Shaver, P. R., Albino, A. W. and Cooper, M. L. (2003) Attachment styles and adolescent sexuality. In P. Florsheim (ed.) *Adolescent Romance and Sexual Behavior: Theory, Research, and Practical Implications*. Mahwah, NJ: Erlbaum, pp. 137–59.

Trevarthen, C. and Aitkin, K. (2001) Infant intersubjectivity: research, theory, and clinical applications. *Journal of Child Psychology and Psychiatry*, 42(1): 3–48.

Trivers, R. (1974) Parent–infant conflict. *American Zoologist*, 14: 249–64.

van IJzendoorn, M. H. and Bakermans-Kranenburg, M. J. (1996) Attachment representations in mothers, fathers, adolescents and clinical groups: a meta-analytic search for normative data. *Journal of Consulting and Clinical Psychology*, 64: 8–21.

van IJzendoorn, M. H. and Bakermans-Kranenburg, M. J. (2004) Maternal sensitivity and infant temperament in the formation of attachment. In G. Bremner and A. Slater (eds) *Theories of Infant Development*. Oxford: Blackwell, pp. 233–58.

van IJzendoorn, M. H. and Bakermans-Kranenburg, M. J. (2010) Invariance of adult attachment across gender, age, culture, and socioeconomic status? *Journal of Social and Personal Relationships*, 27(2): 200–8.

van IJzendoorn, M., Goldberg, S., Kroonenberg, P. M. and Frenkel, O. (1992) The relative effects of maternal and child problems on the quality of attachment: a meta-analysis of attachment in clinical samples. *Child Development*, 63: 840–58.

van IJzendoorn, M. and Hubbard, O. A. (2000) Are infant crying and maternal responsiveness during the first year related to infant–mother attachment at 15 months? *Attachment and Human Development*, 2(3): 371–92.

van IJzendoorn, M. H. and Sagi-Schwartz, A. (2008) Cross-cultural patterns of attachment: universal and contextual dimensions. In J. Cassidy and P. Shaver (eds) *Handbook of Attachment: Theory, Research and Clinical Applications*. New York: Guilford Press, pp. 880–905.

van IJzendoorn, M. H., Schuengel, C. and Bakermans-Kraneburg, M. J. (1999) Disorganized attachment in early childhood: meta-analysis of precursors, concomitants, and sequelae. *Development and Psychopathology*, 11: 225–49.

Vaughn, B. E., Bost, K. K. and van IJzendoorn, M. H. (2008) Attachment and temperament. In J. Cassidy and P. Shaver (eds) *Handbook of Attachment: Theory, Research and Clinical Applications*. New York: Guilford Press, pp. 192–216.

Waskowic, T. and Chartier, B. (2003) Attachment and the experience of grief following the loss of a spouse. *The Journal of Death and Dying*, 47: 77–91.

Walden, T. and Garber, J. (1994) Emotional development. In M. Rutter and D. Hay (eds) *Development Through Life: A Handbook for Clinicians*. Oxford: Blackwell Science, pp. 403–55.

Wallis, P. and Steele, H. (2001) Attachment representations in adolescence: further evidence from psychiatric residential settings. *Attachment and Human Development*, 3(3): 259–68.

Ward, M. J., Lee, S. S. and Polan, H. J. (2006) Attachment and psychopathology in a community sample. *Attachment and Human Development*, 8(4): 327–40.

Warren, S., Huston, L., Egeland, B. and Sroufe, L. A. (1997) Child and adolescent anxiety disorders and early attachment. *Journal of the American Academy of Child and Adolescent Psychiatry*, 36: 637–44.

Waters, E. (1994) Attachment Behavior Q-set (Version 3), unpublished manuscript, State University of New York, Stony Brook.

Waters, E., Merrick, S., Treboux, D. Crowell, J. and Abersheim, L. (2000) Attachment security in infancy and early adulthood. In J. Cassidy and P. Shaver (eds) *Handbook of Attachment: Theory, Research, and Clinical Applications*. New York: Guilford Press, pp. 78–101.

Weinfield, N. S., Sroufe, L. A. and Egeland, B. (2000) Attachment from infancy to early adulthood in a high-risk sample: continuity, discontinuity, and their correlates. *Child Development*, 71(3): 695–702.

Weinfield, N. S., Sroufe, L. A., Egeland, B. and Carlson, E. (2008) Individual differences in infant–caregiver attachment. In J. Cassidy and P. Shaver (eds) *Handbook of Attachment: Theory, Research, and Clinical Applications*. New York: Guilford Press, pp. 78–101.

Weinfield, N. S., Whaley, G. J. L. and Egeland, B. (2004) Continuity, discontinuity, and coherence in attachment from late infancy to late adolescence: sequelae of organization and disorganization. *Attachment and Human Development*, 6(1): 73–98.

Weiss, R. (1982) Attachment in adults. In C. M. Parkes and J. Stevenson-Hinde (eds) *The Place of Attachment in Human Behavior*. New York: Basic Books, pp. 171–94.

Wensauer, M. and Grossman, K. E. (1995) Quality of attachment representation, social integration, and use of network resources in old age. *Zeitschrift für Gerontologie und Geriatrie*, 28: 444–56.

West, M. and George, C. (1999) Abuse and violence in intimate adult relationships: new perspectives from attachment theory. *Attachment and Human Development*, 1(2): 137–56.

Winnicott, D. (1967) Mirror-role of mother and family in child development. In P. Lomas (ed.) *The Predicament of the Family*. London: Hogarth Books, pp. 26–33.

Woodward, L., Fergusson, D. M. and Belsky, J. (2000) Timing of parental separation and attachment to parents in adolescence: results of a prospective study from birth to age 16. *Journal of Marriage and the Family*, 62: 162–74.

Young, J. Z. (1964) *A Model for the Brain*. Oxford: Oxford University Press.

Yunger, J. L., Corby, B. C. and Perry, D. G. (2005) Dimensions of attachment in middle childhood. In K. A. Kerns and R. A. Richardson (eds) *Attachment in Middle Childhood*. New York: Guilford Press, pp. 89–114.

Zeanah, C., Smyke, A. T., Koga, S. F. and Carlson, E. (2005) Attachment in institutionalized and community children in Romania. *Child Development*, 76: 1015–28.

Zeifman, D. and Hazan, C. (1997) A process model of adult attachment formation. In S. Duck (ed.) *Handbook of Personal Relationships* (2nd edn). Chichester: John Wiley & Sons, Ltd, pp. 179–95.

Zeifman, D. and Hazan, C. (2008) Pair bonds as attachments. In J. Cassidy and P. Shaver (eds) *Handbook of Attachment: Theory, Research, and Clinical Applications*. New York: Guilford Press, pp. 436–55.

Zhang, F. and Labouvie-Vief, G. (2004) Stability and fluctuation in adult attachment style over a 6-year period. *Attachment and Human Development*, 6(4): 419–38.

Zionts, L. T. (2005) Examining relationships between students and children: a potential extension of attachment theory? In K. A. Kerns and R. A. Richardson (eds) *Attachment in Middle Childhood*. New York: Guilford Press, pp. 231–54.

Author Index

Abramson, I. Y. 139
Aguilar, B. 103
Aikins, J. W. 185
Ainsworth, M. ix, 7–8, 18–19, 23, 33, 38, 46, 48, 50–1, 88, 227, 230
Aitkin, K. 23
Allen, J. 175, 194, 230
Allen, J. G. 30
Allen, J. P. 57, 80
Allik, J. 136
Alison, C. J. 143, 188
Ammaniti, M. 213, 217
Andrew, A. K. 208
Antonucci, T. C. 94
Aviezer, O. 77, 80

Bakermans-Kranenburg, M. J. 35, 51, 58–60, 205–6, 211, 213
Ballard, J. G. 174–5
Barnett, B. 171
Barnett, D. 208
Barone, L. 121, 196
Bartholomew, K. 61–3, 108, 143, 184, 187–8, 210
Bateman, A. 230
Bauminger, N. 135
Beck, A. T. 149
Beebe, B. 25, 70, 125, 155
Beeghly, M. 180
Beek, M. 230
Belsky, J. 3, 19, 39, 52–4, 90, 113, 117, 126, 204–5
Bennett, S. 230
Berant, E. 230
Berlin, L. 229
Bernier, A. 135
Bifulco, A. 57, 149
Birnbaum, G. E. 116
Bokhurst, C. L. 205
Bomber, L. 181
Booth-LaForce, C. 76, 103
Bosquet, M. 149
Bowlby, J. ix, xii –xiv , 4–8, 9, 11–19, 23, 25, 31–7, 39, 46, 55, 69, 83, 85, 87–8, 93, 142, 156, 158, 163, 174, 179, 202–4, 215–16, 227–8, 230
Bowlby, U. 227
Bradbury, T. N. 144
Bradley, J. M. 93–4

Bradley, R. H. 77
Brandon, M. x
Brennan, K. A. 61
Bretherton, I. 7, 50
Bronfrenbrenner, U. 201
Brumbaugh, C. C. 36, 213

Cafferty, T. P. 93–4
Calabrese, M. L. 138
Carlivati, J. 184, 216
Carlson, E. A. 193
Carlson, V. 153
Carnelley, K. B. 111
Carr, A. 193
Cassidy, J. 9, 17, 19, 35, 126–7, 134, 166–8, 176, 229
Chango, J. M. 135
Chartier, B. 84
Cicchetti, D. 153, 180–1
Cicirelli, V. C. 94
Claussen, A. H. 168
Coan, J. A. 27, 194
Cohen, D. L. 113
Collins, N. C. 85, 88, 116, 144
Collins, N. L. 113, 115
Collins, W. A. 184, 216
Cooper, M. L. 107, 135
Craik, K. 33
Crispi, E. L. 150
Crittenden, P. 42, 44–5, 48, 51, 60, 69, 98, 100, 111, 119, 129, 131, 135, 143, 145, 158–60, 167–8, 173, 175, 177, 182, 194, 211, 214–15, 229

Dallos, R. 121, 148, 230
Davila, J. 144
DeKlyen, M. 163
de Rosnay, M. 74
DeOliveira, C. A. 117
Diamond, L. M. 25, 92, 119
DiLalla, D. L. 173
Dozier, M. 83, 195–6, 206, 221–2
Dykas, M. J. 134

Egeland, B. 149, 217
Elicker, J. 76
Elliot, A. J. 111

Fagundes, C. P. 25

Farber, E. A.   217
Farnfield, S.   51, 159
Fassinger, R. E.   82
Fearon, R. M. P.   52, 117, 180
Feeney, B. C.   89, 113–5
Feeney, J. A.   82, 106, 138, 143
Finger, B.   191
Foley, M.   86, 196
Follete, V. M.   193
Fonagy, P.   21, 22, 28–30, 48, 60, 72, 74, 162, 183, 194, 211, 223, 230
Fox, N. A.   26
Fraley, C.   36, 84, 138, 142, 213

Garber, J.   74
Geddes, H.   181
Gentzler, A. L.   135
George, C.   16, 38, 45–6, 50–1, 57, 75, 97, 104, 116, 118, 125, 145, 153–5, 166–8
Gerhardt, S.   28
Glaser, D.   12, 50–1, 59
Goldberg, S.   71–2, 85, 90, 97
Golding, K.   230
Goldsmith, D.   230
Goldwyn, R.   162
Gottman, J. M.   115
Green, J.   162
Greenberg, M. T.   163
Grienenberger, J.   30
Grossmann, K.   54, 213–14, 229
Grossmann K. E.   94, 229
Guerrero, L. K.   115
Guiducci, V.   121, 196
Gump, B. B.   91

Hadadian, A.   209
Hane, A. A.   26
Harris, P. L.   74
Hautamäki, A.   215
Hazan, C.   85–8, 140
Hazen, N.   175
Henderson, A. J. Z.   188
Hesse, E.   57–8, 60, 158–9, 161, 181, 214
Hicks, A. M.   92, 119
Hinde, R. A.   3, 75, 227
Hinings, D.   x
Hock, E.   91
Hodges, E. V. E.   103
Horowitz, L. M.   63, 108, 184, 187, 210
Howe, D.   x, 175, 210
Hrdy, S.   12
Hubbard, O. A.   10
Huebner, R. A.
Hughes, D.   230

Jacobvitz, D.   54, 57, 175
Jaffee, S.   90
James, W.   6

Johnson, S. M.   116, 230
Johnston, C.   207
Juffer, F.   230

Kagan, J.   203
Kaitz, M.   108
Kasl, C.   172
Keck, G.   177
Kerns, K. A.   135
Kidd, T.   147
Kim, Y.   120
Kirkpatrick, L. A.   114
Klohen, E. C.   87
Kobak, R.   9, 77, 80, 93, 127, 165–6, 170, 175, 180
Koren-Karie, N.   219
Kuczynski, L.   71
Kupecky, R.   177

Labouvie-Vief, G.   149, 214
Larose, S.   135
LeDoux, J.   164
Levy, K. N.   210
Lewis, C. S.   84
Lieberman, A.   38, 229
Liebowitz, J.   74
Liotti, G.   179, 193
Lopez, F. G.   132
Luo, S.   87
Lyons-Ruth, K.   48, 54, 60, 157, 165–6, 195

Macfie, J.   172
Macrae, K. A. M.   209
Madigan, S.   157
Maestripieri, D.   206
Magai, C.   93, 122, 150
Maier, M. A.   108
Main, M.   5, 37, 57–8, 60, 81, 100, 103, 109, 117, 137, 152, 157–8, 161, 165–8, 181, 183–4, 214, 219
Manning, N.   80
Markiewicz, D.   122
Mayseless, O.   78, 80, 102–3, 136, 165
McElwain, N. L.   101, 129
Meadow, K. P.   209
Meadow-Orlans, K. P.   209
Meaney, M. J.   192, 207
Meins, E.   29
Meyer, B.   138
Miesen, B. M. L.   95
Miga, E. M.   57
Miller, J. B.   109
Millings, A.   75
Mikulincer, M.   57, 61–2, 64, 87, 99, 108, 114, 134, 138, 140, 188, 207, 210, 213, 229
Mohr, J. J.   85
Moran, G.   207–8
Moriceau, S.   157

Moss, E. 180
Murdoch, I. 180

National Scientific Council on the
    Developing Child 192
Nelson, J. K. 230
Newman, L. 159, 182, 194
Noftle, E. E. 149
Noller, P. 143

Obegi, J. 230
O'Connor, T. G. 221
Oppenheim, D. 230
Oshio, T. 181

Park, L. E. 134
Parker, G. 171
Parkes, C. M. 84, 148
Pearson, J. L. 219
Perren, S. 122
Perry, B. 25
Pietromonaco, P. R. 89, 140
Prior, V. 12, 50–1, 59

Radke-Yarrow, M. 158
Raikes, H. A. 74, 76, 78
Reis, H. T. 111
Rholes, W. S. 143, 145, 149
Robertson, J. ix, 14
Roisman, G. I. 137
Rovine, M. J. 205
Rutter, M. 221

Sable, P. 26
Sadava, S. W. 210
Sagi-Schwartz, A. 35, 51–2, 80
Sapolsky, R. M. 91, 192
Scharf, M. 80, 107, 136
Schindler, A. 192, 196
Schmitt, D. P. 136
Schofield, G. x, 230
Schoon. I. 72
Schore, A. N. 26–7
Shah, P. E. 159, 215
Shaver, P. R. 57, 61–2, 64, 84, 87–8, 99,
    108, 134, 138, 140, 142, 149, 188, 207, 210,
    213, 229
Shaw, D. S. 193
Sheffield, D. 147
Simpson, J. A. 116, 118, 143, 145, 149
Slade, A. 30, 162
Sloper, P. 207
Soerensen, S. 122
Solomon, J. 50–1, 97, 103, 125, 145, 152–5,
    157, 161, 166–8, 188
Spieker, S. 131, 160, 214

Sroufe, L. A. 33, 73, 92, 184, 203, 216–18,
    229
Stacks, S. 181
Steele, H. 60, 69, 76, 78, 94, 103, 166, 186,
    205, 225, 230
Steele, M. 60, 69, 78, 103, 166, 179, 205,
    222, 225, 230
Steinberg, A. G. 209
Stevenson-Hinde, J. 202–3
Stovall, K. C. 221–2
Stroebe, M. 84
Sullivan, R. M. 157
Suomi, S. J. 206
Susman-Stillman, A. 204
Szalavitz, M. 25

Target, M. 28–9, 48
Teti, D. M. 168
Thomas, A. 203
Thomas, K. R. 208
Thompson, R. A. 74, 76, 78
Toth, S. L. 181
Tracy, J. L. 135
Trevarthen, C. 23
Trivers, R. 75

Van Horn, P. 230
van IJzendoorn, M. H. 10, 35, 51–2,
    58–60, 153, 193, 205, 208, 211, 213
Van Vleet, M. 89
Vetere, A. 121, 148, 230
Vaughn, B. E. 205

Walden, T. 74
Wallis, P. 186
Walsh, J. 75
Ward, M. J. 194
Warren, S. 149
Waskowic, T. 84
Waters, E. 50, 217, 229
Weinfield, N. S. 73, 183, 185, 214
Weiss, R. 80, 148
Wensauer, M. 94
West, M. 166–8, 188
Whiffen, V. 230
Winnicott, D. 28
Wittig, B. A. 19, 25
Woodward, L. 216

Young, J. Z. 33
Yunger, J. L. 143

Zeanah, C. 221
Zeifman, D. 85–88
Zhang, F. 149, 214
Zionts, L. T. 181

Subject Index

abandonment   6, 9, 16, 63, 135–6, 138, 142, 163, 175, 195
ABC+D model   48–9, 168, 214–15
abdicated caregiving   153–4, 189
abuse, child   10, 12, 18, 25, 60, 152–82, 205
adaptive strategies   42, 45–7
adoption   210–23
Adult Attachment Interview (AAI)   56–60, 225
Adult Attachment Questionnaire   (AAQ)   61
adults and attachment   56–65
affect mirroring   28–9
affect regulation   17, 21–31, 80, 194
affectional bonds   12–14, 16, 39, 77, 85, 94
Africa   3, 5
Ainsworth, Mary   ix, 7–8
ambivalent attachments   45–7, 59, 64, 124–51, 158–61, 203
Antisocial Personality Disorder (APD)   195
anxiety disorders   149, 194, 203
anxious attachments   64, 85, 124–51
approach behaviours   11
attachment behaviour   6, 8–20, 25, 37–8, 55
attachment bond   12–14, 19
attachment figures   12, 19, 38, 41, 88, 94
attachment Q-sorts   50
attachment neuroscience   27
attachment patterns   11, 38–54
Attachment Style Interview (ASI)   57
attachments, 'cannot classify'   60, 161
authoritarian parenting   118, 190
authoritative parenting   91, 189
autonomous states of mind   58, 81–3, 95
avoidant attachments   44, 46–7, 59, 63, 85, 96–123, 158–61, 222, 224

balanced attachment strategies   71
behavioural systems   8
blood pressure   120
Borderline Personality Disorders (BPD)   194–5
Bowlby, John   ix, 7–8, 227–8
brain   x, 3, 24–7, 33, 194, 196, 227
broaden-and-build cycle   87

CARE index   51

caregiving   3, 16–8
caregiving bond   13–14
careseeking   3, 5, 89
chameleon self   112
coercive strategies   130–2, 141, 159, 167–9, 175–80, 182
co-dependency   171
cognitive disconnection   125
cognitive sciences   7, 227
compliance   102
compulsive caregiving   159, 166–72, 182
compulsive compliance   159, 168–9, 172–3, 182
compulsive performance   173
compulsive promiscuity   159
compulsive self-reliance   107, 159, 168–9, 173–5, 182, 222
compulsive strategies   167–80, 182–97
conflict resolution   89, 91
conflicted grief   148
constricted caregiving   154
continuity of attachment   90, 211–26
controlling punitive   169, 175–80
controlling strategies   152–82
cooperative breeding   12
co-regulation of affect   23–6
cortisol   25, 93, 175, 191–2, 203
coy behaviour   131
culture and attachment   51–2

danger   5–6, 9, 11, 15, 17–18, 42, 52, 158, 160, 176, 182
deactivated attachment strategies   46, 62, 96–123
defensive exclusion   97, 106, 111
defensive strategies   42–3, 100
dementia   95, 122
depression   149, 157, 172
deprivation, institutional   12, 193, 221
derogation of attachment   110, 195
despair   14–16, 22, 84
detachment   14–16
developmental catch-up   220–1, 223
disability and attachment   207–10
discontinuity of attachment   213–26
dismissing states of mind (Ds)   59, 97, 106, 109
disorganized attachments   47–8, 54, 60, 64, 152–82

dissociation   170, 180, 190
divorce   216
domestic violence   153, 157, 188
Dynamical Maturational Model of attachment (DMM)   48, 51, 159–60, 168, 182, 194, 214–15, 229

earned secure   82, 225
eating disorders   121, 149, 172, 196
emotional intelligence   24, 73–5, 189
emotional lexicon   130, 180
emotional regulation   17, 21–31, 70, 180, 194
endorphins   26
enmeshment   135, 140, 144, 146–7
entangled states of mind (E)   59, 135–6
environment of evolutionary adaptedness   4, 6, 9, 11
epigenetics   92, 192–3, 197, 227
ethnicity and attachment   51–2
ethology   3, 7–8, 227
evolution   x, 3–4, 7, 19, 21–2, 52–3, 78, 182, 201, 227
Experiences in Close Relationships Scales (ECR)   61
exploration   17–19, 79, 132
exploratory system   18

false self   112
fatalism   147
fear system   9, 17
fearful avoidant attachments   63–4, 183–97
feedback   9
felt security   43, 93
fight response   45, 127, 162, 164, 190
flight response   44, 99, 162, 164, 190
foster care   219–23
free-to-evaluate (F)   58, 81
freeze responses   48, 162, 164
friends   80, 103, 112, 186
frightened caregiving   152–82
frightening caregiving   152–82

gender   201–2, 210–11
genetics   x, 3–4, 17, 192, 201–3, 206–7, 227
goal-corrected behaviours   11, 38–9, 75
grief   15, 22, 83–4, 121, 148, 208

Helpless/Hostile (H/H) caregiving   60, 157
HPA axis   25–6
humour   75
hunter gatherers   3–5, 12
hyperactivated attachment strategies   46, 63, 124–51
hypertension   120
hypochondria   193

idealization   59, 106, 109, 196
immune system   91, 191–2
intellectualization   115
internal working model   32–41, 48, 57, 133
intersubjectivity   23

jealousy   136

lifestyle choices   192
looming   155, 157
loss   15, 22, 83–5, 121
love, falling in   85–7, 140

mental health   92–3, 120–1, 148–9, 161, 172, 180, 186, 193–6
mental representations   32–40
mentalization   29–30, 73–5, 83, 93, 120, 164, 183, 189, 193, 218–19, 223
meta-cognition   29, 183
mind-mindedness   29–30
Minnesota Longitudinal Study   185, 203, 229
monkeys   6–7, 206
mourning   15, 148

narrative story stems   50, 104
natural selection   4
nature-nurture debate   201–2
neglect, child   10, 12, 18, 25, 60, 152–82

old age   93–5, 122–3, 149–51, 196–7, 214
organized attachments   45–7
over-regulation of arousal   98, 108, 119

parenthood   89–91, 116–19, 144–7, 188–91
passive attachment strategies   47, 139, 148
peers   75–6, 80, 92, 103, 107, 128, 132–3, 135, 181, 186
perfectionism   102
permissive parenting   129
physical health   91–2, 119–20, 147–8, 191–3
play   17–19, 26, 44, 70, 75, 86
possessiveness   140
Post Traumatic Stress Disorder (PTSD)   164, 169–70, 175
pre-frontal cortex   26
preoccupied states of mind   59, 64, 134–51
Pre-School Assessment of Attachment (PAA)   51
primates   5–7
protest   14–16, 84
psychobabble   137
psychobiology   25
psychological self, development of   27–9, 41
psychoneuroimmunology   92
psychotherapy   224–5
punitive behaviours   166–7, 175–80

reflective function   30, 80, 93, 211, 219, 223, 225
rejection   6, 44, 55, 96–123, 174
relational trauma   155, 175, 178, 182, 193, 205
reproduction   78, 86
reproductive fitness   4
resilience   26, 55, 72–3, 81
resistant attachments   47, 126
role reversal   166, 170
romantic relationships   85–9, 112–16, 140–4, 187–8

sadness   84
safe haven   18–9, 70–1, 85
school   77, 132–3, 181
School-aged Assessment of Attachment (SAA)   51
school-readiness   181
secure attachments   43, 46–7, 54, 58, 63, 69–95
secure base   18–19, 77, 85
segregated mental systems   155–6, 178
self-enhancement, defensive   108
self-disclosure   80, 82, 108, 113, 135, 137
self-harm   157, 194
self-reliance   44
self-report measures   56–7, 61–4, 108
self-soothing   163, 194

self-sufficient   100, 174
separation   14–15, 49–50, 63
SES and attachment
set goal   8–9, 14, 34, 42, 50, 77
sexual abuse   178–9, 193, 195
shock   84
signalling behaviours   10
social class and attachment   52
social support   6, 90–1, 93, 108, 204, 217
social understanding   23–4, 28–30, 73–5
somatization   193
splitting   139
Strange Situation procedure   48–50, 57, 153
systems theory   7, 227

Tavistock Clinic   7
temperament   72, 92, 121, 163, 193, 201–7
threat   55
touch   22
transactional model of development   73, 92, 216, 221–2

uncertain caregiving   124–9, 145–6
Unresolved states of mind (U)   60, 121, 153, 162, 165, 170, 183–97, 207

work   86, 138